M. R. Montgomery

THE WAY OF THE TROUT
An Essay on Anglers, Wild Fish, and Running Water

A wry and luminous account of the principles of fly-fishing—and of the way trout live and anglers fish in the threatened streams and rivers of America. Drawing on a lifetime of experience, as well as historical sources, and—as he puts it—the advice of others, M. R. Montgomery guides us through the heart of trout country. He unlocks the mysteries of running water, from Vermont's Battenkill to the Bitterroot and Blackfoot Rivers of Montana and beyond. He enlightens and delights—with anecdotes of fly-fishing in North America and Great Britain, with the history of this noble and contemplative sport, and with a wealth of up-to-date ecological information and insight into trout biology.

A witty memoir; a learned, merry, and useful guide to the way of the trout.

Since 1973 **M. R. Montgomery, Jr.** has been a journalist with the Boston *Globe*, where he now writes a regular column. He lives in Lincoln, Mass.

•Borzoi Reader

Fishing, 5 ⅝ x 8 ⅜, 288 pages, $22.00
0-394-58063-X/LC 90-53427

The Way of the Trout

THE WAY
OF THE TROUT

An Essay on Anglers, Wild
Fish and Running Water

Principles of Fly-Fishing Drawn from Personal Experience, Historical Sources, and the Advice of Companions, Guides, and Strangers to which are added Anecdotes of Angling in North America and Great Britain, including the Author's Return to the Bitterroot and Blackfoot Rivers of Montana, and Expeditions to New Rivers Created by the Construction of Water Reservoirs and to Old Streams Newly Discovered

M. R. Montgomery

Drawings by Katherine Brown-Wing

Alfred A. Knopf   New York 1991

THIS IS A BORZOI BOOK
PUBLISHED BY ALFRED A. KNOPF, INC.

Copyright © 1991 by M. R. Montgomery
All rights reserved under International and Pan-American
Copyright Conventions. Published in the United States
by Alfred A. Knopf, Inc., New York, and simultaneously
in Canada by Random House of Canada Limited, Toronto.
Distributed by Random House, Inc., New York.

ISBN 0–394–58063-x
LC 90–53427

Manufactured in the United States of America
First Edition

Dedication ToCome

Contents

CONTENTS

Contents

The Way of the Trout

Introduction

*Comments on the purpose, history
and pleasure of angling for trout
with the artificial fly*

In late May, spring seems well advanced in the Battenkill River
valley from Manchester, Vermont, down to Greenwich, New
York. The earliest flowers, daffodils and narcissus, are going
past; the tulips are at their peak. The leaves on the maple trees are
almost full-sized; a pure and pale clean green canopy arches out over
side roads and village streets. May is the beginning of the tourist season, which follows mud season, which follows ski season. Not since
the foliage season of the previous October have so many come to
southern Vermont just to look around.

There are three things that most tourists look at in the valley: an-
tique shops, Holstein cows and people in rubber clothing wading up
to their hips in the Battenkill. These last are fly-fishing anglers, and
they do not do much to entertain the sightseers. A typical fly-fisher
will be motionless, peering at the water, holding a long, thin fishing
rod in one hand and loops of thickish line in the other. The line is
threaded up through small rings set on the rods and advertises by its
unreal colors that it is coated with some modern plastic. The end of
the line droops from the rod as if disconsolate, and floats on the water

in front of the angler. Occasionally, if a motorist pauses long enough on one of the side roads by the river or waits patiently on one of the bridges, he will see the fly-fisher wave the rod back and forth, and then the line will lift off the water and loop out above and behind and then be impelled forward in a second and congruent loop that unrolls and falls on the river. Small drops of water make a temporary mist as the fly line moves through the air. It is a handsome sight, particularly if it is backlit by the sun, when a rainbow may appear over the angler's head. The fisherman will watch very intently while absolutely nothing happens, so far as the visitor can see. At the end of the plastic line (often bile green, but sometimes blue, yellow or mandarin orange) is a thinner piece of line made out of clear monofilament nylon. This is the leader, and it is imperceptible at a distance. At the end of the nylon leader, there is something completely invisible from the front seat of the family sedan. It is a concoction of chicken feathers, fur scraps, fine thread and glue wound about a tiny hook. It is intended, here on the Battenkill, to imitate an aquatic insect called a mayfly; it is a cleverly made artificial fly, just "fly" for short, whence comes the name of this sport of fly-fishing.

On very rare occasions, the visitor may see something splash on the surface out past the end of the visible plastic line. This disturbance is caused by a small fish (by fish-market standards) that is, the angler hopes, swallowing the artificial fly. Tourists are usually amused by the sight.

The angler is almost certainly not amused. His mood, during the day, has progressed from expectation to hope to resignation, possibly all the way to despair. The angler whose fly has fooled this fish is ecstatic, perhaps, or content, fulfilled, elevated, aroused, pleased, even relieved; the whole menu of the happier human emotions may be sampled, save only risible amusement. For this is serious business. How serious it is the spectator would begin to understand if he were to extract and examine the contents of the multipocketed vest the fly-fisher is wearing. An ordinary, garden-variety angler will have small artificial flies that imitate at least a dozen species of mayflies and other aquatic insects: these will include imitations of the juvenile insect—the larvae that live in the stream; and simulacra of the hatching adult as it comes to the surface; copies of the hatched adult that float on the surface before it flies away; representations of the mature insect that returns to the water to lay eggs; even fibrous funereal portraits of the senile insect going to its watery grave. That's just in one pocket.

The minds of anglers are usually as crammed as their fishing vests, although not necessarily with information that will enlighten non-anglers. If there is such a thing as fly-fisher's state of mind, it is composed of vivid recollections, strong views, and more than a hint of pedantry. Fly-fishers are notorious for not explaining what they are doing to their spouses or to strangers. It is too complicated, they think, or else it is like jazz in Louis Armstrong's paradox: if it has to be explained, it can't be. They do talk to, or at, each other. They publish many books on the subject in small editions, they write for and subscribe to magazines of such exquisitely arcane content that the articles make no more sense to the general reader than does a random copy of, say, *The Journal of Renal Transplantation*. Fly-fishermen preach to the converted and fraternize with the lodge brothers. This is a shame, for fly-fishing is a simple, pleasant, fascinating activity, although I would not have thought it was a spectator sport before I moved East, where there are more tourists than there are trout.

I have been and will be one of the anglers waist-deep in the Battenkill, scrutinized by the curious. And I am likely to be the one sufficiently inattentive to the task at hand to wave a greeting. This is because I find it difficult to ignore people when they are staring at me. A friendly gesture seems to take some of the discomfort out of playing the role of scenic view. And I have sat, usually silently, on the fringe of a gaggle of Battenkill anglers in deep discussion over the subtle distinctions between subspecies of mayflies, the many brands of nylon leader material, the styles of fly hooks, the durability of wading gear, the benefits of high-modulus graphite strands in this year's new plastic-resin fly rods. Listening to fly-fishers anywhere in America, you will hear more about manufactured goods than about trout. It is like auditing a conference of renal surgeons: much talk about obscure anatomy and new medical technology, very little about health.

There must be some compromise between the innocence of by-standers and the expertise of these fly-fishers. We shall take this middle way, and talk about the trout itself, speak of anglers, rivers, insects and some of the mechanical devices of fly-fishing. You will see that I am no different from other fishermen—freighted with memories, well stocked with opinions, as chalk-dusted, in spite of all the wading in rivers, as the next pedagogue.

Let us stay with the Battenkill for a while. Not that it is the ultimate trout stream, but because it is so accessible, because it flows through southern Vermont, the playground of the eastern megalopolis. There, surely, more nonanglers share country-inn dining rooms with avid fly-fishers; there more novices have taken up the sport than in any other single valley in America.

We begin with the river, where it is still early in the season. The Battenkill is running high and cold. Like all water, it lags behind the earth, warming slowly in the new year's sunlight. The official, legal beginning of the trout season is a month past, but it is only just under way for the fly-fishers.

There is no crowd of anglers on the Battenkill, no congestion at the pools. This is not a river like so many in eastern North America that have already yielded up thousands of innocent hatchery-reared trout on Opening Day. If you wish, you may fish in the Battenkill using hooks baited with worms, marshmallows or salmon eggs, all treacherous and efficient killers of trout. But there are no tame fish in this river, no government-issue rainbow trout descended from California natives, bred for a hundred generations in hatcheries, ge-netically selected for amenability to factorylike production—resis-tance to disease, rapid growth, tolerance of crowding, docility—fish bred for every quality but wildness.

The Battenkill trout are of two kinds: native brook trout that have been there since the ice went back to Canada ten thousand years ago, and European brown trout that have bred in the river since several people, a hundred years ago, thought America needed British trout

6

to match its English language, laws, customs, and habits of mind. The brown trout have been very successful here and across the nation to where the distant Oregon rolls. They are a little more tolerant of pollution than other trout, a little more able to survive bouts of warm weather in the late summer. Most important to their prosperity, they are not always easy to catch on the artificial fly, nor, except in early spring, are they very susceptible to garden worms, nightcrawlers (the big ones), corn and other more or less digestible lures. The main slaughter of the Battenkill's brown trout is over by late May. The bait-fishermen have had their day. As the river begins to warm and run more clearly, the brown trout and their distant cousins the brook trout have turned to obsessive eating of small aquatic insects and have little interest in alien baits. And, sadly for the serious fly-fishers, the biggest brown trout have long since discovered that other small fish are the best of all possible meals. The large trout not caught with bait in April will be scarcely touched by the summer's fly-casters. The largest trout in the Battenkill are no more interested in small artificial flies than they are in a child's worm dangling under a red-and-white bobber. They resist the attractions of expertise and the lures of innocence.

Still, we anglers return to the river. This is the opening week of the real, the true, the good fly-fishing season; the week when, after a long winter, the summer's first aquatic flies begin to hatch, to rise to the surface, to make themselves known on the boundary between human beings and trout, to show themselves on the threshold between water and air. Even now, in late May, as it has been since the season opened in April, fly-casters will do better if they fish with small submerged artificials that imitate the underwater nymphs, the larvae, the children of the winged flies. This is called "nymph-fishing," and it can be a dreary sport. But by and large we do not go to the Battenkill to dredge the artificial nymph. We go to cast a floating fly, a dry fly, on the dark water, to see the trout come up and take it before our eyes. Even though we release the trout, return it to the river, it is our fish, to be possessed in our mind's eye, to return in our dreamings.

Fly-fishermen—if you allow me a collective noun that is intended to be truly genderless, understanding that women and children increasingly take up the art—are peculiar among the practitioners of outdoor sports in one respect that makes a significant difference: they are almost all interested in the history of the sport. Those who are not, I think, are literally out of the main stream of fly-fishing. The entire game is about anticipation, about predictions based on past experience, whether our own or from something we have read. That is the core value in a sport that is not really and never was, in spite of the best-known angling quotation in the world, "the contemplative man's recreation." Izaak Walton simply could not stop himself from using that phrase as the subtitle of *The Compleat Angler,* but anyone who has read Walton knows him for what he was: a serious, over-eager, scheming, active, vigorous and devious angler. The contemplative part comes afterward, usually with whiskey.

The connection between history and anticipation begins with the autobiographies, published or not, of anglers. No serious fisherman retires until he is incapacitated, and more than one has died from some condition of old age while on the river. There is always a future to angling—or so we pray—for us, for everyone. The past is our vade mecum as we move into the future. Men do give up some other field sports after a while. For many of the most dedicated hunters there will have been, sometime, enough blood. But, although it may involve some killing (and it involves less as each decade of this century passes), trout fishing is always in anticipation of the future, and that expectation is not changed by the occasional fish-fry. Even the greediest anglers put the small ones back, hoping for a substantial meal next spring. And now, when most of us realize that trout are bland and bony and more miraculous outside of the frying pan than in it, we may put back alive all the ones we catch. The hunter cannot return the partridge in the tree, the duck over the marsh, the deer on the heath.

We are interested in how things were long ago and far away because we believe that the ancient anglers would understand what we are doing today and, indeed, have something to teach us. We write, if only in pocket fishing diaries or postcards sent home, about how things are today because we know that tomorrow's anglers will recognize us as kin. We all fish on running water, which comes from above and passes us by, and we are in the same relation to the history of angling that we are to the river. We are all on a floating world.

When the first flush of hatching insects appears on the Battenkill, we are sharing a specific experience that was described five hundred years ago in printed books. We are fishing with the artificial fly in the month of May, a time so closely identified with angling for trout that all the various ephemeral insects of that great and ancient order of beings are simply called, here in America, "mayflies." It is all right to be ignorant of the history, but you cannot speak without using it. It is there whether you know it or not. Let me give you an example from commerce.

In one of the 754 little rectangular bins that tessellate the top of the trout-fly sales table at the Orvis Company store in Manchester, a few hundred yards away from the Battenkill, there is an artificial fly that has been made in one form or another since the Middle Ages. Their marketing name for it is Mahogany Spinner. It sells steadily in the late spring, for it is one of the flies used in that season by anglers attempting to catch the Battenkill's overly sophisticated trout. These trout have seen many pairs of wader-clad legs moving in their stream, and they have seen many artificial flies. Jaded as they are with the annual performances put on by visiting anglers, it is the central miracle of fly-fishing that a few of them remain gullible.

A variant of this ancient lure, subtly tinted to the maker's fancy or slightly modified in color to match a local example of a natural insect, will be found in any fly shop in North America or Great Britain. Across the continent, at the Caddis Fly Shop in Eugene, Oregon, the same artificial pattern, though with a slightly less red body, occupies one of 1,201 bins on the sales table. It is a Dun Brown Henspinner in Oregon jargon. This fly appears in the first angling text printed in English, where it is described as the "Ruddy Fly."

Down the highway toward Manchester Center, and across the road from the Orvis establishment, visitors stop by the Museum of American Fly Fishing, which owns (no one has ever had time to count exactly) some thirty thousand artificial flies. There, you can be sure of it without looking, are several hundred versions of the Ruddy Fly.

These various artificials are all attempts to imitate different genera and families of those mayflies which accidentally share the same adult coloration. The prevalent one in May in Vermont, and in most of eastern and central North America, is *Ephemerella subvaria,* but a ruddy, reddish-bodied, artificial fly will do for at least twenty species of mayflies. Mayflies moult their skins for the last time shortly after they leave the water, and they usually change color then; most reddish flies are meant to imitate the moulted, fully adult insect. When *E. subvaria* first hatches, it is darker and browner; the common American imitation of the newly hatched *E. subvaria,* named after an angler who popularized the pattern in the 1920s, is called a Hendrickson. The fly-fishermen on the river have imitations in their pockets for both stages. Like all mayflies, the adult *E. subvaria* hatches after a short rest—a pupation—the time when it prepares itself to move from crawling to flying, from dissolved to gaseous oxygen. It spends a few hours in the sunshine, and then it sheds the thin, drab skin that had covered it entirely (when it was in the Hendrickson stage) and exposes, in most climes, a body of ruddy brown with nearly transparent wings that look white against the dark river water. Now it is a Ruddy Fly, a Red Quill, or a Mahogany Spinner, to use three names from three different centuries.

When the natural fly has been transformed from the first aerial stage that anglers call the "dun" to what both anglers and scientists may call the "imago," it flies back to its natal stream and dances high over the water near the tops of the arching trees, one of a swirling cloud of myriad *E. subvaria.* Airborne, the flies copulate and the male dies, while the female lives a little longer to lay eggs on the surface of the water. And as the males die, they flutter out of control like crippled World War I fighter planes and spin down to a crash landing on the surface of the stream. The post-coital imago of a mayfly is known to fly-fishers as the "spinner"of that species, and imitations are made to match most of the dying spinners. The natural fly has two pairs of wings, just like an old biplane, and in death they lie out straight to the sides. It floats flat in the surface film of the water like a two-dimensional picture of an insect, robbed of life. This used-up insect is the one so well imitated by the dry fly called Mahogany Spinner. To simplify the definition just a little, a "dry fly" is intended to float on, or barely in, the surface, buoyed up by its inherent lightness, by the surface tension of the water, and by various goos that anglers will apply to it. Even if it sinks (and it will catch trout quite as well when sunk) it is still a "dry" fly. Much of anglers' language is about intention or purpose, and ignores the realities of practice.

An imitation of *E. subvaria* and its similarly colored cousins is mentioned in the list of important flies in the first fishing text in the English language, Dame Juliana Berners's *A Treatyse of Fysshynge wyth an Angle* (1496), an appendage to the second edition of her great text on hunting and falconry, *The Boke of St. Albans.* (The *Boke* is best remembered today by nonfishermen for its list of the resonant terms of venery, the names for a group of animals: an exaltation of larks, a bouquet of pheasants, a knot of toads, a murder of crows.) Juliana Berners may be a nom de plume in the *Boke of St. Albans,* and the addition of the *Treatyse* is almost certainly by a different hand. It appears that the publisher decided to cast a wider net and catch fishermen as well as falconers, archers, horsemen and badger-diggers with a "revised and updated" text.

Whoever the author may have been, the *Treatyse* systematized the world of fly-fishing into a seasonal progression, instructing the reader on which natural fly is to be expected each month of the year and how to manufacture an imitation. It says of the Ruddy Fly: "In the beginning of May a good fly, the body roddyd [ruddy] wool, and lapped about with black silk: the wings of the drake and of the red capon's [is its] hackle." It is still made in this fashion by many anglers. Fly-tiers today would make it thus:

Some fuzzy material, usually the short underfur of a domestic rabbit that has been dyed the appropriate shade, is stuck onto a thin, strong thread with anything from beeswax to flexible glue; the fur is "spun" or "dubbed" on the thread, and the now fuzzy thread is wrapped around the shank of the hook to make the body of the fly. The old anglers might use dyed wool yarn instead of dubbed thread, and many tiers today use synthetic yarns that are more water-resistant and buoyant than fur and wool. If you had to bet on what Dame Juliana's peers used, the likeliest substance would be the underfur of one of the reddish breeds of swine, like a Duroc. Later authors often specify pig's wool. We do not usually think of pigs having wool, but then, most of us don't know much about pigs these days.

Mayflies have segmented bodies (abdomens), although the divisions are not always easily visible. When they are clearly marked (or when the fly-tier thinks they ought to be), a piece of contrasting thread is "lapped" along the body, tied in a spiral that is a fair approximation of natural segmentation.

The wings on Juliana's fly were made with the short webby feathers that lie under a duck's wing. These would be lashed onto the hook at the front, away from the bend, and they would lie down and back along the body toward the bend, an unnatural position for a healthy adult mayfly, but not an impossible one for a broken, drowned adult or for one just emerging, unfolding its wings for the first time.

Her "hackle" is tied on in front of the wings, a narrow chicken's-neck feather (that is, from the hackles of the bird), spun once around the shank of the hook and held in place with a final wrap of silk thread. Hackle, until the twentieth century, was intended to imitate the mayfly's six legs, and the legs are in fact located forward, up under the wings. British hackle, then and now, is a sparse thing, but on classic American dry flies, it is often much denser. Two hackle feathers may be spiraled around the hook, and the individual fibers, numbering in the hundreds, will stick out like a miniature bottle brush. If American-style hackle imitates legs, it certainly overdoes it. This heavier hackle, sticking out all around the hook like one of those lace collars you see in Northern Renaissance oil portraits, not only helps the dry fly float, but also provides a blurry silhouette that could resemble, in the trout's eye, the rapid motion of a fluttering insect's wings.

For commercial efficiency, and with an eye to more exact imitation, different materials and methods have been devised to create modern versions of Juliana's artificial fly. The Mahogany Spinner has a body made from a blend of dyed rabbit fur and polypropylene fibers shredded and mixed together in a food processor. The hackle (remember that a real spinner is no longer capable of flight, of any rapid wing motion, so any presumed function of hackle is irrelevant) has been dispensed with entirely: the Mahogany Spinner, to quote the memorably turgid style of an angling author named Richard Franc (*Northern Memoirs*, 1694), "possesses indigency" of hackle. The spent wings are fibers of pale blue-dun chicken feather, really an off-white shade, which serve well and are somewhat easier to tie on the hook than the barred feathers that come off the flank under the wing of a duck. The two tails, a characteristic of all *Ephemerella* species, are made with single fibers of the same pale blue-dun. (The addition of realistic tail fibers is a nineteenth century invention.) Its small size (the fly would rest comfortably on a child's thumbnail) is accurate, but would startle any angler from Dame Juliana's time or anyone who did not live in the late twentieth century. Small, fine hooks are a modern invention, and matching the artificial fly to the exact size of the natural insect is a twentieth century conceit.

But the ancient anglers would recognize the odd-looking Mahogany Spinner for what it is—a Ruddy Fly—and looking outside the tackle store, they would know the signs of late spring in the Battenkill River valley: the fully unfolded leaves on the oak trees, the daffodils just ending, the lilacs coming to the height of perfection. They would understand perfectly that it was time to fish the Ruddy Fly. But they would probably pick out another version of the fully adult mayfly, a type called the Red Quill. The name comes from its body, which is made of the hard red central stem of a chicken feather, either natural Rhode Island Red or a red gamecock, or something dyed for the occasion, wound on in a tight spiral in place of the reddish wool. The typical Red Quill possesses hackle and has wings like the Ruddy Fly's, made from duck-flank feathers. British anglers might be surprised by the surfeit of hackle and by the uprightness of the wings, but the Red Quill would still look more natural to them than the Mahogany Spinner, unless they had been very acute observers of nature. To be precise, it would look better to them because it would more closely resemble their archetypal idea of what an artificial fly should be.

While waiting for the start of the mating flight, our resurrected anglers would know they should fish with the imitation of the drabber emerging flies of the same species. If they looked thoroughly through the bins, they would find another kind of artificial mayfly entirely, one with wings inaccurately folded back, like Juliana's

Ruddy Fly, but all of it composed of the right dunnish colors. This would be, in modern language, a "wet fly," meaning it is intended to be fished under the surface of the water. If these Lazaruses of angling spoke of it, they would merely call it a fly and speak of "fishing on top" with it, just under the surface film. I suspect they would pick the wet fly labeled Dark Hendrickson from one of the 754 bins, for they would recognize it by its shape and color as the correct one to use during the time when natural flies are hatching. This is the hour, in angler's parlance, "when the fly is on the water," struggling to dry its wings, to fly away, to rest, to pass into sexual perfection, to begin the old dance.

Does the wet fly (and this question begins an argument as old as fly-fishing) imitate the ascending nymph before it reaches the surface or, perhaps, a failed, drowned adult? The answer is almost surely: both. There are modern alternatives to the old choice between wet and dry fly called "emergers," which are fished right on top, in the surface film. These artificials copy the hatching insect at the instant when it is passing from water to air, but I think the old fishermen would ignore them. Typical emergers are post-modern artificials: impressionistic, sort of half-baked, gawky, loosely wrapped, messy things, neither aquatic nor airborne, neither fish nor fowl.

The way the wings are hinged on the natural adult mayfly—they always pivot at right angles to the body—was ignored by fly-tiers for four hundred years that we know of, no doubt for centuries longer. Yet it is absolutely characteristic of the race. Mayflies are very ancient insects whose remains are found full-blown and varied, already highly evolved, fossilized in the Upper Carboniferous sediments laid down some three hundred million years ago. Mayfly fossils consist of nothing more than the characteristic wing joint, but it suffices to identify them. That the wings lie straight out in death is of interest to fly-fishers, who tie many imitations of dying mayflies in what are usually called "spent-wing" patterns. The flies are spent, truly, in the sexual sense. Thus the adjective, like many words used by anglers, carries a double meaning, else they would just refer to the "flat-wing" form.

The extended wing is a sign of the primitive origins of mayflies, for it is a great hindrance to an insect to be unable to fold its wings back over the body and creep through the wildness to feed, to mate in secret, to escape a predator. The later-arriving and successful Hymenoptera can fold their wings cleverly. Thus the bee and the wasp enter their safe nests, find their way into our homes. Termites and ants, the cleverest of all the Hymenoptera, shed their wings after mating and are completely unencumbered as they go about their destructive work. Other insects which are great pests of mankind in their adult stage have wings that can be folded back and covered with a hard protective shell. So are made the beetles that attack flour, the crickets on the hearth, the cockroaches in the kitchen. The most recently evolved of all insects, the bedbugs and fleas that depend on us late-arriving mammals for food and transportation, have dispensed entirely with wings. The butterfly, always innocuous as an adult however pestilent as a caterpillar, has wings on orthogonal hinges like a mayfly's. But the butterfly's closest relation, the moth that corrupts, can fold its wings back and creep into our closed bureau drawers to lay eggs on sweaters or, if we are not careful, on our trout flies.

Happily, the visitor to the Battenkill has no need to study entomology or know that it is *Ephemerella subvaria* that will hatch out on the surface of the water starting around 1:00 p.m. on a May afternoon. If the Latin means little to most anglers (and for some who use it, it is more for social pretension than for scientific accuracy), it means absolutely nothing to the trout. If the tourist is unfamiliar with the famous Hendrickson hatch, to use the imitative name for the just-emerged dun, or does not know that it will be followed inevitably by the Mahogany Spinner-fall, the visitor will find this information on a chalk board by the fly-shop cash register. A list of the flies expected on the water that day is typical signage in all reputable fly-tackle stores fortunate enough to be located near a trout stream. With such information available to us, excellent fishing can be had without knowing, without caring, just who this Dame Juliana was that we should read her.

The dazzling variety in a good fly shop is, here at the tag end of the twentieth century, the very height of perfection. It is fully evolved. To make an analogy, the shopping angler is in the same position as a scientist allowed to dig through the Late Cretaceous era storage bins in the basement of New York's American Museum of Natural History. The paleontologist is confronted with dinosaur fossils showing extreme sophistication in bone structure, in tooth and in nail, indeed, most complicated in tail as well (some tails are long and whiplike, some carry great bony clubs on the very end). Many of the dinosaurs are armored with a hard-plated skin; others have convoluted structures in their nasal bones that mimic the brass-bound cavity of a tuba or a trumpet; there are singing and roaring dinosaurs preserved in the closets. The scientist does not need to know the exact geological source of the bones to understand that this collection is all from the apex of dinosaur evolution, just before the mass extinctions at the Cretaceous-Tertiary boundary. There is too much variety, too much refinement, for this jumble of bones to be from an earlier age in the history of the terrible lizards. (Perhaps you are wondering why I choose dinosaurs as a metaphor for trout flies. We shall get back to dinosaurs before this book is done. Some of the finest trout water in the world is dissolving their old bones, even as you read.) Similarly the shopping angler, casual or expert, is looking at complexity carried to its logical conclusion. Given the nature of fly-tying materials on the one hand, and the regularity of the form and color of the natural flies on the other (nature has variety, but it repeats itself, it is not infinite, and there are no jokes), little is left to be done in the matter of imagining new artificial flies. Real and useful inventions have been scarce for a quarter-century. There are small and important *improvements*, like the various emergers, but no radical changes. There are no entire new worlds to conquer in the manufacture of treacherous lures, and no great leaps forward to be made in the armament of the fly-fisher: rod, reel, line, leader and fly. A beginning angler who is willing to take advice is halfway or more along the path to being a master in the art of catching fish.

One of the phenomena of modern life is that many fly-fishers take up the sport as adults, when they can finally afford the travel it usually requires. Since they have missed their childhood of fishing, some make up for it by either regressing to bumptiousness or else taking the whole activity with a seriousness that might better be reserved for writing legal opinions or conducting genetic research. Many of us will learn the art in organized classes run by mail-order sporting goods companies and tackle manufacturers. Instruction for novice and expert alike is available from Maine to California. Often, the first experience of actually catching trout is under the tutelage of a hired guide while angling on rivers of the best quality. Outfitters, dude ranches and fishing tackle stores near trout water will all offer instruction on the river itself; thus what Izaak Walton called "a brother of the angle" is sure to be available for companionship at somewhere between $150 and $200 a day (Modified American Plan available).

This is because most of us live in complex cities now, and fishing as a sport for urbanites is nearly as organized as downhill skiing or golf. No one walks up the mountain anymore, and even in my old hometown on the high plains of Montana, they have converted the putting surfaces from raked sand to mowed grass. Modernity is upon us, technology assists and assails us. There is transportation by helicopter to the remotest snowfield, the most sequestered trout stream. So far there is no such thing as helicopter-golf, but it, too, will come. Still, there is something fundamentally different—and some of us think also fundamentally better—about fly-fishing for trout that separates it from other vacation amusements of the outdoor persuasion. Skiing is a contest with the mountain, and golf is played against the course. Fly-fishing is about life itself; it is the act of participating in the life history of fish and of the insects they feed on.

I do not denigrate fishing for trout with natural bait, by the way. There are hundreds of thousands of expert fly-fishermen (by their own accounting, I number them), but I have met only two or three people my age who really understood how to fish with a worm, or how to put a live grasshopper on the right model of hook and present it naturally to a trout. The difference with pure fly-fishing, besides cleaner fingernails, is that it encourages the fisherman to spend more time reading and less time digging bait and cleaning fish. Anglers become interested in the geology, biology and fluid dynamics of rivers. The sport and its literature are about water—scarce, coveted, clean water. All devoted anglers, and especially those who fly-fish for wild trout, fall in love with trout country, suffer when it is damaged, agitate when it is threatened. Golfers, by contrast, worry about little that lies beyond the out-of-bounds markers. Alpine skiers, and I have been one, don't worry about anything.

Trout fishing is most especially about *running* water, the most wonderful of inanimate things, infinitely attractive to small children, lovers and fly-fishers. And angling for trout has a cultural history all its own. When lightly borne, this learning enhances our skills and increases our enjoyment.

It must be allowed that the act of fly-casting itself is pleasant, once minimally mastered. It is unlike all other ways taken to put a bait or a lure by a fish's nose. The artificial dry fly at the end of the leader is so light, so air-resistant, that even a professional baseball pitcher would have considerable trouble throwing one more than a foot. Fly-casting is done by rolling out the heavy line in an elongated, moving loop, impelling and controlling it by the lever action of the flexible rod. If we would all just remember that you absolutely cannot "throw" a fly, no matter how often we may use that verb, we would all be better, more consistent fly-casters. Like ice skating or ballroom dancing, fly-casting is a pleasant, continuous, repetitive motion. Like a good golf swing or a dance step, fly-casting has a unique rhythm. You snap the rod back, the line is picked up off the water and forms a loop in the air that unrolls behind you, straightens out and tugs gently with leftover momentum at your rod. You snap (not too hard) forward (not too far), and a loop reappears just over your head and then runs out the length of the line, and (if all is going well) the line straightens out in the air above the river and the rolling loop continues on down the length of the leader until it is straight, too. Then the fly, as far away as it can get, drops (if everything is going very well) softly onto the water. That alone is fun, but it's not over. You get to watch the fly, now a captive of both the leader and the running water, drift on downstream. Such is the pleasure of casting that trout sometimes interfere with the enjoyment of fly-fishing. And certainly the commonest error of all fly-fishermen, even experts who have been to school, is that they cast too often, are too quick to pick up the fly and start another cast. Some are showing off their skill, some just like the activity, some are impatient. The trout is never in so much hurry as the angler.

To be successful, fly-fishers must live in a floating world away from the routine duties and schedules of life. They adjust to the flow of the water, the way of the trout. They are wholly preoccupied with finding a fish that will, for a few minutes, join them in the dance. It is a ballet between partners—angler and fish—and set to the pace of the fly above and the trout below. The water moves, but the world stops. The best of all fly-fishing takes place on the top of flowing water, on the threshold between the angler's world and the trout's. I do not mean it must be done only with the floating dry fly, only that the action is best when it is visible on or near the surface. It was always so. When the world knew only wet flies, anglers loved to see the trout come to their barely sunken lures. When imitations of the nymphal stages of aquatic insects were first made, they were drifted just under the surface to trout espied in the act of feeding. It is as much fun, but considerably more difficult, to fish with bait on or near the surface. The impaled living grasshopper is not as neat a tool as the well-tied imitation. Like the artificial fly, the grasshopper is too light to be cast by its own weight, and it is too fragile to stand much whipping back and forth on the end of a fly line. The artificial-fly man with his durable creations has a great advantage over the bait man, though he will usually deny it.

For all these reasons, when we anglers dream of trout water we seldom dream of fishing with bait or the artificial nymph or the wet fly, for those methods almost always put the terminus of the tackle out of our sight, far down in the alien realm where the trout swims. No, we dream of dry flies floating down the river, of the sudden and visible motion of a trout taking our fly. I doubt anyone dreams of trout taking natural flies; dreams are about involvement, not about spectating. I have never dreamed of dead fish, either. I can close my eyes now and recall with clarity a half-dozen moments when a trout came to a dry fly. My only clear visual memory of a dead fish, and there are more than enough to pick from, is of a cutthroat trout I should have put back. The fly-fisherman's dreams depend on his own artifice, that most human of capabilities, and his anticipation, that most human of emotions. The dream is about the intersection of preparation and chance, the happy convergence of skill and luck. Life itself, we think, is best when it resembles dry-fly fishing.

1

Fishing with Bait

*Thoughts on the instructional
advantages of simplified angling
techniques, with a note on the
aesthetic appeal of trout streams*

How capricious is the memory of anglers! I cannot remember the name of my first dog, my first schoolteacher, or the first girl I kissed—three important beings (in descending order of significance and affection) whom I encountered serially from the age of five to fifteen years. But I remember the correct name of the first trout stream I ever fished. It was and is Lobster Creek, a tributary of the Rogue River in southern Oregon. I remembered it (and I have purchased the appropriate U.S. Geological Survey Land Use Map to confirm a forty-four-year-old memory) because it was the first place in this world that I understood to be beautiful. It still looks lovely and fine as no more than a squiggly blue line on a piece of government paper.

Small boys (I was eight when I saw Lobster Creek) do not easily say that something is lovely or beautiful—it is an age of awe or amusement—and so, as I recall, I had no words for the stream and said nothing. It could not have been the first admirable view in all my eight years. Through the accidental travel of wartime dislocation and the deliberate kindness of relatives, I had already seen the

Golden Gate Bridge from Russian Hill as the first whorls of midafternoon fog drifted between its twin towers. I had seen San Francisco from the Top of the Mark as the streetlights came on, and Glacier Park and Flathead Lake and Yellowstone and the beach at Coronado Island and the Mohave Desert and the redwoods, coastal and giant. Still, the first sight in the world that I understood to be beautiful was this trout stream.

I had been fishing before; it was not the novelty of the thing. At the age of eight, I was already very serious about angling, and would fish for hours. The usual equipment was a borrowed rod with old braided-linen line. An eyed hook would be tied, usually by someone else, directly to the line and baited with bits of raw bacon fat. I always had great expectations of catching fish. Because World War II was under way and my father was gone, my early fishing career was in the hands of women. Neither my mother nor my aunt Mary Duffey Montgomery was familiar with any form of bait other than raw bacon. After the war, my father took me fishing, and I graduated to worms for sunfish and, because we lived near the ocean, to the razor clams sold for bait on Crystal Pier at Pacific Beach in San Diego, and then to the small baitfish, anchovies and sardines and butterfish, used on party boats to catch sand bass and barracuda in the kelp beds that flourished then, and flourish again after a long hiatus, off Point Loma and La Jolla, California. Even when I was too small to be one of the fishermen on the boat—when I was too short to hold a pole over the rail and too weak to crank the reel if I had happened to hook a fish—I was allowed to net the baitfish out of the tank where they were kept alive and carry them to my father. The only trouble I got in was for repeatedly netting the baitfish and then putting them back in the live-well. The deckhands on the boat told me I was going to wear them out. All that was wonderful, but it was not beautiful.

We went trout fishing in Oregon because there had been some confusion about the original and main purpose of the trip, a guided salmon fishing expedition down in the tidal estuary of the Rogue at Wedderburn, Oregon; we had, so to speak, a day to kill. My father had brought his fly rod, perhaps anticipating such a problem, and I had brought my fishing gear, including one of those old tubular-steel telescoping rods. I am sorry I do not own one anymore, for they were fine contraptions for children, and I admit there are still days when I fish for trout in the manner of a small boy. The sections of the rod fit tightly one inside the other, with a guide at the top end of each section, and you could pull out just as much rod as seemed to be the right amount for the task at hand. It seemed that every boy in America had one, once. When I met my second cousins Maurice and Richard (who were named after my father by his niece, my cousin Margaret), they each had one. They lived in Montana, and did most of their fishing in irrigation ditches bordering the alfalfa fields, catching small cutthroat trout that had been diverted from Nine Mile Creek. They seldom pulled out more than one section of the rod, for the ditches were very narrow. It was a clumsy tool, but a flexible one, and I had already soaked a considerable amount of bacon and a few worms with my True Temper telescopic fishing rod.

Technically speaking, it was a collapsible fly rod, meaning that if you had put a genuine fly-casting line on it, you should have been able to cast a weightless fly with it by creating, as I have already tried to explain, those magical moving loops that make it possible to impel a fly, an object with virtually no mass and therefore no momentum, out to the place where the trout live. The whole trick, as anglers know, is to match the weight of the fly line with the flexibility of the rod; it has to balance so that the line will put just the right amount of tension on the rod. Then one can get along with the business of forming and unforming these loops. Except in the hands of advanced fly-casters the line doesn't really move off the reel, it does not start short and get long, it does not pull itself off the reel as it does with spinning and casting equipment. It rolls out like a tank tread or a Caterpillar tractor tread, and you lengthen it bit by bit as you wave the rod back and forth, feeding line out by hand through the guides. Relative to a fixed point on the ground, the bottom of the tractor tread is motionless. Relative to the standing angler, so, virtually, is the bottom of the looping fly line. This was all unknown to me when I owned my True Temper telescopic rod. I had an old fly reel (which is just a winch and

25

storage spool for excess line) and twenty or so yards of saltwater braided-linen fishing line too thin, too light and too floppy for fly-fishing. Even Ted Williams, a noted angler as well as baseball player, couldn't have fly-cast with my outfit.

I understood that fly-fishing was an adult activity. For one thing, I was not allowed to play with my father's fly rods or with his artificial flies. He had returned from Scotland, where he spent part of World War II, with dozens of British trout and salmon flies and a Glasgow-made fly rod intended for salmon fishing, big, heavy, pretty and made of greenheart wood. I still have it. He had his own old American-made fly rod, regular split bamboo, purchased long before fiberglass became the standard material for fly rods. I remember that it was a Montague, the Red Wing model. One of the reasons I remember is that I eventually left it in a bus station and never recovered it. That is the kind of loss that burns brand names into the mind.

The trout and salmon flies were all assembled, in spite of their intrinsic variety, in the same way. Although eyed hooks had been in use for nearly a hundred years, these were made the old-fashioned way, with eyeless hooks. A short piece of leader material was lashed down onto the shank of the hook, and then the fly was tied on over the leader and the hook. The short leader is called a "snell," a word you will never hear spoken in a crowd of modern fly-fishermen. Bait-fishermen still use it, however, and you can still buy snelled bait hooks, though now they always have eyes. My father's were all wet flies, more or less streamlined and hardly fluffy or buoyant, and he kept them in small wallets with soft leather pages, books of flies. The snells on his Scottish flies were made of silkworm gut. Manufactured gut for leaders and snells came from neutral Spain during World War II, but was in very short supply. I suspect most of his flies had been made before 1939.

I was going to fish with salmon eggs as bait. My father bought them for me in the store where he had asked for directions to a trout stream. He gave me a jar of eggs and a package of snelled bait hooks—Eagle Claw hooks with the pouncing bald eagle printed in blue ink on the white paper inside the cellophane wrapper. The eggs were Pautzke's Great Balls o' Fire salmon eggs, dyed a dark red. (Now they come in fluorescent red and shocking pink, and do not smell the same as they used to, not that they ever smelled good.) We were going trout fishing. That was all I knew, having never seen a trout or been to a trout brook or owned a jar of salmon eggs. I was enthusiastic but innocent.

When he parked the car, just a few miles east of U.S. 101, I could not see any running water. We put together our rods and reels. To be precise, I pulled my rod out until all the sections were fully extended—it was about four feet longer than I was. My father put the reel on for me, and I threaded the linen line through the guides. (I probably skipped one; I don't remember, but I still usually miss one when I'm excited about going fishing.) He tied a small loop in the end of the line and poked this loop through the one already tied on the end of the snell and then threaded the hook end of the snell back through the line loop—exactly the same line-to-leader connection that fly-fishermen still use unless they are supersophisticates and insist on retying every leader-to-line connection with less bulky knots. He had some small lead weights, split-shot—round pieces of lead with a slit cut in one side—and he pushed the snell into the slit and then pinched it shut with a judicious bite. I was ready, except for putting a salmon egg on, and I could do that myself.

There are very few places in the world where it is not obvious how to get from the parking area to the brook if the brook has fish in it, and this one was no exception. As we started down the beaten path, I trailed behind, and fell farther and farther behind because I kept poking the front end of my rod into twigs and small trees or, when I was particularly inattentive, straight into the ground in front of me. I was well over forty years old before someone told me that you could avoid this problem by carrying your rod backward, trailing the tip behind you. There are an amazing number of things about trout fishing that no one bothers to explain to beginners.

By the time I got to the stream, my father was already starting to fish. I paid no more attention to him than he did to me. For what seemed like a very long time but was probably no more than thirty seconds, I could not take my eyes off the water. It came down from our left, out of a dark opening in the gray-green forest. In Oregon near the coast, everything is green and gray including the bark of the trees, covered with mosses and lichens, a dark and somber mottled green that begins at the ground and carries up into the trees to a height where the foliage begins. As the stream came out of the shadows, it turned slightly toward us, and it was white where it foamed in the sunlight, dropping quickly a foot or more in small waves into a long, still pool. In the pool, it had no color at all of its own, but was gray where it reflected the bleached logs on the far bank and blue where the sky looked on it. Nearby, the water was clear, and I could look through it and see the small gravel and sand at the bottom, the same as the sand and gravel I was standing on, but all shining in the water. At the tail of the pool, my father was in the creek up to his knees, halfway up his hip boots, casting out over the last deep water before the stream tumbled again into a lower dark pool surrounded and shadowed by trees. I think he must have bought some new trout flies while we were in the store. I have the clearest memory of seeing one, a bushy, floating, dry fly at the end of his leader, showing itself against the bright water. The light was on the gravel at my feet, and the light was on the surface of the stream, and it was dark where the water came from and darker still where it was going, but it was lit and lovely in the sun. Although, as I said, I had never seen a trout, I knew that a trout would be beautiful too.

Sometimes I think about going back to Lobster Creek. It would not look exactly the same, although I know the stream is still there, undrowned by any civil works. Those gray water-bleached logs might be long gone and not replaced by some spring's flood debris. The pool would still be there: it could not have moved up or down across the ledges that made it in the first place. But I think the reason I do not go is because the stream would be so small now. I go back to many places where it is all right if some of them are very small, but not this one. It should always be much bigger than I am because part of its beauty was that it had so much clear, cold water, more water than I could fish in if I lived to be a hundred. I never moved from it all day. It was all I needed, all I could imagine, and it was all mine after my father—admonishing me not to wade in it but to keep my feet dry—went upstream in search of trout willing to take a fly.

I opened the jar of salmon eggs and dropped it, spilling them all out on the gravel. The manufacturer must have expected something like this was going to happen, because it was almost impossible to break a salmon egg jar just by dropping it. You'd have to throw it or whack it with a rock. The glass was as thick as it used to be in cold cream jars, but clear, not opaque white. It takes a while to pick up a whole jar of salmon eggs, or as many as you can, since the gaps between some of the rocks in the gravel bar were wide enough and deep enough to capture stray eggs. By the time I gave up, I had about three-quarters of a jarful, and smelled pretty much like a salmon egg myself. It is a fine and memorable odor if you don't mind a hint of general fishiness. Those days, the eggs came packed with some oil, I suspect it was ordinary linseed oil, for the closest thing to those salmon eggs I ever smell these days is linseed. I'm not too old or too proud to fish with bait, but worms work just as well, and you can throw the leftovers in the creek at the end of the day without committing what surely is an act of littering or pollution, if not pure poisoning: discarding fluorescent salmon eggs.

I always bring some worms when I have company under the age of twelve. You could start a child fishing with the dry fly, just as I suppose you could start a musical child out with a violin, but there's no point in it. The first instrument should produce a recognizable note, whether it's a piano or a harmonica. Worms and salmon eggs and grasshoppers, if you can catch some, are the tin whistles and pianos of trout fishing: if you blow the whistle or strike the key, you get the sound. In educational matters, there is something to be said for simple devices: pianos if you have the room, autoharps, worms, ocarinas, crayons, salmon eggs, soft pencils, fingerpaint, grasshoppers. What you want is some reward, and you want it right now.

I am not a very successful fishing instructor. When it comes to education, being merely well intentioned is not enough. You may think it odd that my father would simply abandon me to my own devices, saving only the injunction to stay out of the water, but I know it was not only well meant but the best solution. You have to pick up your own salmon eggs, after all. And the fish, in the long run, do most of the teaching.

With adults, you can start them out learning how to fish with artificial flies, although I would not recommend following the lesson plan of Izaak Walton. He has probably the most undeserved reputation in all of English literature for being a "companion of the angle," if companionability means due regard for the feelings of a novice. Walton is about twenty thousand words into his text before he shows his student how to catch a trout on a fly, and his method, to put it kindly, is self-serving. When the hapless novice (introduced as Viator, the traveler, but soon called Venator, or student), asks Piscator (Walton) to show him how to fish, Walton takes him at his literal word. "There is your rod and line;" says Walton, "and my advice is, that you fish as you see me do, and let's try which can catch the first fish."

VEN. I thank you Master; I will observe and practise your directions, as far as I am able.

PISC. Look you, Scholar, you see that I have hold of a good fish: I now see it is a trout; I pray put that net under him, and touch not my line, for if you do, then we break all. Well done, Scholar; I thank you.

Now for another. Trust me I have another bite: come, Scholar, come lay down your rod, and help me to land this as you did the other. So, now we shall be sure to have a good dish of fish for supper.

VEN. I am glad of that; but I have no fortune; sure Master, yours is a better rod, and better tackling.

PISC. Nay, then, take mine, and I will fish with yours. Look you, Scholar, I have another; come, do as you did before. And now I have a bite at another. . . .

All in all, I will take the way it was done in our family, which was to bring the student into the trout's neighborhood and leave the two of them to work it out. Another option is to pay Piscator to teach Venator how to fish, but that is a very modern concept.

My father waded up through the pool, casting without any effect, and disappeared into the shaded water upstream. I could not fish as he did with my equipment, and in any case I was spared the anguish of poor Venator: I had nothing to envy. I set about to catch a trout in my own manner. It would have been easier if I had owned a spinning reel (the first ones, all made in France, were just coming on the market). Almost every beginning angler in America starts out with one today. With spinning gear you can store all the line on the reel instead of tripping over it, you can throw small baits and lures a considerable distance with no practice at all (you can even throw artificial flies if you have a little weighted but buoyant float attached to the line). With a fly reel, you have to get the line off the spool by pulling it off by hand, and then you have to figure out what to do with the line—make little loops of it and hold them in one hand is the usual solution, a condition that makes me think a fly-fisherman invented the phrase "all thumbs." I pulled as much line through the tip-top as the rod was long, and decided that was exactly the right amount. I had to use the rod as a kind of extension of my arm—to be honest about it, arms, as it took both hands to hold it—and then swing the line, the snell and the salmon egg out over the water and let them drop into the stream. One nice thing about beginning with such primitive equipment, instead of starting out with cheap but very functional spinning gear, is that you are forced to fish the way Izaak

Walton did. The practice of long-distance casting was inconceivable in his century. Then, too, they fished with a line as long as the rod, although their line was simply tied directly to the tip. They possessed indigency of fly reels in the seventeenth century.

I t took a long time for me to catch a trout. There were no fish in the nearby shallow water, although there may have been some before my father waded up through it and before I started waving my rod over it. I put the salmon egg out as far as I could, and when it settled to the bottom, I could see it glowing darkly red on the pale sand. I realized after a while that if I could not see any fish in the water where I could see my bait, it was possible that there weren't any trout there, and I would have to fish somewhere else. I tried whipping the rod back and forth the way my father did, thinking that I could throw the hook and salmon egg out farther, into the deeper water where I could not see the bottom, where there was at least the possibility of a trout. This attempt at casting only snapped off the salmon egg, which, in spite of Mr. Pautzke's careful preparations, was not nearly so durable as a grape, let alone a piece of raw bacon. I considered taking off my tennis shoes and wading into the stream, but I understood that the rules were not just about keeping my shoes dry, but about doing anything silly or dangerous. I needed a place where I couldn't see the bottom, but one close enough to the bank that I could reach it with my limited casting technique. The narrow head of the pool seemed to have both qualities, under the foam, where the water tumbled down out of the dark shadows. It was all that was available, and perhaps it had trout in it, although, like most trout fishermen to this day, I would rather have angled, or dangled, to a fish I could see.

The murderous powers of a salmon egg on a hook drifting by a trout are not to be underestimated if the fish are small and nearly as innocent as the owner of the salmon egg. Almost every time the bait disappeared under the foam, I saw small twitchings in the line, and then the line would straighten out in the current and gradually sink and slacken as the hook drifted away from the rush of water and settled to the bottom. When I got tired of waiting and lifted the line out of the water, only the hook was on the end of the line, and the egg was gone. I regarded this as a very hopeful sign. It was all working much better than bacon, which seemed to dissolve before anything tried to eat it, and cured hog fat dissolves very slowly indeed.

To be honest, the relationship between the twitching of the line and the disappearance of the salmon egg did not seem to me, at the age of eight, to be one of cause and effect. A biting fish, in my experience, was something you could feel. I learned the meaning of the small movements of the line only after the first trout hooked itself without any help from me.

I have not gotten much better at drifting hidden lures to soft-biting fish. It is just not instinctive with me. I still seldom hook the first fish of the day that mouths a sunken artificial nymph. I have to remind myself, I have to intellectualize, even verbalize, muttering aloud the simple fact that the changes in the drift of the line are upward and visible signs of a downward and invisible fish. It is a kind of angling dyslexia, a small deficiency in reading the water. And like many children and some adults puzzling out a printed text, I move my lips while nymph-fishing, silently reminding myself that even though I cannot see a fish, I will believe the tales told by the line.

When the first trout hooked itself because it had the bad luck to get the hook at too acute an angle in its mouth to spit it out, I did what all small boys do, which is, in shock and surprise, to haul the fish out bodily, derricking it not just out of the water but right back over my head. You can get away with that, bait-fishing for small trout. With serious fish and artificial flies, it's a good way to lose both of them, and I say that with more experience than most people will admit to.

I had seen a lot of different fish before, but I had never seen, or touched, anything like that first trout, all eight inches of it, pink-striped, green above and silver-white below, black-eyed and smooth.

I held it down against the gravel with my left hand (I believe the rod was probably lying unattended, I know I stepped on it once or twice, which made it harder to telescope back together at the end of the day), and I carefully unhooked the trout. The salmon egg was still on the hook. Although I had every intention of eating that fish, I recall being gentle with it, more in admiration for its good looks than out of concern for its well-being. I was in love with trout and the running water they lived in, and I knew it. I had one of my father's wicker creels with an embossed ten-inch rule on the leather trim at the hinge side of the top, and I measured the fish to make sure it was longer than six inches, which was, I had read for myself from a poster in the tackle store, the minimum length of a fish that could be kept. By the time my father came back in the early afternoon, I had seven fish from seven to nine inches long lying in the creel. Every one had come from the same place, the edge of the current at the head of the pool. First one and then another had taken up station within my small but deadly sphere of influence. I talked out loud to myself over the steady sound of the water; I talked to the fish, too. I don't remember the words, now, but I know what I was doing, I was telling us both to pay attention.

My father had not kept any fish. His, he said, were too small to keep, but it was all right for me to keep mine. I found out later that he was planning to plead ignorance of the law on my behalf, for while the general rule for trout was six inches, as I had read, Lobster Creek was a staging ground for sea-run rainbows—steelhead—and to protect the juveniles before they went down to the Rogue River and out into the Pacific Ocean, the length limit was ten inches. I had not intended to begin as a poacher, and my father, who was not always loath to point out the errors of my ways, did not spoil my day.

Even now, I am not disappointed with small fish, although I have caught large ones. And I stayed in love with running water. Given a choice of locations on a small stream, I find myself drawn to any water that comes out of darkness into the light. I waste considerable time in the vicinity of bridges, for example, because I like to see the change in color where the stream meets the sunlight. I still prefer water that is small, and on big rivers I look for the places—which are not everywhere the best places—that have the clear definition, the visible riffle and pool sequence so common to smaller rocky streams. And I still talk to myself, although the language has become more complicated and, on bad days, more barbarous.

2

———

Fly-fishing as a
Rite of Passage

*With a brief note on the
significance of the book* Trout,
by Ray Bergman

It was a long time before I saw another trout stream, though there were rumors of trout in San Diego County, our southern California home after World War II. Forty miles east of the Pacific Ocean, the coastal mountains rise to three and four thousand feet above sea level, and though surrounded by desert, they support many of the common amenities of trout country: pine trees, cold springs, apple orchards, vineyards, lilac bushes and, some years, heavy snowfalls that close the highways. The state of California annually planted a few hatchery trout in streams and in the highest reservoirs.

We went trout fishing only once in San Diego, and it was in all respects a disastrous expedition. Like many talkative children who are also early and voracious readers, I had developed a vocabulary that was remarkable for its occasional use of bizarre words. Just as a child who is allowed to play with anyone, or who has the opportunity to mingle with adults of the wrong sort, will come home with words ranging from blasphemous to scatological, I would occasionally pop an obscure Latinism on one or the other unsuspecting parent. At some point on our drive to the mountain reservoir for what was supposed to be a trout-fishing event, I pointed out to my father that it was a matter of fact that American Indians were not hirsute. I had learned this surprising information not from any Indian (by which we meant, in those days, any Native American) but from an encyclopedia. This interesting word, I understood vaguely (but did not explain to my father), meant that they did not have to shave.

For reasons I did not understand, a moody silence fell upon my father, and it was not improved by the fishing. We learned at the dock that the reservoir had just been treated with copper sulfate, commonly used in those days to kill algae and phytoplankton, thus ensuring that San Diegans would get clean water that did not taste like frog spit. The fish, we were told, would probably be off their feed for a few days. And they were. We caught a few sunfish—bluegill and crappie—which I knew without being told were unimportant fish. For one thing, they had prickly dorsal fins; also, you could feel their scales when you unhooked one. They were bigger than the trout I had caught in Oregon, but they were literally "rough" fish. Trout have scales and fins, but nothing prickly or sandpapery. We gave up, early in the afternoon, and started the long drive home.

"I never want to hear you say anything like that again," my father began without any introduction while gripping the wheel uncharacteristically with both hands. "That is an awful thing to say. Saying all Indian women are prostitutes. I can't imagine where you got an idea like that. Some Indians are very fine people." I could not understand how a factual statement about Indian men had somehow translated into a slander against Indian women, but I had enough sense not to argue. It was a long and glum and luckless ride home. Years later, in college, I learned about the Freudian slip of the tongue, but to this day I have never seen anything written about the Freudian failure of the ear. My father had been raised on the edge of the Fort Belknap Indian Reservation in eastern Montana, and I suspect that words to the effect that all Indian women were whores had at some point been heard by him, even crossed his lips as a boy. We are all savages at ten or twelve. I found out many years later that he had made friends with at least one Native American, another construction man, a Northern Cheyenne from Lame Deer, Montana. In any case, I had rubbed a raw nerve. And as a matter of fact, we seldom went fishing together again.

By the time I was ten or eleven, I was deemed old enough to go party-boat fishing by myself. (This was before the age of liability suits and resulting nervousness about unaccompanied children.) Several times each summer my father would drop me off at the old B Street pier in San Diego, and I would go deep-sea fishing while he went to work. He would pick me up at the end of the day with my gunnysack of kelp bass and sand bass and the occasional Pacific barracuda. Southern California party boats (large enough to take at least a dozen anglers out to sea) were wonderful places for kids and women, as well as for adult males. There was always live bait, which the boat picked up from holding tanks in San Diego Harbor, and that was fun to watch, and sometimes you were even allowed to carry the dip net from the rail of the boat over to the live-tank. The boats would stop and back down into the kelp beds, and deckhands would toss out handfuls of live bait, so that you were fishing near the giant kelp fronds that were the natural cover for the fish, and you had plenty of attractive free-swimming bait to entice the fish even closer to the boat. This made for short, easy casts. I liked it nearly as much as trout fishing, I think, and especially liked the independence. I used to put one dollar in the jackpot for heaviest fish of the day, and I even won it once. I was very short and very fat, but I never got seasick and I did not get tangled up with the other fishermen. I was not a nuisance on the boat, a highly desirable state when you are young.

When I was twelve, I started to grow rapidly and get skinny. My father remarked one evening that I was getting muscles. This was a mistake: they were the same little muscles that had been there all along, but an insignificant bicep (right arm) was becoming visible to him as the fat went away. It was this general improvement in my appearance, as much as simple chronological age, that allowed me to begin my long career as a trout fisherman. In the summer of my twelfth year, I was given a new pair of hip boots (the foot size was two sizes too large, but I would, they said, "grow into them" and that was true, although nothing else grew quite so well as my feet), and I was told that it had been decided that I could go to Montana to visit my uncle Gordon and aunt Ruby and go trout fishing. No one asked me if I wanted to go; I was always pleading to go fishing.

Getting from San Diego to Montana was a complicated trip in 1950. I took the Greyhound bus to Los Angeles, then transferred to a Chicago-bound bus, stayed on it as far as Butte, Montana, then took a local bus to Anaconda, where my uncle and aunt were to meet me. They must have had business in Anaconda, because it would have been just as easy to go from San Diego via Butte right to Missoula, where they lived at 341 Eddy Avenue.

My father loaned me his fly rod, the split-bamboo Montague Red Wing, and a fly line and reel, and a creel. He did not give me any artificial flies or leaders. That was evidently going to be up to Gordon, or up to me, if I spent wisely the four twenty-dollar bills he gave me. The rod was in a round aluminum tube that looked important to me; it had the technological aura of those aluminum suitcases that professional photographers carry today. The trip was a complex rite of passage: budgeting the huge sum of eighty dollars over two weeks and four thousand miles, traveling alone, meeting a relative, going fly-fishing.

I had to carry the rod in its case on the bus, and stow it and the creel on the overhead rack. You never see anyone traveling with a creel these days except in Britain: in the past few years, I have been on airplanes where half the passengers were carrying cased fly rods and olive green hand luggage full of trout gear, but none of them had a wicker creel. The American game seems to have little connection with the traditional ritual of killing, cleaning, seasoning and eating trout. If one eats trout, in this modern era, one does it almost surreptitiously.

My mother drove me to the bus station in downtown San Diego. It was not in the worst part of town, an increasingly common fate of bus stations. As we stopped in a parking lot across the street, it occurred to me I did not know how I would recognize my uncle Gordon.

"You won't have any trouble," she said. "He walks just like all the Montgomerys. All the boys walk the same way."

This was a new thought to me. "How do they all walk?"

"They pick up their feet," she said.

I was familiar with the concept. My father was always telling me to pick up my feet when I walked. I assume his father did the same, although with more effect. It is a truism, not a banality, that in the old days more children did what their fathers told them to do than in later generations. All four of my uncles, like my father, picked their feet up very deliberately, giving them a kind of high-kneed gait, something like show horses.

The next day I was in Anaconda, Montana, having seen Los Angeles and Barstow and Las Vegas, where the bus skirted The Strip in the middle of the night, making it seem like just another small town, and then Cedar City and St. George and Salt Lake City and Ogden and Pocatello. This meant eating pancakes and hamburgers and going to the toilet in strange places without incident. It was on this trip, as best I recall, that I felt first stirrings of romantic, possibly even sexual, desire. In either Cedar City or St. George, Utah, the combination of staying up all night and the clear-skinned beauty of the girl who served me breakfast made me vulnerable to this unfamiliar feeling. I left a tip, which was something I had seen my parents do.

The bus stop in Anaconda was in front of the old, red-brick Montana Hotel. I was the only local passenger. No one met the bus, and so I got my suitcase from the driver, who took it and two flat boxes of movie film out of the luggage compartment under the bus, and I hauled it up to the porch and set it by the railing with my rod case and my creel, which I had hand-carried because they would not fit, by length or by width, in my suitcase, and sat down in a white wicker chair by the front door.

But, I thought to myself, where were the darn trout? The bus route had been through an unrelieved arid landscape. The high country through Idaho and Montana had a few more trees than the vast Great Basin desert that stretches from Los Angeles to Ogden, but I saw nothing resembling trout country—that is, something that looked like Oregon—anywhere near the highway. (Remarkable trout fishing does exist just south of Butte along the highway from Pocatello. It is even better now than it was in 1950, by the way, but it is still not obvious from the highway.) All I could see were a few willow-lined bottoms below sagebrush-covered hills.

I am no longer surprised that my aunt and uncle were late to meet me. Any event in which my aunt Ruby was involved was late in starting. She lived in a house stuffed with furniture and steamer trunks from the basement to the attic. All flat surfaces were covered with boxes and books and albums. Merely putting away the dishes in the kitchen cabinets after my uncle and I had washed and dried them was an exercise in packaging engineering. She treated the automobile as an extension of her house, and she put everything into the car that one might ever need on a simple day trip. My uncle referred to this activity as "getting Ruby ready." Everyone who knew the family agrees: Gordon was the Montgomery with the blessing of the most patience. That was such an unfamilial talent that if he had not so closely resembled his brothers physically, you might have thought Gordon was an adopted child. And by the time I met him, his patience was well honed.

My uncle had no difficulty spotting the only pre-teen on the porch sitting next to a fly rod and creel, but my mother had forgotten to tell me that he was well over six feet, and I had not gotten around to checking the gait of this immensely tall person until he was so close that it seemed unwise to stare at his knees. He did walk like all the Montgomery boys, and I would learn that his characteristic gait was even noticeable when he was wearing hip boots and heading away from me. My aunt Ruby turned out to be tiny (even compared to my mother, who barely saw the long side of five feet) and plump. The other thing no one had told me was that they both smiled like angels.

I cannot remember anything about the drive to Missoula (except that we went by Georgetown Lake, and all I remember about that is the name). I think we just sat in the car and grinned at each other. Gordon was the only childless member of his generation of Montgomerys, and he adopted me, more or less. He was seldom to call me by name, or by my nickname at the time, which was "Butch," but usually addressed me as "Brother," which he deemed a suitable way to speak to a younger person. He had taken a hand in the raising of three younger brothers, and it seemed natural.

My room in the house, then and for many another summer's visit, was in the basement and smelled faintly of natural gas from the water heater. In the attic, for a few years, was the fly-tying room—hot, smelling of mothballs and lacquer thinner. After my aunt managed to fill up the attic completely (the fly-tying desk was wedged in among several sheet-covered pieces of furniture and a dozen large trunks), Gordon moved his fishing equipment and fly-tying materials to a room off the kitchen that had been his office. (Like my father, he was a civil engineer, and did some consulting after his early retirement.) As his office, and a man should have an office, it was the only room in the house safe from Ruby's inability to stop amassing her collection of early Montana artifacts.

On the very first evening, Gordon told me when we would go fishing, and named a day in the future that seemed to me so far off he might as well have said "next month." It was probably just a few days away. We had to get ready, he said. In the morning, he would teach me how to make a leader, and I could begin to learn how to tie a trout fly, and then I would be ready to go fishing. He gave me a book to read. It was, he said, "all in here" and, if I would read the chapter on knots and leaders, we could start with that in the morning. The chapter on tying flies he deemed not useful, because, in his experience, you could not learn how to tie a fly from a book, you had to be shown. Tomorrow he would show me.

I fell asleep with the light on, reading *Trout*, by Ray Bergman. No one reads it much anymore, although when it was new it went through several editions and had been reprinted thirteen times from 1938 until I first saw it; it was revised, enlarged and printed several more times. People don't read it much today because they think everything that wasn't invented last year is out of date, and no one ever read it as literature. Also, the sensibility has changed: Ray Bergman would do just about anything to catch a trout on a fly, and most people, today, will only do what the new experts do.

The difference, in the long run, between fishing like the experts and just plain catching trout is this: the modern angler insists on looking good while casting well; while the old anglers, from Bergman back to Walton, were as devious as road agents. We all want to look like the characters in sporting paintings or like the stars of trout-fishing videos with the backlit fly line uncurling against the blue sky. Modern trout fishing has begun to resemble the ritual of dueling with pistols when there was, as Alexander Hamilton learned to his sorrow, more concern by some participants with the proper location, attire, equipment and behavior than with the object, which was to put a slug in the other person. When angling stories begin to revolve around the smallness of the fly, the weakness of the leader, and the distance of the cast, we are in the post-modern age of trout fishing. Like many post-modern artists, our ego is in the process, not in the art.

3

Making Connections

*An examination of the development
of the modern fly leader, beginning
with the silkworm, to which are
added some comments on the
importance of knots*

A few weeks before I came to Montana, Uncle Gordon had hooked and then lost the largest trout of his life. He seldom hooked a large trout, so losing this one was particularly painful. The first place we went fishing together was the site of the debacle. All he said about it was that he'd "had a bad day" there. Gordon, in fifty or more years of fly-fishing in Montana back when it was good—when heavy fishing pressure meant seeing another car parked by the river, when there were no locked ranch gates—never caught a trout that weighed more than three pounds, was longer than twenty inches. It was not bad luck or ineptitude, although he was overcommitted to the dry fly and that may have played a part in his lack of success. The reasons were multiple, but one of them was simply the quality, the inherent strength, of the fly leaders that he and I started tying on that first morning. Anglers today associate Montana with big trout, even huge trout, and may not understand how someone could fish there in the good times and not succeed. Let me explain the other reasons, besides those clumsy leaders.

First, Gordon did not deliberately fish for brown trout. To him and to many of his generation, the brown was the lowest form of trout life. It was an indicator species, not of quality, but of the decline and fall of Montana. It was not a native, and that was the first strike against it. Second, it survived in water polluted by paper mills, mine tailings, and municipal sewage, and in water warmed by dams. (Most dams built since World War II have outlet systems that actually create cold trout water, but such was not always the case.) That browns thrived wonderfully then and now in clean running water was no excuse for their tolerance of less-than-perfect conditions, any more than the fact that you might encounter the local madam in church meant that she did not spend the other six days of the week in unsavory surroundings. Some nearby rivers, including the Clark Fork of the Columbia which ran through Missoula, carried many five-pound brown trout. This was of no more interest to Uncle Gordon than the fact that piranhas lived in the Amazon. Brown trout were cannibals, and that was all you needed to know about how they had achieved their remarkable size. He knew that during salmon fly hatches and grasshopper season they would take the dry fly, but this was no argument for treating them as real trout. The mark of Cain was on them.

Gordon spent most of his long life on the west slope of the Rocky Mountains, where the native cutthroat trout does not grow to the large size of the heavily spotted, east-slope, so-called Yellowstone cutthroat. (These east-slope-of-the-Rockies cutthroats are also found in the Snake River of Idaho, a tributary of the Columbia, and they are much larger on average than the typical west-slope cutthroat.) This difference in ultimate size is genetic, but the west-slope cutthroats also live in a less nutritious environment. The western Montana streams run through young and rugged mountains and tend to be neutral or slightly acidic waters, "soft" water in householder's terms, good for taking showers and washing clothes but less productive than the nutrient-rich, alkaline "hard" water of the eastern slope of the Rockies, where rivers run through old seabed limestones, dissolving and carrying along the fragile skeletons of ancient plankton, recycling them into abundant new life. Even the form of most west-slope rivers works against large fish, since they are mostly riffle and pool, cataract and plunge, seasonally torrential streams with consequently low growth rates for trout. Trout, especially rainbows and cutthroats, are short-lived creatures—three or four years is a long life—and the western streams cannot fatten them so quickly as the richer and often slower waters of the gentle foothills east of the Continental Divide.

Uncle Gordon hooked his three-pound trout that summer, and lost it after a long fight. My aunt told me about it. Of all the rivers he fished regularly, the Jocko, the Big Blackfoot, Rock Creek and the Bitterroot, he found his dream fish in the least likely place. It was up in Sula Meadows, in the smallish East Fork of the Bitterroot, a river that haunts my memory as it did his, although for different reasons. I know exactly where his big fish was. On the right-hand bank of the East Fork as you walk upstream from the back-road farm bridge nearest the highway, a small creek comes in from the hayfields. Tiny as it is, it has a name: Reimel Creek. I must have jumped it a hundred times. A little thing it was, a couple of feet across at its narrows and as many deep, and in those days it fed into the East Fork just above a deep undercut bank. Usually, when a side stream comes in, it will make a bar in the main stem by washing in sand and gravel, but this creek carried little burden by the time it reached the East Fork. Gordon's trout lay next to the undercut, just downstream from the creek, rising regularly to some very small fly. He cast to it repeatedly, continually turning to smaller flies, tying thinner tippets on his leader, until the fish took. He had it on for what seemed an eternity, and then the fine leader frayed at the hook knot and the fish was gone. He never saw it again.

My aunt, who fished with salmon eggs or live grasshoppers when she fished at all, did not know which fly the fish had taken, or the leader strength. I never asked Gordon for the details. It seemed a private grief that did not lend itself to story-telling. But given the year it happened, 1950, and remembering the state of the art in those days,

I can imagine what he was using. The fly would probably have been an Adams, the only fly we regularly tied in very small sizes. In those days, a hook less than half an inch long, No. 16, was the smallest we used. For the tippet of his leader, he would have had nothing thinner to choose from than a piece of nylon 0.006 inch in diameter, called "5X" in the arcane labeling system of anglers, with a breaking strength in those days of less than one pound. Anyone can lose a three-pound trout on such inadequate tackle. Today, if there were a three-pound trout in the East Fork, an angler would be armed with considerably smaller flies and with much thinner leader material of even greater breaking strength. With today's equipment, my uncle could have killed his great fish. If angling is about that kind of success, the good old days are now.

T he year I started tying leaders at Gordon's fishing tackle desk in the attic, the world was still shifting from silkworm-gut leader material to nylon. Like most serious anglers, Gordon shopped by mail, ordering from the famous Herter's Company catalogue. He owned a complete set of the various diameters of nylon monofilament necessary to create a trout leader along with Herter's instructions, which gave clear charts, tables, and pictures of knot-tying. He did not have to show me how to make a fly leader; he could just open the catalogue to the right page and turn me loose.

I would have to say that nothing in fly-fishing has improved quite as much in forty years as the leader. The American dry fly was already well established, and fly-tying materials were cheaper and possibly better back then when there were more chickens and fewer anglers. Hooks, if anything, have gotten less reliable in the past few decades, with poorer finish around the eye, and inexplicable brittleness. Silkworm gut was an improvement over horsehair leaders, but it was no better made in 1950 than in 1850. Leader material is not something you can create in your workshop, improve in your kitchen (although many an old angler did dye his gut leaders in the hope of making them less visible to the trout, and applied ointments in the vain hope of increasing their strength). The leader has two jobs to do, one entirely mechanical, the other optical and functional. It has to make the transition from thick, heavy fly line down to something small enough to go through the eye of a hook. And it must make the best possible trade-off between invisibility to the trout and sufficient strength to land the fish.

Making leaders is a pleasant activity, not in the least complicated once you have learned three simple knots (two will do). Leader stock, unlike the raw material of fly-tying, is cheap and chemically inert—hypoallergenic. You don't even need special equipment unless you happen to live in the only household in America that doesn't contain a fingernail clipper. And unlike your own artificial flies, the first leader you tie will be at least as good as, and very likely better than, anything you can buy. I have not been able to say that about my trout flies.

For consumers, nylon first replaced silkworm gut in women's hosiery—not in fishing equipment—just before World War II. (I can't think of any consumer product, beginning with the chickens whose feathers are used to make artificial flies, that was ever invented specifically for fishing tackle and then adapted to more universal purposes. In the long run, fishing-tackle manufacturing does not create the wealth required for serious research-and-development laboratories.) Then, during the war, all the available silkworms were dedicated to silk production for parachutes, and most of the nylon went into less delicate articles of war, though occasionally there was enough nylon to produce sheer hosiery. I remember riding in the car with my mother to some nondescript building on the outskirts of Livermore, California, in late 1944 or early 1945, where she queued up for what seemed like hours (I read two comic books and ate a small bunch of grapes, and still had to wait) to buy one or two pairs of nylon hose. I hope it was legal, it certainly had all the sub-rosa characteristics of other trips we took into the countryside to purchase chickens without surrendering ration stamps. The hosiery came fully finished and packaged, unlike the chickens.

The specifications in the Herter's catalogue for tying a compound fly leader—that is, a leader made up of graduated sizes of nylon, with different diameters and breaking strengths—were simple, and the same could be found for many years afterward in post-war fishing books by Ted Trueblood or Ray Bergman. Almost all the pieces, starting with the heaviest at the beginning, or butt, of the leader and continuing down to the finest end, or tippet, were approximately the same length. Here is a sample of the specifications from Trueblood's *The Angler's Handbook* (1947). Starting with the butt section and proceeding through eight pieces to the tippet, one made up a nylon leader this way:

The first five pieces were all 12 inches long, beginning with one of 0.017-inch diameter, followed by strands of 0.015, 0.013, 0.011, 0.010, 0.009 and 0.008 inch. At the very end, the tippet was eighteen inches of 0.007-inch nylon. A filament of only seven-thousandths of an inch was, in 1950, considered extremely light tackle of little more than spiderweb strength.

If you bought a leader like this one in a store, it would be labeled as a nine-foot, 4X leader. Gut and nylon filament were, and nylon still is, labeled with an X-system from 0.011-inch diameter on down to the smallest then available, 0.005 inch—where 0X = 0.011 inch, 1X = 0.010 inch, 2X = 0.009 inch, and so forth. Today, nylon leader material goes as fine as 8X, only 0.003 inch in diameter. (The tradition of using larger numbers for smaller things, which confuses matters, comes naturally from other kinds of manufacture, like that of thread and wire, where the numbers indicate the quantity of diameters required to cover a specific width.) Material too thick for the X-system is labeled with the diameter, given in thousandths of an inch.

The reason for the multiple gradients in the taper of the fly leader had nothing to do with the complicated physics of fly-casting. The succession of small decreases in diameter was necessary because it is difficult to tie two pieces of leader material together if they are of very different diameters. Two-thousandths of an inch isn't much, but if it's a quarter of the total diameter of a filament, it is a huge differential.

The leader has another job to do besides contribute by its fineness and transparency to the deception of the trout. It has to unroll at the end of the cast and carry the characteristic moving loop of a fly line: it has to transfer that energy along its length so that the fly drops on the water at the maximum distance from the rod, and not in a puddle of line and leader coils. If you have a friend who is a physicist, you can have him explain to you the transfer of energy along a flexible cone. Your physicist will almost surely tell you that the energy will be transferred most efficiently if the cone is not symmetrical, if it tapers rather abruptly near its middle, if it is a "truncated" cone. A modern tapered leader, like a well-woven whip, is a truncated cone that transfers the energy of the rod, like the whip handle's, along its length. Unfortunately, the patron saint of anglers is the wrong Izaac, and it was well into the 1960s before anyone thought of consulting Newton, rather than Walton, about how to make a compound leader that really worked.

The reason I was sitting in an attic in Missoula making inadequate and unscientific fly leaders, ones with pieces of filament of graduated diameter but of almost the same length, was the long tradition among anglers of using silkworm gut, the maximum length of which was limited. Silkworms, the caterpillars of the silkmoth, spin their own gut into a very fine thread, weaving themselves inside it, and wait out their transformation into moths inside their own silk cocoon. Man-made silk fabric is spun from the unwrapped cocoon filaments, a single filament of which would be too fine for anything, certainly for catching fish. The makers of gut leader material eliminated the caterpillar from the final step of manufacture. Just before mature caterpillars would have started to build their cocoons, they were killed and their silk repositories removed. Each caterpillar has two silk glands (or guts), and these were stretched by hand and set out to dry. The process (it was a Spanish specialty) amounted to a kind of silkworm pasta-making. Given the natural variation in silkworms and the vagaries inherent in handicraft, some guts were made into longer, thinner strands, some into shorter, thicker ones. Once dry, the gut was hand- and eye-graded for diameter and quality. The finest available gut—from ten-thousandths of an inch in diameter down to six-thousandths of an inch (in angler's jargon, from size 1X down to size 5X)—was manufactured from the stretched strands by warming them, wetting them, and drawing them through a circular die. The best dies were made of drilled diamonds.

The average silkworm gland could be stretched by hand to around two feet, but it could not be stretched evenly to a diameter much smaller than 0X (0.011 inch), a limit imposed by the laws of physics. Whenever you stretch something, it will get much thinner in the middle than at the ends; if you have a thick rubber band handy, you can test this statement with your own eye. The more you stretch, the more pronounced this distortion becomes, and very thin stretched gut was too variable along its length to be useful. (The name for the general rule of diameters along a stretched object is accidentally wonderful when applied to fishing tackle: it is Poisson's Ratio.) The thicker ends would be trimmed, and the average length of gut in all the larger diameters was around sixteen inches by the time it was packaged for sale. Thinner gut, pulled through dies to make drawn gut, would average around twenty-four inches after this final manufacturing stage. You can see where the old leader formulas came from: the makers were simply using the most common material in the most economical way.

When nylon leader material first appeared, it was snipped into gut-lengths and sold in hanks rather than on spools. Even after it was sold on spools, the formula for the compound leader remained fixed in gut-lengths, just as the nomenclature, the X-system, has survived. When one speaks of the "angling tradition," one is sometimes celebrating obsolescence, rigidity and general bugbearishness.

Early nylon was little if any improvement over silkworm gut. It was cheaper but not better. (This was also true in the manufacture of hosiery, as any woman old enough or rich enough to compare silk stockings with nylon stockings will be able to tell you.) The redeeming quality of early nylon was price and consistency. An individual strand, or a length cut from a roll of nylon monofilament (extruded like gut, not woven), would dependably break at, or near, the advertised strength. Gut strengths varied as much as 25 percent in each direction from the average. In the early 1950s, Herter's was still selling gut to those who could afford it and nylon to the rest of us. The preference for silkworm gut, in spite of its variability, was because it was: (a) traditional, and (b) easier to tie knots in. A short comparison table of breaking strengths (in pounds) is worth a glance (the X-value and diameter are repeated for each entry for all of us who, like myself, cannot remember numbers for more than a nanosecond).

Average Breaking Strength

Herter's best gut		Herter's 1950 nylon	
1X (0.010″)	2.9 lbs.	3.0 lbs.	1X (0.010″)
3X (0.008″)	1.6 lbs.	1.75 lbs.	3X (0.008″)
5X (0.006″)	0.8 lbs.	0.9 lbs.	5X (0.006″)

The nylon sold today is a great improvement over the early monofilament. Just as one example—and the ratio is consistent for all diameters—ordinary modern nylon at 0.006 inch (5X) breaks at around 2.4 pounds, a nearly three-fold improvement on 1950 nylon, and it is approaching some kind of manufacturing maximum. In 1986, the Orvis Company introduced a resin-coated nylon leader with nearly double the breaking strength of uncoated nylon—their 5X tested at 4.5 pounds; and they manufactured a truly spider-web 8X (0.003 inch) that rated at 1.75 pounds—half the diameter and twice the strength of the best early nylon.

For centuries, fishing "fine and far-off" has been the ideal. I would say that we are now able to cast farther and finer than we need to, when leaders provide no excuse at all for the refused fly or the broken-off fish. The resin-coated leader material, moreover, has peculiarities that will keep it from being popular with some flyfishermen. It demands that you tie the simplest of knots (unimproved clinch and simple surgeon's and Major Turle's knots made with one turn of the material, not two) because the resin coating is extremely reactive to heat (all nylon is, but this new material is terribly allergic to high temperatures), and the small heat of friction caused by tightening a complicated or wrongly tied knot destroys its strength. At this writing, there is a rumor that the Japanese are going to carry things to another plateau, but I suspect there will be problems with anything much fancier than what is already on the market. In this matter, as in many aspects of fly-fishing (or life, as nonanglers would say), we have entered an era of trade-offs and diminishing returns.

O nce the old formulas for tying leaders were overthrown, and once anglers started experimenting with the possibilities of spooled nylon, several people simultaneously discovered that the most efficient way to transfer energy along a cone was to start out with a long heavy section at the butt, quite beyond the wildest dreams of the most boastful silkworm, and then step down quickly to the thin tippet. This quick step-down is the infamous truncated cone. The same 9-foot, 4X leader in modern dress looks like this:

	Length (in inches)	Diameter (in inches)	
butt section	36	0.021	
	16	0.019	
	12	0.017	
midsection	6	0.015	
	6	0.013	
	6	0.011	(0X)
	6	0.009	(0X)
tippet	20	0.007	(4X)

This leader not only works better than the first one I tied in 1950, but is five times as strong (5.5 pounds, if I use the resin-coated material, compared to 0.9 pounds). The long, relatively stiff first half of the leader, the abrupt step-down, and the extensive and flexible tippet show a physicist's decision, although anglers, depending on how they cast or the effect they desire, may vary these proportions to suit themselves. What is consistent about all modern leader designs is that they take advantage of the variable lengths into which spooled nylon can be cut and ignore the traditional imperatives of the old gut dimensions.

One apparent improvement in modern leader manufacture was (or is, if you insist on buying one) the knotless tapered leader, made of nylon drawn differentially so that it is roughly 0.020 inch at the butt and tapers down evenly to some smaller number, usually 3X or 4X, at the business end. But there are important reasons to stick with the knotted leader, aside from its more efficient transfer of energy. The knots themselves are useful when fishing a "cast" of two flies, that is, one on the end and one some distance up the leader. It is much easier to keep the upper fly in place by jamming its own short leader (the "dropper") against one of the knots. If you tie your own leaders, you can even leave one end of a connecting knot sticking out, and tie a fly on the excess. When you are nymph- and wet-fly-fishing, a leader knot will keep a small lead weight like a split-shot from sliding down against the fly. If you are using one of the floating strike-indicators that have become popular, a knot will help keep it in place. And anyone who has fished enough will someday have a trout rise to a leader knot. This is not to be sneezed at, though it may be upsetting. At least you have located a trout that's looking up, and that is half the battle.

Another reason has to do with casting. The first step in casting a fly line is to put some useful tension on the rod as you pick the line up off the water. With a short line (and I hope before we are done to convince you to fish sometimes with a very short line), the leader knots actually assist you in putting tension on the rod, for they drag against the surface of the water as you pick up the line at the beginning of the backcast. Experienced and expert fly-casters—and there are hundreds of thousands of them—may laugh at the idea of "loading" a rod with a little bit of line and a knotted leader, but there are more good fly-casters than fly-fishers. Expert trout fishermen (by the time they reach that elevated state) find themselves casting no more than a leader on many occasions.

When nylon replaced silkworm gut, knot-tiers, whether they were making leaders or attaching flies to tippets, quickly discovered that gut, for all its expense and inconsistency in diameter and absolute breaking strength, had one great advantage over nylon: when gut is wet (and you always soaked it before using it, which is why you carried leaders in wallets with damp chamois-cloth pages to keep them soaked), it deforms slightly as you tighten the knot, increasing the amount of contacted surface and thus the friction within the knot. The trouble with nylon monofilament is that it is very hard and almost perfectly round, and two round surfaces (be they cylinders crossing each other, or spheres abutting each other) meet at an infinitely small point. (One common method for piercing cell walls in biological research is to shake the microscopic cells in a suspension of little round glass balls.) It is difficult to get round, hard nylon to deform, to grip itself in a knot. Nonanglers seldom encounter so miserable a material to tie with as monofilament nylon. The closest thing in ordinary life is hard polypropylene twine, which doesn't tie nearly so neatly or easily as old-fashioned cotton. For the elite classes, another good example is water-skiing tow rope. Although nylon monofilament isn't perfectly round, and doesn't cross itself at exact right angles in a knot, its qualities of hardness and roundness make for knots that don't share much surface area and tend to slip.

For a few years, in the 1960s, you could buy flattened nylon leader material, the idea of it being to increase the surface area of contact in a knot. This material (Platyl was one brand name) was a prolate spheroid in cross section, like a football looked at sideways. (It is a rugby ball that is an *oblate* spheroid, no matter what you read in your local sports pages.) Flattened leader material went the way of all poor solutions. It is even surprising that it was attempted to begin with. The nineteenth- and early-twentieth-century angling authors all warned readers against using anything but the roundest of natural gut. When a knot is tied in a flattened filament, the leader always flexes back and forth in the same direction, right next to the knot. It wears itself out by repeated bending at the same place and in the same arc, like a paper clip in an idle executive's fidgeting hands.

The best solution when tying nylon was to increase the number of turns in all the standard British knots for tying gut. Their "blood knot" for joining two pieces of leader material together was increased from two wraps in each direction to as many as five (an excessive number, by the way, three or four will do) and is called a "barrel knot." Properly tied, it does make a neat, cylindrical knot, and increasing the number of turns merely makes it a longer barrel, not a fatter one, which is all to the good. Their "water" or "surgeon's knot," once nothing more than a simple overhand knot tied with both pieces of material held parallel, had to be doubled for nylon. Major Turle's knot (still the best for tying flies to leaders, but not so popular as it should be because it is slower to tie and harder to untie, and if there's one thing we like to do, it's change flies all the time) had to be doubled as well. Most of us turned to tying flies on with the half-barrel, or "clinch" knot.

Benjamin . . Drawings

ART

On the general theory that knots are hard to learn (Henry Thoreau was over thirty before he learned the difference between a square knot and a granny knot, and was amazed at the improvement when it came time to untie his boot laces), most printed instructions for tying nylon leaders recommended the use of the barrel knot from one end to the other. Now it is true that the doubled surgeon's knot makes a clumsy blob in the large diameters near the butt of the leader, but it makes a neat, consistent, and even stronger knot than the barrel knot when you get down toward the tippet (say, from about 0.009 inch [2X] on down). And it is almost impossible to tie a faulty surgeon's knot, even in the dark. Yet, although it was once the standard leader knot, it virtually disappeared with the advent of spooled nylon. The reason is simple: with the barrel knot, you can tie one piece to another without first cutting the pieces to size—you can use, for both sides of the knot if you're in need of amusement, the loose ends from two fat spools of nylon. That is the way I measured my sections in Missoula in 1950. I tied the knot first, then cut the added material to the proper length.

Once anglers stopped buying leader material in pre-cut hanks, they forgot the surgeon's knot and spent many an unhappy moment, either with cold fingers or fingers shaking in excitement or fingers disappearing in the dusk—on very bad days, in all three conditions at once—trying to tie a new tippet on with the barrel knot. I do not laugh at Thoreau and his square knot. I was forty-eight years old (and obviously not paying much attention) before I learned how to tie the surgeon's knot. For years I fished with tippets that, after changing flies and cutting out wind knots, were nipped down to six or seven inches long before I would stop and put on a new one. Spools of tippet material used to die a silent chemical death in my fishing vest before I used them up. For a few years, I felt foolish about staying ignorant of the surgeon's knot, and then a guide on the Big-horn River told me that he had learned a new leader knot at a summer workshop for master anglers. "Better and easier" than the barrel knot, he explained, as he showed me the venerable surgeon's knot.

Gut, always tied wet, was effectively stronger than early nylon; it may not have been absolutely stronger, but it was more flexible wet, less subject to breakage due to brittleness. Nylon loses strength when it absorbs water, which is one of the reasons it is manufactured with a hard surface. But the harder the surface, the more heat of friction you get when you go to tighten the knot, and heat absolutely destroys the strength of all nylon, resin-coated nylon in particular. If there is one rule of tying knots, particularly with small-diameter coated nylon, it is that you cannot spit on it too much. This is usually referred to in instructions as "lubricating" the knot, as though everyone knew what the word intended. Women anglers have more trouble tying knots than they should, until they figure out what the word means and make up their mind to do it. I have had several store-bought top-dollar leaders break at a knot well up and away from the tippet, where the material should have held ten or fifteen pounds. I doubt that anyone sitting in a factory tying leaders at piecework rates (and that is how it is done) has the time or capacity to lubricate all the knots.

The other uses of spit are less critical but still effective. There's nothing like it for cleaning fish slime off a dry fly. It must be the enzymes. For large dry flies (on a day when you are being very careful) a slight chewing action improves the performance of the saliva. Spit on the fly (chew if necessary), wash it vigorously in the stream, and squeeze it dry with a bit of your T-shirt that you have pulled out from between your shirt buttons (another common male advantage on the stream) or with a facial tissue (a female advantage, nine times out of ten). Lastly, neatly applied spit works fairly well at getting the tippet to sink, which is sometimes important, especially on still water.

M y uncle Gordon never mentioned spitting on knots. But sitting in the attic with good light and all day to tie, you could be careful enough so that it wasn't absolutely necessary. He did show me the trick of chewing on a fly. They don't taste as good as they used to—not nearly so many hints of mothball and arsenic and borax on the palate as they once offered. Trout themselves taste just as good. I must say, though, I have recently caught trout in water that did not encourage me to chew on the fly. Once I would fish in any stream where there were trout, but no more. It is not fear of infection or snobbery. I simply have no interest in running water that isn't fit to be chewed off a fly.

Gordon was a good fly-tier of the old school, and when I write "school," I mean it almost literally. He did not invent flies; there were so many good ones, he would say, that it was best to copy the successful patterns from books—and from friends. His regular fishing companion, Ashley Roche, a retired U.S. Forest Service warden who lived across the street, would occasionally create a new fly, but Gordon stuck with the standard, published patterns unless one of Ashley's turned out to be exceptional.

I am the last person in the world to give written, oral or demonstrative lessons in fly-tying. If Gordon tended to stick with the established patterns (in the sense of dress patterns: the popular sizes, colors and silhouettes), I take it one step further and buy almost all my flies now, relying even more directly on the opinions of the real experts. It is fun to catch a fish on a fly you tied yourself, and I miss it. But I would also miss gardening, reading, writing and watching baseball on television.

Anyway, I have no special talent for making small things with large fingers. Lack of handiness, of fine muscle control, is no impediment, by the way, if you really want to tie your own flies. When I met Ashley Roche he was already suffering from severe rheumatoid arthritis in his hands and had to use his thumb, index, middle and ring finger simultaneously just to hold the scissors or the thread-bobbin as he tied material onto the hook. It took him about twenty minutes to tie a simple pattern, but he had all day and all winter.

What amazes me still is that when I first sat down at Gordon's desk I thought I could learn to tie flies. I knew I had less small-muscle skill than the average child; teachers had been pointing it out for years. I had never been able to color my coloring books neatly, couldn't play the piano (lessons were unavailing), and had the handwriting of an illiterate copying a language he didn't read—I printed in a mixture of capital and lowercase letters that looked like the hand of someone trying to disguise his writing in a ransom note.

It used to be a truism of angling writers, starting with Walton, that the art of fly-tying could not be explained in print. This is not true anymore, at least not after someone has shown you how to do it once or twice. The reason you can learn how from books now, and could not back then, is that the materials are standardized—everything from thread to feather to tinsel to fur has a nomenclature accepted by all authors—and because the writers today are people who have derived part of their income from teaching fly-tying. There is nothing like the failures of pupils to force the instructor to reflect on the inadequacies of his language. I have never presumed to teach the art. Any fly shop worth visiting has people in it who tie flies and will sit at the vise and demonstrate (although not on Saturday mornings or weekday lunch hours, when things are busy). Tackle shops have excellent books of instruction explaining special techniques and the various patterns. Even failing eyesight is no excuse. I wear some flip-down magnifying glasses now on the river, most especially at dusk when my eyes refuse to see hook eyes and thin leader. Fixed or movable magnifying lenses are stock-in-trade for fly-tiers.

I won't even argue that patience is a necessary virtue for making your own flies. I was no more patient than the average twelve-year-old. I would only say that you should learn how to tie one fly at a time and stick with it until you are satisfied. Be like the hedgehog, who has only one trick but knows it well.

4

Learning to Fly-fish

*A narrative of the difficulties
encountered by the novice, with
comments on the unusual habits of the
Columbia Basin cutthroat trout
(Oncorhynchus clarki clarki)*

Aunt Ruby turned out to be a Christian Scientist. I discovered this on the day we finally got to go trout fishing. We began by packing the car with all sorts of sensible things including an old, pre-propane Coleman portable stove, the kind with two burners and a generator. A Coleman generator was a coil of tubing over which one poured a little white gas and then lit it to get the tubing warmed up properly so that the liquid gas would vaporize before it reached the burners. The possibility of setting everything on fire while lighting the generator was always high. On one occasion I saw my father carry a flaming Coleman stove out of our house when we tried to use it during a power outage. Gordon's stove was similar to the very dangerous paraffin stove in Kipling's *Just So Stories*, the one where the rhinoceros gets its skin: "A cooking-stove of the kind that you must particularly never touch."

The purpose of the stove was to cook the trout for lunch. We also packed canned corned beef as reserve protein, along with bread, potatoes, onions, bacon (and bacon grease), eggs, jam, lettuce, tomatoes and bottled dressing. Then we packed Ruby's watercolors, paper and easel. I never saw her paint a picture in my life, but we always took the watercolors just in case. And the last two things I carried to the car were the Bible and two copies of *Science and Health with a Key to the Scripture*, one in English, one in German. I rather fancied the German volume, which was printed in black-letter type, because the third word of the title was *Gesundheit*. This was what we said at home when someone sneezed rather than "Bless you." Ruby occasionally taught beginning German at the University of Montana in Missoula and kept her hand in by reading *Wissenschaft und Gesundheit mit Schlussel zur Heiligen Schrift*.

We sat three across in the front seat of Gordon's 1949 Ford sedan. The trunk was filled with boots, creels, rods and lunch gear, including a folding table and three chairs, while the back seat was wholly occupied up to the bottom of the windows with everything from the watercolor equipment to changes of clothing and berry-picking baskets. He drove, I read the day's verses from the Bible, and Ruby read the explication of the text from *Science and Health*, first in English aloud, and then to herself in German, followed by silent prayer and meditation. This took about half an hour, by which time we were well shed of Missoula, halfway to going fishing, and fairly reeking of holiness.

On the first day, and whenever Ruby came along, we proceeded directly to the place where we would eat lunch and got Ruby settled. What with the stove, the table and chairs, the watercolors, the books, the crocheting gear and the berry baskets (which got no more use than the paints), this took a few minutes. That day we went to a little camping and picnicking spot called Spring Creek Campground which still exists by the side of Montana's state highway 93. The highway runs south, upstream, paralleling the Bitterroot River from the Clark Fork in Missoula to the headwaters of the East Fork of the Bitterroot at Sula, Montana. From there, it heads over the Lost Trail Pass to Salmon, Idaho. The campground is on the East Fork, just north (downriver) of the spot where Warm Springs Creek comes into the river. If you stop there this summer, I know you will like it, although I can no longer recommend the drive wholeheartedly.

In 1950, Montana 93 was the best highway I had ever seen. The Bitterroot valley was all good hay country, although the toll on the river from irrigation draw-down was significant between the towns of Darby and Hamilton, and still is today. Back then, before anyone lived in the valley who did not have business there, as they say, the road was lined with cattle fences, and the ranchers, almost to a man, ran purebred Herefords, the white-faced red cattle. Behind the fields, above the grazing stock, the very young and very rugged Bitterroot Mountains loomed over the west side of the valley—knife-edged, snow-capped even on this hot August morning. As we approached Conner and the campground, the mountains pinched in on the river, and the cattle and alfalfa disappeared, replaced by ponderosa pine and firs. It was travel-poster Montana, I suppose, but no less lovely for being so obvious an advertisement.

Once Ruby was settled, Gordon and I went fishing, right at the campground. The camping area sits on a gravel flat left when the East Fork takes advantage of the landscape and meanders, looping east, away from where in modern times the highway has cut a reasonably straight line up through the valley. People have a tendency not to fish at campgrounds on the assumption that any place so easily reached is soon fished out. I sometimes think that Gordon enjoyed fishing through the campground because it gave him the possibility of an audience for his evident skill. (The only other sign of vanity I ever noticed—and it was really just a way to tease someone—was the way he would towel his head dry out in the backyard after taking a shower. John Petersen, his good friend who lived next door, was as bald as a cue ball.) A few families were tent-camping and trailering at Spring Gulch, and one or two children were fishing with salmon eggs, in sight of their parents. I pitied the children that first morning because they were not fly-fishing.

We walked down to the lower end of the campground, where the river swings back to hit the edge of the highway. Short of asking you to imagine what it would be like to carry a six-gun and waltz along covering Wyatt Earp's back in Tombstone, I'm not sure I can explain just how important, how manly, a boy can feel when, clad in hip boots, a creel strapped over his shoulder and bouncing on his hip, carrying a genuine fly rod, he walks down to the river behind his uncle. I have crossed a lot of thresholds, but I don't recall taking bigger steps.

We were going to fish upstream, through the campground, and then have lunch. There is a simple reason why anglers like to move upstream, given the choice, and that is because the trout invariably face in the direction from which the current comes. This bit of information has exaggerated the importance of fishing upstream, of casting so that the floating fly lands above both angler and fish, but it has a kind of simple logic that keeps most of us from thinking the problem through.

Scientists have complicated theories about what exactly the world looks like to a trout, but the conventional wisdom is that trout are able to see all things at once, but only to the side, forward and above, not to the rear. Whatever a trout's vision is, it is more like a general scan of the world than ours is, more like a sweeping radar than a telescope. In 1950, the science of angling with the artificial fly (or the *Wissenschaft auf Angeln mit kunstlichen Fliegen*, as Ruby might think of it, if it was a day to keep up with German) was to fish upstream with the dry fly and then return downriver with a wet fly, and this had been the orthodox notion for nearly a century. What had not been thought through was the equally obvious truth that there is nothing so different between showing a trout a fly on top of the water and showing it a fly under the surface as to require that we fish up dry and down wet. The rules were divorced from reality, and to this day there are private fishing clubs whose local rules absolutely prohibit fishing downstream, as though it were an ethical issue.

So you understand my education in fly-fishing, I will tell you the flat truth that my uncle Gordon was not only a patient soul but as kind and generous a man as lived in Missoula, maybe anywhere. When it snowed he shoveled his walk and then the sidewalks (he lived on a corner lot, and this was no small chore) and then the neighbors' sidewalks and front walks and porches if necessary. Aunt Ruby, who never gave away anything in her life except at Christmas time (the furniture stashed in the house was just one example of her hoarding), was equally good-hearted, but she just didn't act on it as often. I say this so you will know that the way my uncle showed me how to fly-fish was not even conceivably mean-spirited and, I think now, was the best way to go about it.

"You start here," he said, "and I'll start up there, and we'll fish upstream until we get to the bridge." Just above the campground, and visible from any part of it, the highway bridge crosses over from the west to the east side of the river. The bridge is new and much improved since 1950, not quite so narrow as to make meeting an oncoming logging truck a nervous moment. Floods destroyed the old bridge and toppled many of the large conifers in the campground. Still, the river bends where it always did, cutting into its own east bank across from the campground, slowly chewing at the granite foundation of Coyote Peak. Rivers are very old, compared to lakes, and live much longer and stay in their course if you leave them be.

And so he left me, and walked up the bank to the next likely spot and waded out into the river and began to cast. Most fishermen— and Gordon was no exception, and neither am I, unless I am being unusually thoughtful—wade first and fish second. I watched him for a minute and then took my first step into the Bitterroot. I fell in. To be precise, I stumbled to my knees, which, because of the nature of hip boots and the depth of the water, meant I filled them both up. In the East Fork, as in most of western Montana's freestone tumbling rivers, you can seldom keep your footing against the current if you wade in as deep as your knees (standing) or your waist (kneeling accidentally). Wading out so far that your head would be underwater if you fell in was understood to be a bad idea. That is one reason that chest waders, in 1950, were regarded as death traps in Montana. They seemed not only likely to drown you if you went in over the top, but something of an affectation, like a too-big Stetson.

I am not a clumsy person, but I have fallen into as many trout rivers as most people have fished. I keep forgetting that water, although it is fluid, is incompressible, and you might as well be hit by a rolling oil barrel as by a swift-moving mountain stream. On days when I don't fall in, I usually trip over a root or a bit of abandoned barbed-wire fence on the way to the river, because, unlike the older generation of Montgomery boys, I never learned to pick up my feet. I wear chest waders now with a belt on the outside and carry a wading stick. Still, at least on purpose, I seldom wade in over my knees.

The one advantage to hip boots over waders is that you can get the water out without taking them off. That day, I went back to the bank, sat down, and raised first one foot and then the other to let each boot drain. No one showed me how to do that. Some of these minor techniques of fly-fishing come naturally, although learning by trial and error is inefficient.

I started upstream, wading carefully, feeling ahead with my upstream foot, waving my father's fly rod. The line and leader—all together I had no more than twenty feet out through the rod tip—had minds of their own and flopped on the water and caught on the bushes behind me. I stumbled in the current and backed out to the bank when it got too scary to wade. Sometimes the fly floated, and I watched it with pleasure; sometimes it sank or drifted along in a tangle of leader. I didn't so much as see a fish. If I hadn't been fishing, if it had been something equally frustrating like piano practice, I would have cried. But I wasn't the least bit miserable. It was obsessive fun. The sun came down on the water and the water sparkled, and I had a clear vision that I had lived to the advanced age of twelve years for the purpose of going fly-fishing with my uncle. Catching a trout was inevitable. The fish would be given to me, I thought, like all God's gifts, in good time—preferably before lunch.

When I got to the bridge (like almost all bridges in the world it had a deep pool underneath it), Gordon was across the river, on the opposite side from the campground, throwing a fly up into the shadows under the bridge. I could see that it was easy to wade across. The deep pool shallowed up quickly, and the river riffled over a gravel bar that began on my bank and shelved evenly across the river, nowhere more than a few inches deep. On the far bank, in summer's low water, the gravel stepped up into a beach twice as wide as the river. It was the first place all morning where I could imagine casting without catching the fly in the bushes and trees that closed in on the water below the bridge pool. And so I crossed, and sat on the sun-heated rocky ground and waited for my uncle to stop fishing. There was enough room in the pool below him that I could have fished, but I did not know whether that would be all right, so I waited.

I sat on that same gravel forty years later, and the pool looked exactly as I remembered it. Gordon was long dead, and I could only imagine him standing in the shallow water, the fly line unrolling before him, the end of the line and the leader and the fly disappearing into the shadow under the bridge. I do not remember whether he caught a fish there. In fact, I have no clear memory of seeing him actually land a trout, there or anywhere. We fished together, but apart.

As the river turns and drops into the pool under the bridge, the current favors the outside of the curve (water, like anything set in motion, tries to continue in the same direction) and the water pushes hard against the bridge abutment. For the first few feet at the head of the pool, the pressure is too great, and the resulting current too heavy, for a trout to hold there. But in summer's low water the tongue of the river pulls away from the bridge foundation, and a steady current with very shallow and gradually diminishing standing waves comes down the middle of the pool. As the pool widens, the waves subside into a barely visible roiling of the surface. Between this current and the concrete bridge abutment you will find one of those classic pieces of trout water—the soft water, the easy water just at the edge of the main current. This one, shaded by the bridge, was the best of all places to find a trout, because, given a choice, most trout will spend the hours of high sun either very deep or in shadow. If you go there, you will find a fish; I know it, I have done it recently. Everything along the Bitterroot valley has changed except the physics of running water.

Gordon stopped casting and waded out of the pool, saying, "Well, Brother, you can try it for a while." Fish were rising when he came, and he thought they would rise again "on the far bank, just below the bridge." He would go help Ruby get lunch started (lighting a

Coleman stove was a man's job), and I should come down pretty soon.

Even for me, it was possible to cast without tangling in the brush, so I did the other thing you do when you are small, which is let the fly drop too low on the backcast. It popped on the rocky bar behind me and came off. I did not notice this immediately, and for a few minutes I cast nothing but the leader. I went to lunch fishless, something that never happened again on the East Fork of the Bitterroot. In those days the only trout in the river were cutthroats, and they were and are a vulnerable fish.

After lunch (corned-beef sandwiches; Gordon had caught several fish from the campground section of the river, but we decided to save them for supper, "just in case"), Gordon and I drove up to Sula Meadows, where we fished for a few hours. It wasn't going to be dark for a long time, but the sun, even in August, disappeared quickly behind the steep hills west of the campground, and we would have to pack up Ruby and start home before the end of the afternoon. Ever since that day, I have spent most of my time fishing from midmorning to midafternoon. I have seen trout jump in the high sun and at dusk, and it is better in the light. It is true that fishing is best from sunset to pitch-dark, since it is an hour of increased movement, both of trout and of the aquatic insects they feed on. There is a changing of the guard underwater, a scurrying of nymphs as the daylight feeders retire and the nocturnal ones begin to roam. The fishing is better, but only if you have gone to the river solely to kill fish or take a large trout unawares. Fishing at dusk can be good for the ego and may even be necessary in warmed and heavily pounded water. But I do not do it. With the sun gone, I find myself fishing in my own darkness.

Sula Meadows is not a popular place to fish anymore. I will tell you how it was then, and what I learned about it, so that its memory will not disappear. Sula is a post office, a store with a gas station, and a private campground tucked in behind the store. We always called the ground about the river above the store "Sula Meadows," although, on a topographic map, it is properly "Ross's Hole," named for Alexander Ross, an official of the Hudson's Bay Company. (Sula was Ursula Thompson, reputedly the first white child born in the area.) Ross's Hole is the end of the line for the Bitterroot River, surrounded on the west by the steep and glaciated Bitterroot Mountains, on the east by the gentler Pintlar Range. Lewis and Clark, searching for a way through to the Pacific, winter camped in Ross's Hole. A Charles Russell painting shows Lewis and Clark meeting with their friends the Flathead Indians, sometimes called the Bitterroot Indians, in the snow-covered bowl where the mountains close in at the head of the river. (The painting hangs behind the speaker's chair in the Montana House of Representatives.) The Flatheads were the Montana branch of the larger Siwash nation, some of whom, on the coast of British Columbia, did practice a deliberate flattening of the fore head, binding the child's skull against a cedar board. The Hudson's Bay men, recognizing the linguistic kinship, named the ones near Missoula "Flatheads." Meriwether Lewis, who called them "our beloved Siwash," found them honest, generous and peaceable, a pleasant discovery after his encounters with the more hostile Indians of the Great Plains.

Ross's Hole is the only meadow on the East Fork of the Bitterroot—everywhere else the river tumbles precipitously from pool to pool, closed in by steep hillsides and sheer cliffs. But for about three miles as the river runs—just two on a straight line—the East Fork meanders through Sula Meadows with none of the haste or turbulence of an ordinary western Montana freestone creek. There, where we parked at the old farm-road wooden bridge in the meadow, it flowed quietly. It looped and straightened, looped again, cutting under first one bank and then the other on the outside of the curves. Barbed-wire fences came near to the river's bank, sometimes, where the water had cut the bank back, to the very edge. In many places the river was too deep to wade. You had to get out and make your way in the hay land. Moving up- or downriver meant climbing over or crawling under the same fence a dozen times a mile.

That first day, I stayed near the bridge. Gordon was headed upstream, around the bend, and I was supposed to fish from the bridge up and down, but no farther, he asked, than I could be seen from the bridge, so that he could find me when it was time to go. I'd have plenty of good fishing within sight of the bridge, he said.

In Ray Bergman's *Trout* (which I had been studying for days), as in all proper instructional books on trout fishing, a number of diagrams indicated where trout lived. In the East Fork at Sula, the places where trout should live seemed to be within my reach. The trout under the bridge by the campground were where the diagrams taught us they should be, but it had been an impossible task to throw a fly across the pool. Here in the meadows, I thought, were Genuine Ray Bergman Places Where Trout Lived, and in a river even narrower than the one-lane country road that had brought us the last mile. It was a boy-sized river.

In trout-book diagrams, the fish live at letters: there is a fish at A and another at B and a third at C. In very likely places or complicated ones, a trout may even be found at D, E and F. The first one I caught, not long after Gordon had disappeared behind some willows upstream, was not even at G. This first experience with the perversity of real trout, as opposed to Bergman trout, made me skeptical for years about what could be learned from book diagrams. Catching that fish was something like hitting a small jackpot the first time you put a coin in a slot machine—bad instruction in the unyielding law of binomial probability. It was not entirely my fault, because the illustrations in books are of ordinary trout, which for most authors means European brown trout, the fish on which the first authors practiced, the trout now found, sometimes to my sorrow, in most of North America.

My fish, which measured at least nine inches (the leather hinge of my new creel had an eight-inch rule printed on it), was a cutthroat trout, and although this fish is a close cousin of the more predictable

TROUT Book STyle Diagram

ART

and better-known rainbow trout, it is peculiarly adapted to small, tumbling mountain streams. If you look at rainbows and cutthroats in cross section (something that ought to be done in the imagination, as actual surgery is messy and the results inconclusive) you see a subtle difference. A cross section of an ordinary rainbow is symmetrical about both its horizontal and vertical axes—the oval of the cross section could be flopped or inverted without your noticing. But the cutthroat is slightly wider below the center line and noticeably flatter on the bottom curve of the oval than it is on the top. It is shaped, to be blunt about it, a little more like a sucker or a whitefish than a rainbow trout or an Atlantic salmon. This flattened curve across the belly has a function; the cutthroat can squeeze itself down a little closer to the bottom than other trout, and that puts it down at the point where the power of the running river is mitigated by friction. (For the same reason, but much more extremely, nymphs that live on rocks in rapid water are very flat, often four times as wide as they are deep.) My fish was living happily in the dead center of a riffle, not at *A* in the cushioned water in front of the rock, or *B* in the quiet current behind the rock, or *C* where the current slackened next to the deep bank. It was at nowhere, in the middle of featureless riffled water, exactly where it wanted to be.

If I had not lost so many flies in bushes and trees and broken so many off on gravel banks and snapped so many off from making the other usual mistake of beginning fly-casters—moving the rod forward before the line has straightened out behind, which makes a satisfying bull-whip "crack" as it breaks off the fly in midair—I might even have caught my first fly-rod trout on my own fly. Something usually happens to keep people from being able to make that boast. The fly the trout took was one of the half-dozen Gordon gave me at lunchtime after I confessed to being entirely bereft of flies. Unless we had a reason to try something else—a noticeable hatch of some particular insect, or the prediction of one—we fished with one or the other of two dry flies most of the time. We started with one of two and changed when it seemed like a good idea or when an identifiable fly started to hatch, whichever came first.

ART

One was the Adams. I didn't learn how to tie that pattern well enough to use my own until the second summer I fished with Gordon. The other, which I could tie, was an all-purpose thing that we called a hairwing. Sometimes we tied it with a tail, in which case it didn't represent any living thing, but still caught fish. Most of the time we tied it tailless in fairly large sizes—anglers' hook sizes 10 to 14. An insect (or an artificial) in sizes 10 to 14 corresponds roughly to the range of lengths of household cockroaches. Our hairwing, when tied without a tail, imitated the larger caddis flies and the smaller stone flies. The body was made out of clipped muskrat fur, which you stuck to the tying thread with beeswax and then wound around the shank of the hook. The wings were soft deer hair, if you wanted them to flare out and stand up, or else squirrel tail for a laid-back look. Deer hair is hollow, and when pinched down by the tying thread, tends to crimp and stand up off the hook. The hackles were either reddish brown or a grizzly speckled gray (Rhode Island Red and Plymouth Barred Rock, in chicken-growers' jargon). I usually mixed the hackle, spinning one brown feather around the head of the hook in one direction, and then spiraling the gray feather in the opposite direction. This covered up some of the sins of general clumsiness, and made a fly that floated well.

Professional tiers never, in my experience, spin hackles in opposite directions. Most of them stick to single-feather hackles (money saved on material and time saved in tying); and if they use two feathers, they spin them both at once in one direction (time equals money). A few modern fly patterns call for a mixed hackle, and the Adams is the best known of these. I got the brilliant and really quite successful idea for mixing the hackle on the hairwing the easy way: I got the directions for it and the Adams mixed up in my mind.

Before Gordon came back, fishing a wet fly downstream toward the bridge, I had caught three trout and lost four flies: one hung up in a willow across the stream, two snagged and broke off in the high hay behind me, and one just disappeared. I was having a perfectly happy time. My second trout was living at *C*—across the river and right next to the undercut bank. I caught it when I cast too far, which was a new mistake, and the fly hung up for a moment in the grass that drooped down to the water before it gently fell onto the surface. It was the best cast, for effect, that I made all day. It did not occur to me, considering that the trout were living right next to the bank, to go over on their side of the river and see what could be done about them from there or to pay serious attention to the bank on my side. I had a picture in my mind of how one fly-cast for trout, and it meant standing tall and casting far off, as the Montgomery boys did. That the river was only fifteen or twenty feet wide and that I was only about five-foot-two did not change the rules, only the dimensions.

We got back to Missoula before dark and cleaned trout on the back lawn. I knew how to clean fish, and gutted all of them. Gordon dealt with the details and hosed down the trout, leaving bright sparkles where the porch light shone on the green-black grass. I had been converted to a fly-caster. I had found out what fishing was supposed to be. From that day, all trout and all rivers would be compared to cutthroats and the East Fork. I thought then, and for many years, that if ever things went badly for me I could always return to Sula in August.

5

Trout Country

*Notes on the relative rarity
of suitable trout water,
considered as a biological and
geological phenomenon*

Although I did not know it when I was twelve—I didn't
know much—the East Fork of the Bitterroot River had
the character of ideal trout water. It is not (and never was)
the best fishing river in western Montana, although it is good, or the
most beautiful, although it is lovely. But it has another quality. It is—
and I wish I had a less pompous word for it—an *archetypal* stream,
the very essence of what running water has been since the beginning
of time and what running water is going to be when the next convul-
sion raises new Rocky Mountains. The East Fork begins on a moun-
taintop and flows to the Pacific Ocean, and it is the business of rivers
to bind the sky to the sea.

Its headwaters come from the west slope of the Pintlar Range, at
the very Continental Divide. From there it runs west and north, gathering in waters from the partly lovely, partly much-abused, Bitterroots. A raindrop falling on the East Fork's side of the divide will end
up, via the Clark Fork of the Columbia River, in the Pacific. And the
next drop from the same cloud falling a few feet south and east will
go via Pintlar Creek, the Big Hole, the Madison, the Missouri and the

Mississippi, and reach the Atlantic's Gulf of Mexico. It is proper for running water to begin as far from the ocean as possible, and you cannot get any farther from either ocean, measured along the river's run, than the Pintlar divide.

It is not an old river, for the Pintlars and the adjacent Sapphires and Bitterroots are young mountains, but it is older than any lake in Montana. Rivers are usually more ancient than lakes. They keep themselves young by scouring down their beds in flood, and they eventually bury the lakes below them in silt. Sula Meadows, where we fished, had been a lake once. It is a valley partially filled in with debris flows and rock slides, and looks, except for being so much larger, like the meadows of all Montana streams, although the smaller meadows are usually the work of beavers. The contours of the valley floor upstream from the Sula post office are too regular to have been formed by mere debris flows. At some time, the narrow pass—where the East Fork meets Camp Creek near Montana 93—may have been blocked by landslide or glacial debris. With a lake formed, there was time for sedge grasses and lilies to grow and decay and cover the gravel with the thin coat of level topsoil that made Sula Meadows good hay country, before and after the white men came. And long before that, the whole drainage of the Clark Fork was dammed by the Bull Lake glaciers, and the entire valley was a lake whose surface rose to nearly five thousand feet above modern sea level. In those days, if that were the last eon in which it was flooded, Sula Meadows would have been a bay at the farthest southwestern edge of glacial Bull Lake. The levelness of the meadow, exposed after the lake drained, allowed the East Fork to cut meanders through the hay bottom, keeping just enough channel open to slide on down toward Darby and the big Bitterroot.

When lakes die, and they always do, they leave rivers running through them after they have choked on their own detritus. Although even the shallowest lake will outlive generations of human beings, its relatively short life means it cannot have the biological intensity of running water. Very few lakes in all the world have produced unique species, and few have as many varieties of plants or animals living in them as a single mile of the East Fork, or any good river. There is too much sameness in a lake, and too little time, to fill all the possible evolutionary niches. Great and ancient lakes do have a few unique genera in them—Baikal in the Soviet Union and Nyasa in Africa come to mind—but most lakes do not. For the purpose of evolving unique new life, lakes are failures, evolutionary dead ends.

Fly-fishermen imitating winged adult insects on a lake usually carry one or two artificial midge flies (buzzing midges are a lakeshore specialty, as picnickers know), mosquito imitations, and copies of the commonest local lake-borne mayflies. After that, anglers must imitate baitfish with streamers or lacustrine amphipods with "shrimp" flies. They are reduced, in short, to fishing wet.

But in a mile of a good trout stream, you can rely on finding a dozen kinds of mayfly, another dozen of the net-spinning and free-living caddis, and several stone and salmon flies, dragon- and damselflies, dobson and alder flies, more kinds of midge than any lake will see, and a varied menu of mosquitoes. Running water also brings wayward terrestrial food along its entire length and, if it is not too broad, its entire width. Every trout living in running water has eaten ants, grasshoppers, caterpillars, beetles and crickets, food rare or unknown to the vast majority of lake-dwelling fish.

The world over, stream insects seem to have sprung up in the high, cold and rapid headwaters. The most primitive ones are found there still, along with their more complicated and specialized descendants. The primacy of cold mountain water is inferred from the distribution of mayflies, caddis flies and other forms of trout food. Warm and still waters have their own hundreds of species of mayfly and caddis, because both insects are marvelously adaptive. But of the larger grouping, by families within the orders (caddis are of the order Trichoptera—*tricos* = hair, *ptera* = wing—"with fuzzy wings") an interesting pattern develops. Of the twenty-two families of caddis in North America, every one is represented by genera and species in cool running water; twenty of the families have warm-stream members; only seven appear in lakes; and only three families have produced a species adapted to temporary ponds. The distribution of the more than eighteen hundred distinct species of caddis is roughly in the same proportion as the distribution of the families, the largest number are most widely found in cold trout water—both streams and mountain lakes. Many fewer species occupy warm or slow-moving water, temperate lakes or seasonally flooded ponds.

Much the same happens with the various types of stone fly and mayfly. Of approximately five hundred species of stone flies in ninety-two genera, only three or four live in lakes, and they are restricted to elevated, cold, large lakes that maintain high oxygen levels. The enormous variety of mayflies have representatives everywhere from high cold streams to muddy-bottomed rivers at sea level, but many families are found only in cold streams. Lake fishermen across America are familiar with the speckle-wing quill, the most widely distributed cold-lake mayfly, and all trout lakes have an abundance of one or two local species. But it is a river, and particularly a river with a variety of pools and riffles and gravel and mud and rock bottom, that shows you, in a single season, the authentic variety of the mayfly.

Compared to the insects of rivers, trout are newcomers. Like all freshwater fish, they arose in the oceans and have only lately adapted to running water. When the first trout in the world reached a river's headwaters, it found the river already stocked with flies. The sea origin is not forgotten in the racial memory of trout. Every landlocked trout has its seagoing cousins still, close relatives who spend time as temporary residents in sweet water—living in rivers as juveniles before going back to the sea, and again on their return as spawning adults. In the East Fork, the native trout is the green-hued, lightly spotted west-slope cutthroat, and there are sea-run cutthroats all along the Pacific Northwest coast. Rainbow and brown and brook trout all have tribes that run to the salt when they are big enough to compete for and profit from the richer foodstuff of the ocean. And as they age, river-locked trout behave more and more like their seagoing relations. They shift from a diet of insects to a diet of other fish, including their own young. They seek quiet, deep pools and cease fighting the current. All older trout are carnivores and have the teeth to prove it; the dentition of small trout is little more than a pleasing roughness to the touch. The brown trout gets more and sharper teeth and gets them sooner than rainbows and cutthroats: it has deeper urges to go to sea and forage on shoals of small fishes.

The adaptation of trout to their insect diet is at once compulsive and imperfect. Trout have no philosophy of insectivorianism. It is true that they will devote themselves fanatically to a single species of insect (all too often a very small one, and quite unlike any artificial insect you happen to have with you), but this is a matter of circumstance and convenience, of necessity combined with obsession. The real or artificial minnow is the best bait in the world for any trout big enough to swallow it, unless that trout, for that hour, has temporary and compulsive ideas about the superior nature of small mayflies. Trout are also imperfectly adapted to swimming in running water, which is not a criticism of the creation, but the beginning of insight into how to catch one, even in small and slow-moving meadow streams.

In lakes, trout live in schools like other fish. They move in concert, maintaining a spacing that pleases them, a distance of their own choice, not one dictated by currents or structures. It is like this also in the ocean, with the exception of those hours of the day when tidal currents sweep over bars and reefs and points of submerged land. In moving water, whether periodical as in the ocean or constant as in rivers, fish do seek those places where they are sheltered from the force of the flow. If they are hungry, they choose a place where there is a balance between the energy expended to resist the current and the energy acquired when that same current delivers them food. How much they need shelter depends on their efficiency as swimmers and predators. Tuna seem almost oblivious to tides, and so do salmon as long as they are in the deep ocean; but the fasting salmon, conserving energy in fresh water on its way to the spawning ground, soon adapts and becomes troutlike. I have seen salmon that were just out of the salt water playing in the stiffest currents like children holding their hand out the window of a moving automobile, apparently enjoying the rush of water against their fins. But after staying a few days or traveling a few miles upstream, they avoid the heavy water.

The partial evolution of trout from ocean-dwellers to riverine fish is apparent in their growth and ultimate size. As an absolute rule, all record fish come from lakes, where they can grow on a diet of plankton, crustaceans (the "scud" of fly-tiers), insect larvae and especially on other fish, all this without spending energy running the treadmill of flowing water. The effect of rapid growth and a diet of lake organisms on the eating quality of trout is also remarkable. Some river fish are good eating, but not all. People with a choice will put back stream-bred trout and go to the lake when the urge to kill and eat fish is irresistible.

Both anglers and scientists assumed for many years that large trout—the "Loch Leven" brown trout of Scotland and the "Kamloops" rainbows of British Columbia and Idaho, for two examples— were separate species, or at least different subspecies, from their smaller riverine relations. While that is possible, it is not necessary for some trout to be genetically different from others to grow to monstrously different proportions. One of the classic examples of environmentally controlled size is that of the giant trout of Lake Tahoe.

When the gold rush reached the High Sierra a little more than a century ago, a commercial net-fishery sprang up to supply the miners with enormous trout taken from Lake Tahoe and its outlet, the Truckee River (with no significant inlet streams, Tahoe's trout went downstream to spawn). This race of inland cutthroat trout was so remarkable in size that they were regarded as a unique genus. Damming the Truckee for sawmills reduced their breeding grounds and trapped the last spawning fish in a short reach between the lake and the first mill. If you want a clear example of how recent concern for endangered species is, how modern is the concept of fisheries management, reflect on the fact that the very last giant cutthroats were gill-netted out of Tahoe the year I was born, 1938. They were slaughtered, hung on poles, weighed, photographed and sold.

Today, we know that the Tahoe trout are the Lahontan cutthroat, a subspecies named after the extinct dry lake in Nevada that was once their home. Though presumed to be extinct, Tahoe's trout were found in tiny Independence, California, the headwater of the Little Truckee River. They were much smaller than the Tahoe fish, because Summit Lake is higher, colder and less productive. These little cutthroats were marked—heavily spotted, especially on the tail—like the missing Tahoe giants.

The state of California is trying to reestablish Lahontans, although not in Tahoe, where their niche in the lake is now filled by alien, planted rainbow trout and kokanee salmon and where the Truckee is unavailable for spawning because of a water-control dam at the lake's outlet. A dozen years ago, a transplant of hatchery-reared Lahontans to an artificial lake by North Tahoe's airport started out well. It was a new lake without competing trout, and the Lahontans grew to several pounds in weight in a few years, attracting fly-fishermen from all over California. But upstream was a vacation-home development and a golf course, and the golf course ponds were filled with bluegill sunfish. In one ordinary Sierra flood, some of the golf course bluegills were washed down into Lahontan Lake, and they subsequently overran it in the prolific manner of sunfish everywhere, outcompeting the trout for space and food. The same flood washed a few Lahontans over the reservoir dam into the stream below, a tributary of the Truckee already stocked with brown trout.

I may have caught the last surviving Lahontan in that stream. It was living happily a few hundred yards below the dam in a long, deep pool also occupied by a half-dozen brown trout. I have never had a clearer lesson in the vulnerability of cutthroat trout compared to their cousins the brown trout. Like most water coming out of a lake, the stream was very clear and cold, and you couldn't get within ten feet of the river without seeing brown trout scurrying to cover, either diving to the bottom or moving under the brush that lined the banks of the pool. The Lahontan cutthroat simply waited, poised at the seam where the fast water slid along the quiet water. It was this indifference to human contact that gave the fish its charm. You could scare it; I managed to do that the first day, slapping the water with a badly misjudged cast. But it was not inherently suspicious of mere movement, for it had spent its entire biological history, however many thousands of years, under the impression that large things that walked on the bank were deer or antelope or elk and could be tolerated up to a very close point. Brown trout, when they were transplanted to America in the late 1800s, came from rivers and lakes where fishermen had harassed them for centuries. Our imported browns, in a variation on Darwin's theme, were shaped by the principle of the survival of the wariest.

When the cutthroat turned to take a natural nymph that was rising up to the surface, I could see the black-spotted tail and the crimson slashes on the lower gill cover that give the species its common name. I went back to the vacation home where we—I and my wife and her entire extended family—were staying (it was on the edge of the golf course that built the ponds that stocked the bluegills that ruined the lake) and talked my brother-in-law Frank, who had just taken up fly-fishing, into coming down with me to the river below the lake. We parked at the end of the road by the gate to the Sanitary Landfill (sometimes I think I have spent too much time fishing in rivers next to dumps), climbed the fence and went down to the pool. Frank had caught fish on a fly, but not in places where everything was so perfectly organized for instruction. The water was clear, the light was aligned so that you could see the cutthroat without polarizing glasses (with them, the trout was as visible as a mouse on a pool table), and I suspected that this fish would be innocent enough to offer itself as a curricular example.

In that mood, I tied on the biggest, brushiest, ugliest fly I owned, gave the rod to Frank and told him to catch the fish. He did not, but he got the intellectual content of the lesson down perfectly. The trout flinched a little when the fly landed, and eased out into the current toward it (he had cast just a little short of the perfect line). The cutthroat tipped up by rotating its pectoral fins up and back. This lowered its tail and raised its head into the perfect attitude to give it a clear look up and forward. And it just drifted downstream tailfirst, matching the movement of the fly. Then it rotated its fins a little farther back, flicked its tail, planed up the current to the surface, opened its mouth and tried to eat the fly. All it got was some deer hair, which it spit out. And then it swam back up to its original lie, and the three of us, the instructor, the student and the lesson-object, repeated the process two more times. My brother-in-law had never seen such a performance—and many fishermen never do because they usually have to fish farther off and in darker water. Something, either the repeated casting or the recurrent mouthful of hair, put the fish off its feed, and it swam deliberately away from our side of the pool and disappeared into the shade under the far bank. The next day, I caught it on the first cast with a small artificial caddis, killed it, and ate it for lunch. I told myself that this trout was going nowhere except into someone's frying pan. I reminded myself that the survival of animal life is in the species, not in the individual. I argued silently that this particular fish was merely an artificial creation of the state of California. I still felt guilty.

It was not the rarity of the fish that disturbed my conscience. Field biology and fisheries-management science will produce more Lahontans to be stocked in more and better places than this insignificant outlet of a small flood-control dam. What I had done, I think, was ignore the sanctity of the river. It was a piece of water as artificial as the flies we floated on it, depending as it did entirely on the dam for a constant flow of cold water. (Not that I sneer at artificial things. The word was once a compliment, signifying the artifice of the maker.) But any running water, regardless of quality, is rare stuff. Flowing cold water suitable for trout is scarcer still. There was little physical similarity either in the stream or in the fish to my beloved East Fork or the west-slope cutthroats of my youth. But I should have seen the spiritual identity, if not the simple physical grace of a trout in trout water.

Of all the water on the face of the earth, less than one-half of one percent is in lakes and rivers. The rest is in oceans, in snowfields, or locked underground. And of all surface fresh water, most is in the lakes. At any time, less than one one-thousandth of one percent of the world's water is flowing, and much of that is warm or muddy. The amount of water suitable for trout is so small as to be all but unimaginable, so trivial that no one has attempted an accurate estimate of the percentage. The great rivers of the United States begin as trout water: whether you travel from Manhattan to the Adirondack source of the Hudson or from New Orleans to the Minnesota source of the Mississippi, you travel hundreds or thousands of miles before you reach trout country. Unless chilled by dams or replenished by spring flows, trout habitat ends within a few dozen miles of the source of rivers. Even man-made trout water, created by the outlet of dams, is precious. I should have let the trout be, not for itself, but for what it represented, for the grace it signified.

6

The Invention of
the Dry Fly and the
Artificial Nymph

*A commentary on the rise of the
modern industrial state and its
influence on trout fishing*

F ly-fishing as we know it today in all its complexity and
subtlety is inconceivable without running water. By fly-
fishing I mean, as it is so precisely defined in the Maine fish
and game laws, the "artificial fly, cast and retrieved in the customary
manner." It was not necessary to create the art of fly-fishing to catch
trout that live in lakes, though someone would surely have invented
a feathered lure, imitative of baitfish, that could be trolled behind a
moving boat—the clever streamer flies of Maine's lakes are famous
examples of that development in the history of the sport. But
streamer flies (their feathers, especially when wet, stream out behind
the hook) are really just more accurate, more lifelike, imitations of
baitfish no different in anything but materials from the plastic or
wood "plugs" cast with revolving-spool or fixed-spool tackle; the
lifestyle of trout (and landlocked salmon) in lakes is rather monotonous, and useful streamer flies are numbered in the tens. Useful dry,
wet and nymph patterns for riverine trout are counted by the hundreds, however, because the more complex ecology of running water
spurred anglers to perfect their sport by adding the artificial fly to

their armament centuries before the baitfish-imitating streamer was invented.

Fly-fishing came into being because there are times when nothing but an artificial fly will catch a stream-dwelling trout. Indeed, timing is the essence. Fly-fishing is about the task of using every hour of the angler's time on the river to the greatest advantage (or to none; such days happen to the best of fly-casters on the best of rivers, but we speak of happy possibilities always, when we speak of fishing). The first use of the artificial fly, and the dry fly in particular, was in streams. It later spread to still waters, not the reverse. It began with stream-locked trout and then was applied to sea-run fish, sea trout or salmon, after long experience with the year-round residents. The only exception to this rule, as far as I can tell from the literature, is the adaptation of minnow-imitating streamer flies, lures meant to be trolled behind a moving boat, to versions made especially to be "cast and retrieved in the ordinary manner." Both the trolling fly and the shorter, castable versions of it were an American contribution, one of the few that can be pointed out. British anglers invented artificial minnows by the hundreds, but they seem all to have been metal or wooden lures.

It is worth looking at the oldest-known record of fishing with the artificial fly, the often-quoted commentary of Aelian (A.D. 170–230) on the Macedonians. (The translation from the original Greek is by O. Lambert, *Angling Literature in England*, 1881, with slight alterations by William Radcliffe, *Fishing from the Earliest Times*, 1926.) In this account Aelian specifies that the Macedonians angle in high mountain streams for fish "with speckled skins." Aelian (and his readers) knew of the use of living insects as bait, but, he explained, that tactic would not work because of a natural fly "peculiar to the country."

"These flies," he writes, "do not escape the observations of the fish swimming below. When then the fish observes a fly on the surface, it swims quietly up, afraid to stir the water above, lest it should scare away its prey; then coming up by its shadow, it opens its mouth gently and gulps down the fly, like a wolf carrying off a sheep from the fold . . . ; having done this it goes below the rippling water." This is all very well understood by the Macedonians, Aelian continues, but, "though the fishermen know of this, they do not use these flies at all for bait for fish; for if a man's hand touch them, they lose their natural colour, their wings wither, and they become unfit food for the fish. For this reason they have nothing to do with them, hating them for their bad character; but they have planned a snare for the fish, and get the better of them by their fisherman's craft."

These Macedonian fish were, in modern jargon, "selective feeders," and when the natural flies were on the water the ancient anglers, as do modern fishermen, found their ordinary baits useless. And there is no doubt that they were trout. Aelian's "river called Astraeus" is the modern Aliákmon River, which rises in the central Píndos Mountains near the Albanian border and flows northeastward to Salonica. The Aliákmon has just thirty species of native fish, and the only surface-feeding spotted fish is the southern species of the brown trout, *Salmo trutta macrostigma*, with great black spots scattered along its lateral line. To catch this trout, Aelian explains:

> They fasten red [crimson red] wool round a hook, and fix onto the wool two feathers which grow under a cock's wattles, and which in colour are like wax. Their rod is six feet long and their line is the same length. Then they throw their snare, and the fish, attracted and maddened by the colour, comes straight at it, thinking from the pretty sight to get a dainty mouthful; when, however, it opens its jaws, it is caught by the hook and enjoys a bitter repast, a captive. (Translator's brackets.)

Not only is this the first record of fly-fishing, but it is almost certainly a record of dry-fly fishing with an old and not much used technique called "dapping," that is, bouncing or tapping the surface of the water with a natural or artificial fly. Note that the line is no longer than the rod, which would prevent any deep-swimming of an artificial fly and restrict the angler to fishing on, or just under, the surface film. The artful device was probably not very large (though the manufacture of very small hooks is modern, any society that can make a needle can make a fairly fine hook), and the fly's wing feathers were taken from where they grow smallest, from the very top of the cock's neck, under the wattles.

While Aelian's account is the oldest known record of fishing with a specific artificial fly, it may be deduced from his text that fly-fishing itself was not a Macedonian invention. Aelian mentions the specific red-bodied, pale-winged fly as "a Macedonian way of catching fish." He makes no point of emphasizing the uniqueness of fly-fishing itself. Elsewhere in his *Natural History,* Aelian gives a list of the accessory tackle used to fish with hooks (as opposed to nets or snares or spears), including what sounds like the ordinary stuff of any fly-tier's desk, beginning with dyed horsehair in various colors, and "the straight bristles of swine, and thread, and much copper and lead . . . and feathers, chiefly white, or black, or various[ly colored]. They use two wools, red and blue." It would go much too far to read everything into these haphazard notes from the third century A.D., but you could tie an awfully nice weighted nymph with a little lead wire around the hook, some boar's bristle, blue-dun wool segmented with a spiral of horsehair, and a few variously colored feathers. What strikes a modern angler the most, however, is the location of the Macedonian gambit: running water.

ART

While trout in lakes do rise selectively and obsessively to hatching and egg-laying insects, it is only on the stream that the angler is regularly driven to using flies, whether natural or artificial. The phenomenon of the hatch, of a truly generous outpouring of hatching aquatic insects, is one of the most obvious events in nature, comparable to a swarming of bees, a flocking of swallows, a migration of wildebeest. If you are fishing for trout when the hatch occurs, the consequences are unmistakable.

The Invention of The Dry Fly and the Artificial Nymph

. . .

One June day in 1989, I was spending a few days on the Big Hole River near the town of Wise River, Montana. Due to a drought, the main river was virtually closed to the taking of fish. (Montana had a terrible drought that year, and emergency regulations were begun and then carried forward into 1990 as "Centennial regulations," marking the beginning of the hundred-and-first year of Montana statehood.) I was staying in one-half of a duplex motel cabin, next to four anglers from Alabama who had never even heard of fly-fishing or of catch-and-release fishing. They came to the Big Hole by mistake. At the airport in Butte they had asked for directions to a trout river, and did not realize that they were ascending into the rarefied and sophisticated world of catch-and-release fishing amidst gentlemen anglers. Not to worry: the tributary of the Big Hole called Wise River was open to general angling, and they would get up every morning, take their spinning rods and small bass lures and locally purchased worms, and go up the Wise River and catch eating-sized trout. But this worked for them only until two in the afternoon, when the first hatches of mayflies started.

That someone should acquire wisdom on a river named Wise is an accident of history. The Big Hole was originally supposed to be named the Wisdom River, a name that survives in the largest town (two gas stations) on the river, Wisdom, Montana, and the Wise River is its diminished remnant. The Big Hole, the Beaverhead and the Ruby (the last named for the garnets in the local mountains) are the three major tributaries of the Jefferson River, and Lewis and Clark tried to name them after President Jefferson's major virtues: Wisdom, Philosophy and Philanthropy.

The drawling Alabamans were by far the best company of all the trout fishermen who stayed in the motel cabins and ate the dreadful food in the owner's barroom. They were so happy to be in Montana and catching fish that all the sophisticated angling talk and petty complaints about the quality of guides and superfluity of anglers did not stop them from trying to be sociable, trying to swap fishing stories. I realized, after a few hours, that I was the only one in the place willing to talk to four bait-fishermen.

I ran into them the next night, a few miles down the river in the village of Dewey, where the food was better, although the general conversation still revolved around very small dry flies (No. 16 Adams Irresistibles, to be precise). The four rebels were eating their trout for dinner—the owner of the Dewey barroom had cooked them at no charge—while all the fly-fishermen were dining on the only protein staple on the menu, T-bone steak. I remarked that it looked, from the evidence on their plates, as if they had had another good day.

Well, they had a good morning, they agreed. And then one of them said, "I think we saw what you call your 'hatch.' Is that when all them little bugs come down the water?" I said that's just what it was. "Well," he said, "that sure put an end to our fishing. Trout were jumping all over the place and we couldn't touch one after all them bugs started." So, two thousand years later, the five of us found ourselves discussing what may be called "the Macedonian complaint."

I saw them again the next morning, when we were all packing up to leave the small comforts of Wise River. I was headed up the river and over the Lost Trail Pass to the East Fork of the Bitterroot, to see how things were going there. They were bound for Butte, to turn in their rent-a-wreck and fly back to Alabama. They were taking each other's pictures, and I took one of all four of them lined up in front of the cabin, under the elk antlers. I asked if they were coming back sometime, and they said next year, and one of them asked me if it was hard to learn how to fly-fish—how did you do it?

"It's just like learning to play golf," I said. "You need some equipment and some lessons and a place to play. It's just no mystery at all to learn." Not being very philosophical at eight in the morning, I didn't add that all the mystery started *after* you learned how.

The refinements of fly-fishing all spring from the Alabamans' problem, the Macedonian dilemma: there are times when nothing but an artificial fly catches trout. The elevated, aesthetic, artful purpose of fly-fishing was in the beginning simply to kill trout; it was an adjunct to existing methods of angling, not more difficult, sporting or

genteel than worms, minnows and maggots. The ancient writers—
Walton, Cotton, and Richard Bowlker—give descriptions of how to
maintain a steady supply of maggots, or how to find and keep the
best varieties of worms, that are clearer and more detailed than anything they write about artificial flies. Walton, in particular, has a
countryman's unmistakable, almost sensuous, pleasure in the art of
keeping maggots (known as "gentles") on hand for those months of
the year when fly-blown carcasses were not easily found in the gut-
ters and byways:

> . . . if you desire to keep gentles to fish with all the year, then get
> a dead cat or a kite [a kitten?], and let it be fly-blown; and when
> the gentles begin to be alive and to stir, then bury it and them in soft
> moist earth, but as free from frost as you can, and these you may
> dig up at any time when you intend to use them: these will last till
> March. . . .

Bowlker's *Art of Angling* (the first edition written by Richard
Bowlker, the subsequent ones by his son Charles) has the distinction
of being the second most oft-printed book on the subject, failing only
by inferior literary reputation from surpassing Walton's *The Compleat
Angler* in number of editions. There is a certain refinement to every
detail in Bowlker, who published nearly one hundred years after
Walton (Richard Bowlker in 1747, Walton in 1653), a sophistication
that reflects not only a century of progress in angling techniques, but
a century of increased wealth and industrialization. No longer is the
avid fisherman sent out to find a dead cat and bury it. Bowlker is a
consumer, not a scavenger. The things he uses can be purchased;
they are the products or by-products of commerce and industry:

> For this purpose you are to get a beef's liver, lights, lungs, or a
> sheep's head, but livers are the best; after it is scored with a knife,
> hang it up and cover it [with a cloth], but not too close, for the flies
> will blow it better covered than hanging in the open air . . . take
> down the liver and put it into a barrel, box, or large earthen pot,
> and there let it remain till you think the Maggots [even the euphe-

mism "gentles" has disappeared over the century since Walton] are
of full growth; then take a sufficient quantity of bran [the hulls of
milled grain], in proportion to the largeness of the liver, and throw
it into them, and in three or four days the first brood of them will
come out of the liver into the bran, and there scour themselves;
then, in three or four days more, take a stick and run through the
liver, and hang it across the barrel or pot, when the latter brood will
soon drop out into the bran, and scour themselves fit for use. If you
are willing to preserve Maggots all the winter, you must get two or
three livers about the beginning of November . . . these are to be
managed in the same manner as the other, only kept somewhat
warmer till they come to their full growth, and then throw in a
good quantity of bran, which will preserve them from the frost in
the winter, keeping them in a cellar or some dampish place in the
barrel or box they were bred in; thus you may keep them till the
end of February, and use them any time at your pleasure.

With one small change, this exact method was in use in Missoula
when I was a boy. The local maggot growers had to get started in
October; by November, carrion flies get scarce in Montana. I never
met a man fishing for trout with maggots. It was a bait reserved for
the winter whitefish season, when old men fished the Bitterroot
through natural openings in the ice where the constricted current
kept some water open, usually below bridges. Whitefish are bottom
feeders by the look of their rubbery lips and down-turned mouths,
although in summer they are avid eaters of natural and artificial flies,
much to the dismay of trout anglers who have not learned to tell the
difference between the splashy way a whitefish rises and takes the
bait and the more purposeful and efficient rise of a trout. (The rise-
form, the characteristic splash, of a whitefish is distinctive. It is long
and oval, quite unlike the round hole left by a gulping or sipping
trout. One of the less offensive nicknames for a whitefish is "stiffy,"
which somehow captures the elongated rise, something that would
be made by dropping a stick, as opposed to a pebble, on the water.)
Whitefish were supposed to taste better in the winter, either fresh or
smoked, and the maggot-men who sought them used small wet flies
in bright colors with a maggot impaled on the hook.

However disagreeable was the art of keeping bait, the most effete anglers showed no real preference for fly-fishing until the Victorian era in Britain, or until after the American Civil War. Even the most artificial (that is, cleverly made) fly was understood by the old writers to be a specific lure for a particular moment. The ancient and universal example is the Blue Dun—the most famous fly in the history of angling. There is nothing quite as rare in nature as a true blue-dun feather—blue-gray with brown highlights—and the production of a neck of blue-dun feathers has been the object of both chicken breeders and kitchen alchemists. One reason for its scarcity is that the pigment blue is unknown in any bird. The blue color we see is refracted light, not inherent color. It is an illusion, like much in fly-fishing.

The natural fly imitated by the Blue Dun is one of the earliest important mayflies of the year in Britain, coming off the water as early as March. That it is a mayfly (in American terms) is clear from Bowlker's description:

> As he swims down the water his wings stand upright on his back; his tail forked, and of the same color as his wings. He appears on the water about ten o'clock in the forenoon, and continues till about three in the afternoon, but the principal time of day is from twelve till two; the flies then come down in great quantities. . . .

A Montana version of the Blue Dun—a natural fly that could be imitated with a dry fly made with wings and tail of dark blue-dun chicken feathers, tied in a mayfly shape—had poured down the river at the party of Alabama bait-fishermen. It was the mayfly called the blue-winged olive—a darker version of the British insect imitated by the Blue Dun fly—that they watched float by and ruin their fishing. The original Blue Dun, by the way, had a hint of yellow mohair in its mingled gray and tan fox-fur body, which is not a bad idea for any of the Blue-Winged Olives, although they are usually tied with simple gray muskrat-fur bodies. The ultimate and best fur for Blue Duns and Blue-Winged Olives is clipped from near the urine-stained private parts of the male or female fox. Yellow mohair creates the same effect when mixed with untainted parts of the animal's pelt. Some tiers use yellow silk thread as the core around which the muskrat or mole fur is spun, and if the fur is applied sparsely, the yellow tying thread shows through and gives the desired effect.

I suspect that if you could have raised some eighteenth century angler from his sleep and handed him any darkish modern Blue Dun fly you could find, he would have managed to take a few fish out of the Wise River during the hatch that confounded my Alabamans, even if he were forced to angle with a hickory rod and six feet of horsehair line tied directly to the tip-top. But, unlike modern anglers, who are devoutly either fly-fishers or ordinary bait-and-lure men but seldom both, the old ones would not have wasted half their day. Bowlker's advice on the Blue Dun fly is very clear, and the men from Alabama followed the first half of it exactly: "Your morning's fishing, till the flies come on, should be with the worm or minnow." While waiting for the hatch, and the opportunity to fish with dry flies, expert fly-casters will fish during the morning with an artificial nymph, which is progress in cleanliness, if not in angling sophistication.

The old English flies were intended to be fished just in or just under the surface film of the river water. We call the old patterns "wet" flies, but we miss the point if our only purpose is to distinguish them from the high-floating dry fly, which did not come into use until around the middle of the nineteenth century. That the ancients usually fished with flies on or near the surface is obvious from the nature of the tackle—lines little longer than the rod—and from the advice to the beginner that he must make sure that the fly lands on the water before the line. You can close your eyes, after reading the careful instructions in Bowlker, and see the ancients reaching out with the rod, dapping the fly down on the surface. Also, the old authors describe the trout biting the fly, an action they expected to see because it took place high in the water, if not on the surface itself, and near at hand. Charles Cotton, who added the useful fly-fishing information to later editions of *The Compleat Angler,* is perfectly clear about the nature of "Fly-fishing, or fishing at the top." It certainly was not dry-fly fishing as we know it today, but neither did it resemble the kind of nymph-and-streamer dredging expeditions that characterize modern sunken-fly fishing. Until the twentieth century, there was no such thing as a weighted fly or a fly line deliberately meant to sink well below the surface. That the ancients were fishing in or just below the film is also clear from the description of hooking the trout. When Cotton's pupil pulls the fly away from a fish, the master says: "Why now, let me tell you, you lost that fish by your own fault, and through your own eagerness and haste; for you are never to offer to strike a good fish, if he do not strike himself, till first you see him turn his head after he has taken your fly. . . ."

They still fish so in Britain, with flies just below the surface, and you will meet British anglers who insist that what they are doing is dry-fly fishing. On the Derwent River, at the great Cavendish estate of Chatsworth, I watched a gentleman fishing upstream through a riffle that headed a deep pool shaded by an oak. He was casting constantly, short throws directly across the current, and dragging the fly with a tight line. He was, he told me a few minutes later, dry-fly fishing, and had two brace of trout (that is, four) and a brace of grayling in his creel, all taken on the dry fly. I told him I had been fishing with the nymph and had done almost as well. He said, firmly, that "nymph-fishing was too clever for me." There was an odd dactylic accent on the words "too clever." He spoke with just the metric beat that we might use to say that someone was "too clever by half."

We sat on one of the benches ubiquitous along the banks of British streams, and he offered to give me one of his best local dry flies, a Badger and Ginger. It was a small two-toned fly. The body was dark peacock herl, and the front half of the fly was pale palmered hackle, the back half a bright, gingery red. To "palmer" means to wind a feather along a hook so that its individual fibers stick out like a miniature bottle-brush. (Badger hackle does not come from badgers. It is plucked off chickens with two-toned feathers—a dark tan next to the central rib of the feather, a creamy yellow at the outside edge—the two colors resembling those of a good badger-hair shaving brush. The chicken source is the Wyandotte, or one of several unclassified breeds of gamecocks. Ginger is a reddish-yellow, quite bright color common to gamecocks and to the wild jungle fowl that in temperate climates populate zoological gardens.) I gave him a Western-style caddis fly imitation, after he said that the river often had good hatches of "sedges." It should work perfectly for him, even if he fishes it "wet" by my standards, "dry" by his, because many female caddis flies come back to the river and swim down into the water to lay their eggs. I dropped his Badger and Ginger in a glass of water at the hotel that evening, and it sank like a stone.

(*ic aracford*)

ART

P almer," whether noun or verb, is a nice British word that has no resonance in American English, and is only used in the United States by fly-tiers. It is about as obscure in its transference to angling argot as any word in English. Palmers were pilgrims to the Holy Land, who carried palm fronds as souvenirs, as proof they had been to Jerusalem. Spring was the beginning of the pilgrimage season, so noted in the General Prologue to Chaucer's *Canterbury Tales:*

The Invention of The Dry Fly and the Artificial Nymph

> Thanne longen folk to goon on pilgrimages,
> And palmeres for to seeken straunge strondes.

From the idea of pilgrimage, of wandering, the British began to call the various ambulating hairy caterpillars "palmer-worms." In America, we call the mobile hairy caterpillar that plagues our deciduous trees a gypsy moth with the same idea in mind. The original palmer flies were deliberate imitations of caterpillars. Many good, even great, trout and salmon flies are "palmered," whether or not the tier is the least bit interested in imitating a caterpillar. The fine feather fibers that stick out when the hackle feather is wound spirally around the hook add that quality of movement and light-refraction that characterizes all great trout flies, whether wet, dry or nymph. Fishermen over the age of forty will remember that there was once a great movement to use various plastic materials for fly-tying, particularly for the wings of dry flies and the bodies of nymphs. Clear, rubbery, "natural-looking" vinyl was touted as the ultimate imitation of the chitinous exterior of semitranslucent insects. The fad lasted until they ran out of suckers, and I don't mean fish. The purpose of the artificial fly is to create the illusion of life, not the imitation of it.

Any discussion of nuances in dry-fly fishing would have meant nothing to my companion on the Derwent. To him, as to Cotton, who had fished the same river three hundred years earlier, it simply meant fishing on top.

A consistent theme through all the angling authors before the 1880s is that the artificial fly worked best on overcast, windy days. It still does, by the way, although the great advances in dry-fly- and nymph-tying somewhat mitigate the effects of glassy surfaces and bright sun. The general explanation of why one had greater success in such weather was that it drowned many natural flies while they were trying to hatch, and the artificial sunken fly—in or below the film—was a fair representation of nature at that moment. That is probably true, but the motivation of trout is not entirely determined by any one factor. Trout are like people. A friend of mine who combines interests in human psychology and fly-fishing says that the behavior of both fish and people "has multiple causes and is overdetermined." Whether you are fishing wets, drys, streamers or sunken nymphs, the hours with cloud cover and a breeze will average out to being better times than high sun and calm. A riffle on the water, whether generated by the stream or by the wind, obscures the leader and the hook and activates the feathers of surface and sunken flies. For the hours of glassy calm, more delicate, high-floating, flies were developed.

The Industrial Revolution spurred the development of the true dry fly in Britain. The growth of factory cities and the sprawl of urban marketplaces and suburbs polluted streams like the Thames above London, once a famous trout and salmon river. At the same time, railroad transportation made distant waters accessible. For most of the population, angling ceased to be a near-home activity. And the wealth of Britain, though badly apportioned between capital and labor, created that peculiar institution called "vacation" for managers and owners. Such leisure time for the upper classes is a phenomenon of early industrial growth. What had been a backyard entertainment for the masses became the focus of travel for the relatively wealthy, and in the jargon of travel agents, trout rivers became "destination resorts." The angler (or poacher) lucky enough to live by a river can pick his day and wait for the dark and windy hour. The London stockbroker, headed for leased trout water in Hampshire or Derbyshire, cannot promise himself the weather needed to fish his Badger and Ginger palmer fly just under the surface. Gentlemen anglers were no different then from what they are now. And like the young professionals of today, the anglers of the last half of the nineteenth century wanted it all, and they wanted it that very day.

The dry fly became popular on the chalk streams of Hampshire because it took fish on calm, bright days. The British have never gotten very good at tying flies that float well. Their chalk streams move slowly and have none of the bright riffles and standing waves of a good Montana or Adirondack trout river, and their flies are as effete as the mowed lawns that edge the Itchen and much of the Test. I stopped in Hardy's Venerable Tackle Shop on Pall Mall in London and looked at their dry flies. Without exception, they were tied with unimpressive soft hackle feathers and floppy wings. They were really wet flies made to stand up and float, not floating flies, and they looked very much like the models in any 1930s American trout-fishing manual. Clipped deer-hair bodies, for instance, would have been as out of place in a Hardy's fly drawer as someone actually wading in the Test or the Itchen. One crosses a British chalk stream on the numerous footbridges, or else one stays where one belongs, on the bank where your fishing ticket is valid. Prohibitions on wading are not silly on a small, slow-moving stream. It is not nice to scare fish, to stir up the mucky mud of the streambed, to trample the watercress maturing toward tea-time sandwichhood.

The pressure on Hampshire rivers to produce trout for visiting anglers to kill and to take home led directly to the invention and near-perfection of the dry fly, so as to increase the number of opportune days in a vacation. The cleverness of the new technique and the increased number of successful anglers then led to that curse of angling everywhere: the artificial hatching and rearing of catchable trout. Just as the Industrial Revolution made vacations possible, so it made the art of fish-rearing practical as a supplement to natural reproduction and growth in the destination rivers. Raising fish in hatchery conditions requires everything from chemical disinfectants to manufactured fish food, and most of all it requires the mentality of a factory manager to operate the rearing ponds. By the beginning of this century, angling in Britain and the eastern United States was a closed and complete system: a man whose wealth and leisure depended on manufacture or trade rode a mechanical conveyance to a river filled with trout produced by that combination of science and craft we call technology. It was an odd, even sad, coincidence: humankind, in the same century, developed the accurate imitation of the natural fly and then used it to catch artificially raised imitations of the true and wild trout.

Certainly, the first style of dry-fly fishing was simply to use the winged wet flies and the unwinged palmered flies on the top—that is, fishing the fly dry, as opposed to fishing with a fly made to float, to stay dry. The writers of the midnineteenth century understood that fishing dry extended the reach—the killing power—of a man who had already paid dearly for the rights to fish. He had not only invested his time and expenses for travel and lodging, but paid a substantial fee (or joined a club with expensive annual dues) for the right to fish. Virtually all trout fishing in Britain is on private water and has been for centuries; so it is with hunting. You may remember that the basic fight between Robin Hood and the Sheriff of Nottingham was over who owned the deer in Sherwood Forest. Under Norman forest law, imposed after 1066, fish and game belonged to the sovereign, and the right to take them was doled out, sparingly, to the king's friends and relations. Even with parliamentary democracy, landowners retain the once-royal prerogatives. Anglers who have purchased or rented fishing rights cannot be denied their several brace of trout.

D ouble-named Francis Francis published his *Book on Angling* in 1867, just at the time when fishing with an ordinary artificial fly *in* the surface water was about to turn into the art of fishing a specially made dry fly *on* the surface. Francis was not a dry-fly purist, and neither was anyone else in his day. His most quoted sentence explains much about the age, and I draw the reader's attention with italics to Francis's metaphor of angling expertise: "The judicious and perfect application of dry, wet, and mid water fly fishing *stamps the finished fly fisher with the hall mark of efficiency.*" In just three hundred years, we have come an enormous distance from Walton's Venator and Piscator, from his milkmaids' songs and lavender-scented sheets.

On many waters in Britain, from the late nineteenth century until after World War I, anglers were required, either by river-keepers' rule or by club regulation or by the equally powerful coercion of social approval, to fish only with the dry fly. In addition, they were required to cast it upstream. The British reason for upstream fishing had nothing to do with the fact that most of the time that is the best way to cast a dry fly. By limiting anglers to upstream fishing, the keepers were assuring that the angler could approach the fish closely enough to determine its size. The British had, and still have, very little faith in the recuperative power of trout. They thought a caught fish was a dead fish whether you released it or not. Upstream fishing made it easier to limit angling to casts over fish that met the water's minimum size for killing. Also, especially on the smooth waters of Hampshire chalk streams, catching and releasing a small fish would tend to frighten the preferred victims, to "put them down," as fishermen say.

When the art of fishing with the artificial nymph was invented, it was slow in being adopted on club waters, even though the ancient and honorable rule of dry-fly-only was then less than fifty years old. Fortunately for the success of nymph-fishing, the artificial nymph can be, and often should be, cast upstream to a rising fish, just as if it were a noble dry fly. Soon the pressure to use this new and deadly technique became too great to resist, and the British took a tack which they usually associate with less forthright cultures: they called the artificial nymph, although it usually is sunk down several inches under the surface, a "dry fly." It is still against social and contractual rules to fish downstream on the Test and Itchen, but the nymph is now the choice of guides and club anglers, exactly because it, too, is stamped with the hallmark of efficiency.

Casting the wet fly (by which I mean patterns recognizable as traditional wet flies) upstream and letting it drift down naturally with the current (the "dead-drift" of angler's speech) was the first step in the development of nymph-fishing. This was the subject of the seminal work by G. E. M. Skues, *Minor Tactics of the Chalk Stream*, published in 1910. It was well into the twentieth century before flies were commonly made so as to resemble actual nymphs. In the modern exact imitations, wings are dispensed with (sometimes replaced with short pads that represented the folded-up and encased wing of the adult-to-be), bodies are tapered to match the shape of the natural, and hackle is limited to the merest suggestion of legs, breathing tubes or external gills. A few whisks of fibers, rather than the small bunched tails of traditional wet flies, represent the short tails characteristic of most nymphs. Skues began this work of exact imitation, summed up in his *Nymph Fishing for Chalk Stream Trout* (1939). It was further perfected by a professional angler, Frank Sawyer, a full-time river-keeper, who was in search of a fly that would work when a customer absolutely needed to catch a fish. His book *Nymphs and the Trout* (1952) modestly documents his own inventions and describes the trials of a man trying to improve fishing success for his clients while obeying the moral order imposed by dry-fly fanatics.

The transition from wet fly to nymph was due not entirely to individual inventions like Skues's and Sawyer's, important as they are, but also to subtle and continuous modifications of the old wet-fly patterns, including alterations made by that great modifier of flies, the dentition of a brown trout. A well-chewed wet fly soon becomes more formless, more nymphlike. The great popularity of one of the oldest wet flies known to the angling literature, the Hare's Ear, was its very simplicity, and when sparsely tied with small wings it is still a fair imitation of an emerging mayfly nymph. It is now always tied with gold tinsel spiraled through the hare's fur, making it the Gold-Ribbed Hare's Ear of commerce, and it is usually tied without wings, as a nymph. But nothing has improved on the raw material it was made from historically—the short, bristly hair from the mask (the face, not the ears) of a proper British hare. My friend Tom Rosenbauer, who labors for the Orvis fishing tackle company, uses hare's mask fur to make a very modern "emerger" for the Battenkill River's Hendrickson hatch. An emerger is a representation of the most ephemeral moment in a mayfly's life, just as it splits its pupal skin in the surface film and begins to crawl out as a matured mayfly. It is at this point in its life—struggling, half-formed, all knees and elbows—

that trout most like to eat the mayfly. It would not be unkind, or demeaning to Rosenbauer's skill, to say that his "emerger" rather closely resembles a well-masticated wet fly.

The old wet-fly patterns, consisting of a ribbed wool or fur body, a pair of wings tied parallel to the shank of the hook, and a wrapping of soft hen-hackle fibers just behind the eye of the hook, are hardly outdated. The process of emerging, the act of achieving full-blown fly-ness, is a continuum that covers all stages from pure streamlined nymph to, one supposes, a fly with one wing fully extended and the other still half-trapped in the pupal shuck. The old wet patterns serve well as emergers, provided that when they are used there are natural emerging flies struggling to the surface. For all the new patterns that have been invented, the old Dark Hendrickson wet fly will still take trout, even in the Battenkill.

Young, scientific and well-read fly-tiers stick with the standard wet fly on occasion. As I write, I have before me artificials representing three life stages of the western green drake (very comparable to the British mayfly or green drake of Duffer's Fortnight in size, shape and color) tied by Tony Hill of Alsea, Oregon. His nymph is biologically sound, a classic exact imitation of the nymph as it might have been tied by G. E. M. Skues or Frank Sawyer, or as it has been tied more recently by Ernest Schweibert, author of *Trout* in two exhaustive volumes. Tony's dry flies come in two forms, a bushy, hairwinged pattern for fast and riffly water, and a beautiful adaptation of the delicate thorax style popularized by Doug Swisher and Carl Richards (authors of *Selective Trout*), this latter form to be used on still pools and back-eddies. In short, Tony Hill's nymphs and dries are state-of-the-art, post-modern and informed by biology. But his emerging Green

ART

Drake, which he recommends using even during the height of the hatch should the trout refuse either of his dry patterns, is simply a sparse, well-tied and old-fashioned wet fly—a green-tinted Dark Hendrickson. In the last decade of the twentieth century, Hill is tying, fishing and selling a fly that Juliana Berners would have recognized and listed in 1496, that Charles Cotton would have sat and tied at stream-side for the education of hapless Venator in the 1670s. What more can you ask from a sport than that it should survive unchanged over time? Well, almost unchanged. There will always be such temporary aberrations as rules requiring the dry fly, or such silly amendments as calling a nymph a dry fly.

I have fished the Test and the Itchen and played the game of upstream casting to the rising fish. It is a pointless rule now, although cherished as tradition to the point of absurdity. The fish in those rivers are much the same size, all products of fish-culture, raised to the proper heft to impress the vacationing executives who make up most of the clientele. Only a few are wild trout, identifiable by their small size, bright color and extreme agitation. The stocked-out fish you cast to so religiously weigh at least a pound and a half, usually more, and are fat as pigs, as full of fight as you would expect considering that they are nearly terminally obese. Still, to preserve the illusion that one is in search of a proper fish, one casts upstream to visible fish. Like all stocked trout, they are as likely to be in a silly holding spot as a natural one, and fishing blind on the great flat runs of the rivers would be as efficient as any other method.

This can be easily proved. After you have sighted a fish and cast to it properly, you are allowed to continue the drift of the nymph long past the point where your alleged target has been feeding, and you are permitted to hook the next trout downstream when your fly finally arrives in his lair.

Once, when Robin Gow, my instructor and good companion on the Test, was otherwise occupied (feeding a soft drink to a visiting pony), I took one trout by deliberately fishing downstream with a nymph. The trout was about a foot under the water and no more than five feet downstream from the spot where I stood on the bank. Three pounds if he was an ounce, and we took his picture on the bank before putting him back (it was a male, judging by the shape of the underjaw). I had to reel part of the leader back into the guides on the rod to make my equipment short enough to put a nymph in front of his nose; I had to recreate a Macedonian's rig. I used one of the nettle plants on the bank to shield myself from the fish's uninterested vision. Izaak Walton and every author before this century would have approved of the whole procedure, just because it was so devious. (In the year just past, it has come to my attention that this technique is now taught by such famous instructors in fly-fishing as Dave Whitlock, author, illustrator and adviser to the L. L. Bean mail-order company. I have been told it is properly called "The Short-Line Nymph Technique." Fly-fishing is all pretense, and some of it is pretension.)

The rivers of Hampshire are very beautiful, and worth a trip if you are already in England. They do not offer easy fishing, and if the trout turn to sipping tiny flies, it can be frustrating fishing. But it is not altogether real and not at all natural. A river where the occasional wild trout is easily differentiated from the stocked fish is not the place for me. I would rather use The Short-Line Worm Technique for the native trout of Wise River, hip by thigh with my friends from Alabama. The angler who cannot use his tackle to connect with wildness has little to remember from his day on the water.

7

The Household
Science of Trout

*A discussion of the effect of
moving water on the behavior
of trout and anglers*

In manuals of trout fishing, running water is usually regarded as a problem for the angler to overcome. And while it is true that flowing rivers create difficulties for the fly-caster, these are trivial compared to the problems faced by the trout. We think of rivers and streams as the natural environment of trout and presume that they have the advantage over us, but that is not true. All fish, so far as we know, evolved in the ocean and only lately (in geologic time) began to occupy the rivers of the world. Trout are not perfectly adapted; they are successful river dwellers, but they are made vulnerable by running water, even by gently flowing British chalk streams and their American counterparts, the spring creeks of Pennsylvania and the foothills of the Rocky Mountains. The craft of fly-fishing preys on their weaknesses; we anglers depend on the river to make trout available to us. Even in English rivers where one is obliged to cast only to rising fish, or visible fish lurking underwater, the trout are not randomly scattered over the waterscape.

Trout that have moved out of the ocean into running water are exiles and lead desperate lives. When Ishmael was sent into the wilderness, his curse was this: "His hand will be against every man, and every man's hand against him." So it is with all river trout. They live amicably with their neighbors in lakes, and we know that they school familiarly in the open ocean. They are different animals in the river, where every trout competes against all the others for the limited places where life is possible.

The main problem is their strength. Trout, to put it bluntly, are not very good swimmers. Their endurance is minimal, their speed is greatly overestimated by the awe-struck angler. Put them in moving water, and they are at such a disadvantage that fly-fishing is not only possible but lethal. Just as rivers sort their substrates—rocks here, gravel there, and sand farther on down—so the rush of water sorts the animate fish and places them where they can be found.

In Japan, where nature has been closely observed by artists and poets for centuries, the symbol of fortitude and strength is the carp. In America, we are not used to thinking of goldfish as heroic, having spent too many years looking at them in the tanks at the back of five-and-dime stores. But on Boy's Day in Japan families hang the wind-sock banners of carp on the boys' houses to tell the world that they have sons and to remind sons that they have a world to face. Japanese artists paint carp leaping waterfalls and breasting currents as they struggle upriver. In short, the carp of Japan is the indomitable leaping salmon of the Western world. Pacific salmon struggle upstream in northernmost Japan, but they are not held in the same esteem as the valiant carp, possibly because the provinces of Aomori and Hokkaido became integrated into the empire only in the late nineteenth century.

When a researcher decided to measure the endurance of fish, he picked a rainbow trout as the primary test object for the usual economic reason—there is financial support for game-fish research. He chose a goldfish as the comparison, a cheap and available example of the qualities of nonsporting "rough" fish. To his surprise, the goldfish could swim farther and longer than the trout—by a factor of three. Fish accumulate lactic acid, the by-product of work, in their muscles much more rapidly than mammals do, and dispose of it even more slowly; the lactic-acid production of trout is twice as fast as in gold-fish and three times as slow to recover to normal levels. His trout swam faster than his goldfish, which should not surprise us. How-ever, the speed of goldfish is not really tested by pulling one out of a five-and-dime store's tank and bringing it to the laboratory. When spawning, the mirror carp (the generic goldfish) is an astonishingly active fish. The male dashes at the female, butts her, sometimes to the point of injury, bullies her into spewing her eggs. I have seen the released pets of Cambridge, Massachusetts, residents spawning in the water hazards at the municipal golf course at Fresh Pond, and these great overgrown goldfish, fretful with lust, moved with more speed and vigor than any trout I have ever encountered.

In short bursts, trout move fairly rapidly, but not so fast as we imagine. Measuring the speed of a startled brown trout in a scientific apparatus, another researcher has come up with a maximum speed of 440 centimeters a second. Rainbow trout anglers like my uncle Gordon would sniff at brown trout, but there's no reason to assume that rainbows are very much faster (although no one has taken the trouble to prove it), even if they are typically a little more stream-lined. Anyone who has caught the various species of trout and also hooked Atlantic salmon is well aware of the faster speed of salmon. In the same apparatus a startled Atlantic salmon was timed at 800 centimeters a second.

This not being a metric country, some translation is necessary for the American reader. If the salmon could keep it up (and he can't) his maximum speed is the equivalent of 480 meters (525 yards) a minute or almost 18 miles an hour. That is roughly the speed at which competitive collegians run the 400 meter (and once ran the 440 yard) dash. Human sprinters reach speeds of about 23 miles an hour in short races, far beyond the capacity of a salmon. The humbler trout, which also cannot keep up to speed for more than a few yards, never goes faster than 8.22 miles an hour. That is not even as fast as a hip-swinging human race walker can move. Competitive race walkers average almost 9.3 miles per hour over distances as long as

20 kilometers (12.4 miles). Fly-fishing for almost anything would provide more excitement than trout fishing, if speed was the criterion. One is reminded of Rudyard Kipling's humorous short story of "Dry-fly Fishing for Cows." He claimed to be astonished at the relative speed, compared to a trout, with which his accidentally hooked heifer tore line off the reel. Cows, in fact, run even faster than salmon.

So, the trout is a fish blessed with neither endurance nor speed, trapped in a riverine world that requires it to expend effort simply to maintain position, let alone to feed. It is the balancing act inherent in the trout's precarious existence that makes it so vulnerable to predation by fly-fishers. Some experimental evidence suggests that trout prefer to live in water moving at around half a mile an hour, but this is questionable, since they obviously thrive in lakes where the water is still. It would be better to say that trout confined in an artificial raceway will seek slow-moving water, and show some preference for that slight movement over a more imperceptible flow. (Trout earnestly defend their chosen spot in the river, a subject I will take up later, but it is worth noting here that the trout who gather in the half-mile-an-hour water in the researcher's raceway do not defend territory. They school up. You can eliminate territoriality in an experimental stream simply by slowing the flow of water. Trout also do not defend territories in lakes or the quiet waters of beaver ponds.) What the angler has to remember is that the trout will prefer to expend as little energy as possible while holding position, and it will, when feeding, stay as close to the source of food as possible. It lacks both the quickness and the stamina to race long distances after small mouthfuls.

It is this desire for easy water that motivates trout to live in a limited part of a stream, and motivates angling authors to insert diagrams showing trout living at *A* and *B* and *C*—in front of rocks and behind rocks, at the heads of pools, under logs, between the branches of sweeping trees (like the one from which poor drowned Ophelia fell, the willow that grew "aslant a brook") and beneath undercut banks. Those are places where trout live, although not all of these sites, at any season or time of day, have the second quality a trout desires: access to a steady supply of food.

All structure in a river—that is, all deviation from a featureless underwater terrain—has some potential for holding a trout. The structure most often neglected in the past but now well known among the scientific angling set is the simplest one of all, the bank. Water flows down a chute at an average speed—useful for calculating volume also, as in the standard measurement of river volume, cubic feet per second—but it does not flow consistently. It flows fastest in the center, where neither the friction of the bank and bottom nor any turbulence caused by structure interferes. The arresting power of simple friction along the bank and bottom creates what is called "laminar flow"—meaning a series of smooth currents of increasing speed as you move away from the edges toward the center. Laminar flow has become, by misunderstanding, the term applied to the slowest of the laminations, the current immediately next to the bank. More than one guide has told more than one uncomprehending customer to "cast to the laminar flow," as though this were either correct or common English. The effect is well known to small children, even if they have no word for it. We all learned about it the first time we floated stick boats down a gutter: they invariably drifted into the impelling center, we inevitably followed, and we came home with squelching shoes.

The importance of the bank, regardless of any other structures it may feature—undercuts, tree roots, rip-rap, sweeping trees and caught-up logs—is well understood out West, where guides on large rivers spend many hours boating customers just an easy cast away from the shoreline. It can be amusing, if you are easily humored, to watch a section of river where both wading and floating anglers are working. If the river is large and fairly even, flowing straight along without much bend or change in depth or interesting rocks and eddies, the float-fishermen will all be looking at the river edge, casting right up to the grass, bouncing flies off the bank. The wading fishermen will be in up to their waists, throwing flies out to, or past, the course taken by the drifting boats. Most guides are careful not to interfere with wading fishermen, and ask their clients to stop casting until they have passed the pedestrian anglers. As soon as the waders and the floaters are separated, once again the floating fishermen cast to the bank, the wading fishermen cast toward the middle of the river. So it happens every summer along Montana rivers, and countless more, on the Yellowstone in Paradise Canyon, the Missouri below Holter Dam, and the Bighorn at St. Xavier on the long, flat run above Sedge Bar. No one, in this modern age, wants to make short casts. The last time I was out West (and I am not a good big-fish fisherman) all the trout over two pounds came while I was wading or walking, not floating, and all of them were living within a few feet of the bank on my side of the river, some within six inches.

When I was young, I was not fond of fishing in the Big Blackfoot River, south of Missoula. My uncle took me there many years before it was made famous by Norman Maclean in *A River Runs Through It*. It was too big, too brawling, too vast to be understood by a boy and, sometimes, by grown men. My uncle Gordon and his friend Ashley Roche fished it hard, wading to their capacity, making long casts. So it is done by Maclean's ill-fated brother in *A River,* and so, I am sure, it will be done and photographed when the film of the novella is made.

The Blackfoot is not the river it used to be. There are problems in the headwaters, logging and its associated siltation of the streambed, new mines and old ones, with the inevitable acidic pollution from exposed sulfur-bearing rocks and the industrial acids used in extracting minerals from crushed ore. And there are boaters now; it is an easy river to run in a rubber raft, and joyful families float past the occasional summer trout fisherman. The mine drainage is being addressed by public and private groups, the logging scars will heal themselves someday, and the boaters—well, they are only a distraction, not a menace. I fished it a few years ago in the heat of summer, in the least likely time of the year, and caught enough trout to make the rumors of pollution seem greatly exaggerated. Fly rods, of course, are poor measures of the health of a river, although usually they underestimate, rather than exaggerate, the population of trout.

It was a very odd day. Here I was angling during what may be the nadir of the Big Blackfoot (assuming things will improve), and I caught trout after trout, some to fourteen inches, at least one over sixteen inches. Sadly, because all lost opportunities are melancholy, I caught every single fish by casting to water within a rod's length of the bank. They were all rainbows (the insistent brown trout has captured some, but not all, of the river), and all took big attractor dry flies—Royal Wulffs, Trudes and Bombers. They were living and feeding where their ancestors held some forty years ago, and they were taking flies so large and floatable that the twelve-year-old I was then would have had no trouble casting and following the drift of the lure. I seldom wish, as it is said, "that I knew then . . . ," but I did that day.

B esides needing slow-moving water, trout like to be near the food supply—the strand in the current that is carrying insects downriver. Their world is not perfectly organized, and the places they rest and where they feed are not always spheres that overlap. A trout that is not feeding is of no interest except to an otter or an osprey. So, in addition to holding close to some structure that mitigates the pressure of the current, a trout of concern to anglers—a feeding trout—is going to be as near to the food supply as prudence and stamina permit. The food of interest to fly-fishermen is either floating or sunk, and floating insects are by far the easiest to see and imitate. The surface of almost any fishable stream or river is braided with one or more ribbons of foam mingled with leaf-litter and isolated bubbles. On very good days, these braids of current carry hatching and egg-laying insects. Call them "bubble lines," "foam lines" or "drift lines," they are indicators of where a natural insect is most likely to be. (They are harder to see in fast-moving, riffly water, which is one of the reasons not enough fishing effort goes into those interesting places.) Some drift lines are sterile from the angler's point of view. A

good foam line in the middle of uninterrupted fast water may not
have trout anywhere near it, no matter how many floating insects it
has captured. The fish may not be willing to fight the main current
regardless of the many insects swept along in it.

The ideal foam line may be a point of concentration in a slow pool
or in a big, backward-swinging eddy. It may be immediately next to
a bank or skirting by a log; it can divide around a subsurface or out-
standing rock. At these places, the drift line is doing what the books
promise it will: it is showing you the natural place where trout and
insect are likely to be most proximate. Such places must be fished
carefully, but not to the exclusion of everything else.

Just because you are fishing in the drift line you should not assume
that you have dissembled completely. One of the things we forget, in
this modern world of sophisticated artificial flies and fine leader material, is that we seldom completely fool a trout, especially with the
dry fly. If you think about your own fishing, you remember some
differences between the way trout rise to the natural fly and the way
they take your artificial. Reflect, if you will, on how often the rise of
a trout to your fly is much splashier, noisier, bolder, perhaps more
irritated than the rise-form to the natural insect. It can be difficult in
some slants of light to see a small trout fly, even if you are standing
up in a drift boat. For me, it is becoming difficult to see trout flies in
low light, and on rivers with free-rising fish and steady insect
hatches, trying to guess which rise goes with your fly is frustrating.
The Bighorn River has the most fish per mile and, in high summer,
the most continuous fly-hatches I ever hope to see. I hooked a few
more fish in slanting backlit conditions, and even managed a few at
dusk, by regarding any unusually noticeable rise as one to my artificial. There is something slightly angry looking about many rises to
imitation bugs.

Once in a while, and this is truly infrequent, a big, old, smart trout
will come up and very gently and very thoroughly inhale a fly without excessive commotion. I once saw a trout make a very large Joe's
Hopper (No. 8 3XL) disappear into a vortex on the Missouri. Not a
bit of the fish broke the surface; the trout's mouth opened under-

water, creating a vacuum, and there was suddenly a hole in the river and the fly fell into it. I didn't strike, I just stared, and the fish managed to figure there was something wrong with the grasshopper before I understood that this calm, businesslike moment meant a trout had eaten a very expensive fly. (The fly cost only $1.75, but the entire price of presentation, not including opportunity costs, was more than a thousand dollars.)

Often we cannot see any relationship between the places where trout eat terrestrial insects that just happen to fall in the water and those places where the trout, and the fly-fisherman, expect to see a conveyor belt of aquatic insects coming down a drift line. My missed fish was ten feet away from the nearest foam line, but not in a totally unpredictable place. The Missouri between Helena and Great Falls is often lined, sometimes on both sides, with civil works—highways and railroad tracks. The contractors placed broken granite rock (rip-rap) where their construction impinged on the river, to keep the current and the winter's ice from scouring out their roadbeds. Although the rip-rap seems almost featureless, it does break up the current by friction and creates holding water for trout. Someday I'm going to get on the railroad bed and walk it for a mile or two, dangling a grasshopper imitation just out past the rip-rap. This will look silly to anyone but the fish.

In slow-moving meadow streams, rare and wonderful places, you quickly realize that drift lines aren't everything, compared to the comfortable, nearly current-free water that runs next to the bank and even under it. Flint Creek, a small brook that comes out of a reservoir in Philipsburg, Montana, and works its way down to the Clark Fork of the Columbia at Drummond, parallels one of the main roads into the headwaters of Rock Creek, a river so famous that it was almost fished to death in the early 1980s. Flint Creek isn't famous and never will be: it is too small to hold trophy trout, and the trout it does hold are browns, of which you can get all you want in Montana without going out of your way. If it was within a hundred miles of a big city, Flint Creek would get fished down to a nub—it would require and deserve special catch-and-release regulations—but in Montana it's just another place to play with the fish. It does have something special about it, though. Unlike most meadow creeks in cow country (and I mean everything from Vermont dairy herds to Washington beef), it hasn't been trampled to death. Next to kids with worms, grown-ups with 7X leaders, and acid water, the biggest enemy of trout in North America is the cow. Where Flint Creek has a meandering meadow character, three or four miles south of Philipsburg, the cows are fenced well back from the creek bottom, and the banks are beautifully undercut and overgrown with grasses and a few (not too many) willows. The reason the cattle are fenced out seems to be that the meadow beside the stream is loaded with blue flag iris, poisonous to livestock. I had never thought of toxic plants as a fisheries-management tool, but there they were, one June day, protecting the river better than any game warden or biologist or fish-releasing angler ever could.

The fishing was so good it was either boring or exhilarating, depending on your mood. I was ecstatic. My friend was satiated quickly by ten- to twelve-inch brown trout—but he lives there. Such disdain protects many of Montana's small brooks from overfishing. You could raise a fish on every cast that fell within two inches of the undercut bank. If the fly hung up for a moment in the drooping grass, so much the better, so much surer the take. You could not touch a fish (except for five-inchers) anywhere else: not under the foam line, not at *A* in front of the rock, *B* behind the rock or anywhere but under the bank. And from there, they wouldn't come more than four inches to eat. This was one of the very, very rare days when the fish seemed to take the fly without that characteristic extra motion. But it was June, and the water was still cold, and the first fly-hatches of the year were on, and everything looked good and natural to the trout.

O nce in my life, I have fished where all the trout did in fact live and eat at the *A* and *B* spots of an illustrated fly-fishing manual. I don't mind telling you where, because the Little Blackfoot is also not a river that will ever approach the popularity of a Madison or a Big Hole or a Beaverhead, for unlike them, and like Flint Creek, it does not produce large numbers of big trout. By the time summer vacation comes, it is well drawn down for irrigating hayfields. When it is in good shape in June, late enough for the trout to have recovered from the winter, all the Serious Anglers are chasing salmon-fly hatches around the Rockies, and the Little Blackfoot is just a stream you see out the car window from Montana 10, the cutoff highway between those two famous rivers, Rock Creek and the Missouri.

Some of the Little Blackfoot has been altered by highway construction, and most of it runs over a sand-and-gravel bottom without much structure or feature to it—not exactly a riffle and pool river, more of a flat run and deep hole river. But there is just enough structure to make it a place to learn how to find fish. It would be a good place to take a novice, someone not yet committed to the dogged pursuit of three-pound trout.

The Little Blackfoot valley suffers from some of the traditional Montana blemishes and still has most of the virtues. There are house trailers, sand pits, a mine near where the river drops into the Clark Fork, but it still has cottonwoods and hayfields with beaver-slide hay-stackers, the ones that pull the hay up an inclined ramp to the top of the stack. It even has a barroom. And it has one of those large, modern Montana rest areas with trailer parking and running water in the restrooms. Montana must spend more per capita on public comfort than any state in the union. The rest area, downriver and northwest of Avon, is at the end of a sweeping curve in the road. The highway impinges on the river, as they all did before 1975, when stream-protection laws were written, and the west bank is rip-rapped for nearly a mile. The river next to the highway is one long gentle glide without deep pools. The streambed material is firm sand and gravel, and most of the rocks in the river bed seem to be pieces of rip-rap that got away from the contractor—they are all on the highway side of the stream. And every one of them has three fish: one in the soft water in front of the rock, one clinging close to the side of the rock where the friction creates a gentler area of flow, and one behind the rock in the seam between the divided current. I say three, but there is almost surely a fourth fish on the other side of the rock, though you cannot and need not cast to it.

It is a long wade upstream between fish, but the bottom is so even, and the current, even in June's higher water, so gentle that you have no trouble prospecting your way upstream, and the fish will come to any small dry fly, not always taking, but showing themselves. From the rest area downstream, the highway climbs up and away from the river, and the water has its original character still: meanders, curves, deep pools overhung with willow and box elder, even one wild apple tree that marks a deep pocket directly across from the upstream end of the rest area. Here the fish are closer together and the deep pools hold dozens of smallish brown trout. Everything works as if the authors of trout-fishing manuals had designed their books to match this particular stream. Again, it is the consistent sand-and-gravel bottom—lacking the rocks that create turbulence and drag in riffles, slowing the water into pockets of trout habitat—that seems to concentrate the fish at more obvious places: just below bars at the heads of pools, underneath sweeping branches. The sandy soil of the valley doesn't lend itself to undercut banks, or the fish would be there, too. All the trout are browns, the archetypal trout of angling authors (all the British ones to this day, and all the East Coast Americans after the turn of the century, by which time brown trout were well established in New York and Pennsylvania), and they behave properly. As the British would say, they know their place.

But the wilder Rocky Mountain streams still hold trout that do not follow the rules. When the first angling writers reached the West Coast after the Civil War, they were astonished by more than the unusual abundance of western trout—rainbow, cutthroat and bull. What struck them most was that the fish did not know their station in life. Amidst a mishmash of bad information written about the biology of western species by G. O. Shields (under the pen name Coquina) is a gem of information not always included in the works of modern experts. He was familiar only with brook trout (the avalanche of stocked brown trout had not already changed the biological landscape of the East Coast), but his comment on the preferences of the cutthroat is worth quoting:

> The habits as well as color and shape of the Rocky Mountain Trout vary in different waters, but in all cases are widely different from those of the eastern Brook Trout. The latter loves to hide under a log, a drift, or a rock, while the former seeks an open riffle or rapid for his feeding or lounging ground and when alarmed takes refuge in some deep open pool, but rarely or never under a rock or log. *Fontinalis* [the brook trout] is a lover of dark, shady nooks, while *Purpuratus* [as he pedantically names the cutthroat] always prefers the sunniest parts of the lake or stream. The eastern Trout feeds till well into the night, many a basket being filled with him, after the shades of night have drawn over the water; while his mountain cousin usually suspends operations promptly at sunset. (Author's punctuation, reprinted in *American Game Fishes*, Chicago, 1892)

As far as the cutthroat's preference for sunlight and riffles is concerned, Coquina is correct. It is interesting how one can forget early lessons after a steady diet of brown trout and brook trout. Most of the dozens of cutthroats that I caught as a youth were feeding steadily in riffles and runs, well out from the bank, seldom hiding under sweeping branches, and as eager at noonday as any other time. What appears, from the angler's eye, to be an inhospitable and featureless riffle will often hold a surprising cutthroat or rainbow. Cutthroats take advantage of the smallest pockets or soft spots in the flow, or the slower laminar current on an otherwise unremarkable bottom, and they come up unexpectedly, unpredictably. They appear to have little interest in living at *A* through *F.* I think this is one reason they are so vulnerable compared to brown trout: cutthroats will live and feed in water where it is enjoyable to cast a fly, water with a single consistent surface current, water without overhangs, eddies, mixed currents or glassy calm, all of which make drifting a fly less than easy, or make it impossible.

A few years ago I stopped in Livingston, Montana, on the Yellowstone River, and fished for an hour. I had driven over the river on the interstate highway a half-dozen times in two years, always headed for some distant place, and never thought that it would repay any brief encounter. There are three or four first-rate fly-tackle stores in Livingston, all tributes to the fishing as much as to profitability, for tackle stores are usually run by people who have given up financial advantage for the privilege of living in the good country. Like most first-time visitors to Livingston, I went to Dan Bailey's, on Main Street, although a few years too late to meet the eponymous Bailey. I purchased a license, two leaders, a half-dozen flies appropriate to the season, and asked if there was a place I could fish for an hour or so before I had to get back on the interstate and go to Hardin.

The fellow I spoke with has since left the employ of Dan Bailey, Inc., for which I am sorry, because he was just the kind of sales clerk one prays to encounter in fly-tackle stores. He gave me very clear directions to an island in the middle of the Yellowstone, just upstream of the interstate bridge, told me which bank to fish (the far bank of the channel on the east side of the island), and wished me well. "It will occupy you for at least an hour," he added.

Where I came upon the river, after parking across the road from the landmark gravel pit (mining, including the production of sand and gravel, is a sacred industry in Montana), a long riffle dropped into a deep hole, and fish rose visibly just as the water deepened in the pool. On the first cast (an attractor pattern from Bailey's, either a Royal Wulff or a Trude, I'm not sure now) I hooked and eventually landed what was, until then, the largest brown trout I had ever seen. It was nothing spectacular by Dan Bailey standards, about three pounds, not nearly large enough to merit one of the plywood silhouettes with the angler's name and fly written on them that line the walls of the store. After that, I caught a series of whitefish, none of which I cast to deliberately, all of which came rushing up out of various deep holes to take the fly.

I had not been able to fish the far side of the first hole properly, since the main current was too swift to allow the fly even a foot of natural dead-drift as I cast across it to the far bank, so I waded across well above the hole and started down toward it. Some anglers are too lazy to reel in their line while they're walking, and I'm one. So, to keep from hanging up the fly while I was working my way down the gravel shore, I just kept roll-casting it out into the riffle, left-handed, my stream-side hand.

ART

(I am hardly ambidextrous, barely dextrous, but the roll-cast—throwing a rolling loop into the line while the line is lying on the water, turning it all over and dropping the fly neatly at the end—is the easiest cast to perform with either hand though the hardest to learn. It violates reason, goes against nature, to cast a fly line without picking it up and first rolling it out behind your head and then bringing it forward. And the sudden snapping motion of roll-casting is contrary to the gentler rhythm of ordinary back-and-forth fly-casting. I had read a dozen descriptions of it, sort of learned how to do it, and never thought much of it except as something I tried when the bank or the trees pinched in so close behind me that ordinary casting was impossible. All the instructions agree that you leave all the line lying on the water, bring the rod tip back until it is pointing directly over your head, and then snap the rod forward. This throws a big, circular loop in the line which then rolls out. You can find diagrams of instruction in any how-to manual. The missing ingredient in most people's roll-casting is the manner of bringing the rod down and forward after you're cocked and ready. Lefty Kreh, a fishing expert whose reputation is totally deserved, explains it this way: you bring the rod down as if it were a hammer you're trying to break a rock with, and you stop it with your own muscles just as quickly and firmly as if the hammer had struck the rock. It is that abrupt, muscular stop that makes the cast work.)

The riffle I was roll-casting into was so rapid it amounted to more of a chute or a cascade. It supported small standing waves, and looked to be dropping about a foot in every ten. And, while I was watching my footing and mechanically roll-casting, a very large cutthroat trout ate the fly. I didn't see it happen, which remains a great disappointment. It is still the largest cutthroat I've seen, not counting the ones in Busch beer television advertisements. (The beer commercials are filmed in the Snake River country of Idaho, the only place west of the Continental Divide that harbors cutthroats of the same subspecies, *Oncorhynchus clarki lewisi*, as the ones in the Yellowstone.) It filled the distance between the top of the rod's cork handle and the first guide: 23½ inches. If it didn't weigh four pounds, I don't weigh 145 with my waders on. It took the fly as Coquina said it would, in bright 11:30 A.M. sunlight where it was "lounging" in a riffle or run.

It was not the first place, or the last, where a trout has taken a fly in small—by which I mean six- or eight-inch-high-standing waves. There is a funny reason for this, and it requires a diagram:

Trout will very seldom battle a current to rise to a fly (salmon will, but they're crazy, anyhow), but the same physics that creates a standing wave gives the fish a little escalator up to the top. The downstream current, striking the bottom at an angle (or hitting a rock), splits in two parts. The larger current continues downstream, the second deflects toward the surface, creating the back-pressure to hold up the standing wave. A trout can get on the escalating current and take an energy-free ride to the surface. The cutthroat, slightly more flattened ventrally than other trout, shaped more like a whitefish than a salmon, will sit right on the bottom beneath surprisingly swift currents.

I had to get going, to quit fishing. Usually I take ten or a dozen "last" casts, but nothing better could possibly have happened after the amazing cutthroat, so I waded across, got in the car and decided to stop by Dan Bailey's to say thanks. It was lunchtime, and my salesman was out. A serious young man was doing something on a personal computer (Bailey's has a substantial mail-order business; I suppose he was working on that), and I ah-hemmed and shifted my weight until he looked up and asked if there was something he could do, and I said, no, but I had just had the best hour of fishing in my life and I wanted to stop back and say thanks to the store for putting me on to it. And he said: "Really." Not being very good at quick responses, I simply walked away.

I related this episode to my friend Joe Caton, a guide on the Bighorn River south of Hardin, as an example that Montanans didn't always seem to be as friendly as one remembered them to be. "I wouldn't let it bother you," he said. "The guy was probably from Colorado." Montana has its peculiar prejudices, and the alleged rudeness of Coloradans is one, comparable to the alleged stupidity of any person or any animal from North Dakota. If you are ever in Montana, you may have to suffer through the joke about the North Dakota coyote that got caught in a leg-hold trap.

I have nothing against Colorado. I would have guessed Boston, if I'd had to. But the friendly index has gone up considerably at Dan Bailey's since then, because nobody can stay in retail without agreeing to put up with grateful strangers. In several subsequent visits, I have gotten nothing but good advice there, and in the Orvis dealership around the corner and from all of Montana's fly-shop owners and clerks. In the long run, the flood of visitors sorts out the employees, just as water sorts out the materials of a streambed and dictates the location of trout. When you're asking for local information it helps to mention that you're not going to keep any fish. Good tackle stores are even more dependent on running water with trout in it than the angler is. Anything you can say without getting maudlin that indicates your respect for the river is likely to be rewarded with better answers to your questions. In the long run, it will help to stop back and say thanks. You might even buy a leader and a couple of flies. You can always use a new piece of string and some imitation bugs.

8

The Stocked-Out Trout

*A brief history of the rise of trout
hatcheries, with an analysis of the differing
behavior of artificially raised trout and
wild trout, from which is deduced the reason
it is imperative to stop the pernicious
practice of adding man-made fish to rivers
populated by real trout*

Human behavior is a poor guide to understanding the mind of a trout, of which even the most sagacious is an animal of very little brain. The most important thing about a trout's brain is not its size (in the good-old-boy style of the more cynical outdoor writers, always described as "the size of a pea"). The interesting thing about a trout's brain, if you trepanned one, is that it is clearly divided into four separate hemispheres controlling different functions. The optic centers are located within the largest pair of hemispheres, and although the optic nerve is the main input to this area of a trout's brain, the trout's optic hemispheres also control its voluntary muscles. A trout is truly "all eyes," something to be remembered when approaching the water.

However intelligent a fish may be, it does make sense to think of a trout as a conflicted being, one suffering from a life of continuous approach-avoidance dilemmas. As I have said, the trout finds a place in the river where it can balance two needs: to approach food and to avoid current. When it is resting, or hiding from some real or imagined threat, it will balance maximum security against the effort required to stay in the safe location. Life in the river is brutish and short; any trout that reaches three or four years of age is both a trophy for the angler and a fish that has succeeded in resolving a Benthamite calculus of benefit and (energy) cost. Like anyone learning to fish, I found that likely places held likely trout, but I always thought the fish chose to be there; I did not know, in my innocence, that they simply had to be in such places, or that they struggled amongst themselves to capture and keep the good water.

Since Cotton, bookish anglers have written that the largest trout occupied a mild current adjacent to the most favorable and continuous food supply or, when in a dour mood, a gentle flow in the most secure and sheltered spot. What they did not know, and blessedly had no reason to ponder in their age of natural abundance, was that trout were jealous and possessive about these feeding and resting stations. Trout are territorial, although the word has a certain etymological problem when applied to water. If you like making up new words, trout are "aquatorial" or, more accurately, "torrentorial" or "fluvatorial," because they defend preferred places only in moving water.

The ability to occupy and defend their positions depends not merely on raw strength but on a well-developed social system. Like a flock of chickens, trout raised in wild rivers have a pecking order that develops during infancy and is, at least at the beginning, independent of size and strength. River-born trout establish a chain of relative dominance before they have begun to differ visibly. As they mature and move from the shallow edges of the stream to take up feeding stations in the food-rich flow, they sort themselves out by their previously established pecking order, and the dominant troutlet takes the best spot. During the past century of modern fisheries management, no attention was paid to this rigid and complicated pattern of behavior.

It was ignored for the simple reason that until the 1970s trout management consisted entirely of rearing and stocking additional trout to satisfy the growing horde of anglers. Like the modern fishing tackle factory, which has replaced the solitary craftsman's workbench, this management was a creature of the Industrial Revolution. It had both the mentality and the capability of a first-rate frozen-pea or automobile-tire plant; and, as will happen with manufacturing processes, the side effects were misunderstood for generations. It was not that anglers of the late nineteenth century were fond of stocked-out trout; as soon as the fish-culture farms and state hatcheries began cranking out widget-trout, these imitation wild fish were scorned for aesthetic and gastronomic reasons. You might wonder why anyone would eat such a dubious fish, but the idea of catching and then releasing trout, even offal-fed hatchery trout, is a post-modern concept. Charles Hallock, venerable editor of the United States's largest sporting magazine, *Forest and Stream,* in an elegiac editorial in December 1879 on the increasing numbers of stocked trout encountered in club waters near New York City, passed judgment on the practice with two sad sentences:

> In those future days, not long hence to come, some venerable piscator, in whose memory still lingers the joy of fishing . . . will totter forth to velvety edge of some peacefully-flowing stream, and having seated himself on a convenient point in a revolving easy chair, placed there by his careful attendant, cast right and left for the semblance of sport long dead. Hosts of liver-fed fish will rush to the signal for their morning meal, and from the centre of the boil which follows the fall of the handsful thrown in, my piscator of the ancient days will hook a two-pound trout, and play him hither and yon . . . and when he has leisurely brought him to hand at last, and the gillie has scooped him with his landing net, he will feel in his capacious pocket for his last trade dollar, and giving his friend the tip, shuffle back to his house and lay aside his rod forever.

For the public fisheries manager after the turn of this century, hatchery trout became the source of income on which his budgets depended. Managers assumed that the relationship between killing trout and selling fishing licenses was direct and proportional. And as the rivers of the United States continued their long decline—polluted by industry and the curious modern invention of the flushing toilet, warmed by innumerable power and irrigation reservoirs, blocked by milldams and sluiceways, and most of all, devastated by mining, forestry and farming practices—the hatchery replaced natural reproduction where that was impossible and attempted to supplement it where fishing pressure seemed to require additional quarry. At first, public hatcheries concentrated on providing fry and juvenile fish, hoping that water marginally suitable for natural reproduction would nonetheless be adequate for rearing abundant infant fish to catchable size. But except in remote ponds and large reservoirs, where stocking is still an asset to the fishery, the survival of juvenile factory-fish until they were of a size to fill the angler's creel was questionable. Fisheries managers had neither the technique to assess this "recruitment" nor the leisure to wait for it to happen. With improvements in hatchery technology—in trout food, in water-tempering and in sanitation, including antibiotics and disinfectants—it became possible to rear large numbers of trout to frying-pan size and better. Thus was born put-and-take fishing, particularly in rivers that were only suitable for trout in the cooler months of spring and early summer. Most of us who fish on the East Coast became dependent on the hatchery. Fish and game agencies had developed a product that could be sold immediately to the license holders. (A friend of mine in one state fisheries department refers to stocking as "point-of-sale merchandising.") And, even where nature was already supplying what should have been a sufficiency of trout, hatchery fish were used to supplement the river's production, to provide increased entertainment for the customers of guides and outfitters.

It was many years before this practice was questioned by anyone but snobs, that is, by anyone but anglers who could, by accident of geography or wealth, afford the luxury of catching (and eating) wild trout. I was twenty-one before I saw my first hatchery trout. Some Montana rivers were loaded with them when I was a boy, but my uncle had long since learned how to avoid such inadequate quarry.

The earliest scientific demurrer of whom I am aware was Professor W. C. Kendall, of Syracuse University, who in 1924 wrote an article, as scientists will, about "the need for more research" on stocking-out programs. The questions he raised were a good foundation, although Kendall, too, was unaware of the importance of territoriality to understanding a stream fishery. Close readers of his article will note that he was interested more in the competition among races of fish than in intraspecific aggression and competition, but such concerns about racial differences typify much biological and anthropological thought in the 1920s.

To summarize Kendall: first, it is a mistake to stock exotic species of fish in waters where there is a sufficiency of self-reproducing species. (The rainbow trout, being more hatchery-amenable than native brook, cutthroat or feral brown trout, was and is the fish-culturists' favorite.) Second, even if there are good reasons for transplanting species into water already occupied by other species, you do it at your peril unless you understand the cultural needs of all the fish involved and "the delicate question of their inter-relations and the possible disturbance of the balance established by nature." Finally, he wrote, stocking can result in an overuse of the available food supply, with disastrous results for the entire fish population. And that is another important issue, since in running water, only that portion of the food supply is truly "available" which is located where it can be reached by a trout without undue expense of energy. Even if stocked trout cannot eat all the bugs in the water, they can still consume too many of the smaller number of insects coming down the river in the strands of water accessible to a trout.

Kendall's questions were insoluble in the 1920s (neither electro-fishing techniques for population census nor scuba-diving for behavioral observation had been invented), and they were left unresolved until the 1960s. The first, tentative suspicions about the value of putting hatchery trout into good trout streams were raised when managers tried to justify their factory system by intensely studying the survival of their hatchery fish. In the early 1950s, R. B. Miller, in the Province of Alberta, Canada, observing the results of adding hatchery cutthroats to a stream that already had resident wild cutthroats, found that the planted fish suffered high mortality and lost considerable weight immediately after stocking. Although he could not prove it by direct observation, he theorized that this decline resulted from conflict between hatchery and resident fish. He did not inquire as to the effect of the conflict on the wild residents, it being an article of faith until very recently that any wild fish could hold its own against any Purina Fish Chow graduate. Several experts in the 1960s discovered that hatchery trout survived much better in streams that held fewer native trout and surmised that "detrimental social interaction" made stockers more vulnerable in well-populated streams. For these reasons, the states of Michigan and Wisconsin reduced their stocking programs in a few selected "wild trout" streams in the 1960s. The fishery managers intended to use their hatchery output in the most economical and efficient way. Nationally, managers continued to believe that stocked trout were necessary to satisfy the demands of anglers and especially the high demands created by tourism, including guiding, outfitting and float-tripping.

In the early 1960s, when I was studying at the University of Oregon in Eugene, I fished every chance I could on the McKenzie River, a large and scenic mountain stream that comes down out of the Cascades and joins the Willamette at Springfield, Oregon, a paper-factory and sawmill town on the east side of the Willamette. I quickly learned the difference between stocked trout and wild trout. And except on very good days, we all caught mostly hatchery fish. They were handsome—Oregon has always grown about as good a hatchery trout as any state or federal program produces—but they were pale, pink-striped instead of red-striped, and had rounded tails, their fins either eroded by constant circular swimming in square hatchery ponds or nipped down by their thousands of tank-mates. They were easier to catch, easier to fool with ordinary skills and pretty-good flies. The occasional wild trout I caught—bright and red-sided, with sharply edged fins and noticeably larger eyes—stood out in the creel, which was where all of mine ended up. The limit in the 1960s was ten fish a day, none over fourteen inches, the idea being to preserve the larger native fish for natural breeding stock. The stocking was, and still is, largely the work of the McKenzie River Guides Association, whose members would haul a stock-out boat down the river through rapids and pools, letting the trout escape throughout the river, most of which was unavailable to bank anglers and all of which was the guides' for-profit territory. Guides everywhere wanted stocked fish, but only on the McKenzie, I believe, have they played so active a role in the process.

The McKenzie, heavily stocked, was an odd river to fish in. You did find fish at *A* and *B*, but you were likely to raise a fish almost anywhere, especially stocked ones. We always fished with two flies on the same cast, one at the tail end of the leader, another on a short dropper three or four feet up the leader from the tail fly. When we hooked a fish on the end fly, we would use its tension against the line to lift the fly on the dropper off the water by raising the rod high, and then, dipping the rod tip up and down, bounce the dropper fly on the water's surface. It was a kind of fish-aided dapping, and it usually worked. Sometimes you would see two or three fish—planted fish, it always turned out—following under the dangling dropper, chasing it across the river. It never occurred to me that there was anything unnatural about the McKenzie and its trout: it was so much larger than any stream I was acquainted with that any oddness was, I thought, a function of its size and depth.

In fact, my good days on the river were simply a result of large numbers of nervous, hungry, wandering fish. If you put catchable-sized trout in a lake, the average annual mortality at the hands of anglers will be around 20 to 30 percent of the total. When you put the same product in a river, where territoriality drives their behavior, up to 60 percent of them will be caught in a season and nearly all the rest will die some quasi-natural death by the following spring. The forks of the Bitterroot, when I knew them as a boy, were unsullied by stocked trout. It was a long way from the hatchery, and the main stem of the river could accommodate all the production.

Thirty years ago, big rivers were a mystery to fisheries biologists. Small streams were studied with electrofishing: the fish in them were temporarily paralyzed by an intermittent pulse of direct current at moderate amperage and high voltage, netted, counted, measured and released. Repeated surveys gave biologists a reasonably accurate idea of stream fish populations. But in rivers too big for electroshocking, managers had little to study except the contents of angler's creels. In manufacturing terms, the only quality control was destructive testing.

The obstacle to studying live fish in a big river was that it wasn't easy to generate enough electrical current to stun them while floating along in boats filled with portable generators, net-men, shocking crews and biologists. It required the development of small, reliable power sources, and it also required figuring out a way to shock the fish without killing the investigators. The amount of amperage it takes to stun a trout in a small brook is enough to be dangerous to a fisheries worker who falls in or develops a leak in his insulating rubber waders. In a big river, it's enough to kill one instantly. Electrofishing stream surveys are not everyone's favorite way to earn a living. Even in very small streams, electrofishing is not 100 percent effective. It is not a question of just turning on the juice, but of using the intermittent electrical current to steer the fish toward the waiting netter. In the easiest of conditions, with the best equipment and skilled personnel, biologists might capture 30 percent of the resident trout. In large rivers, only 5 to 6 percent of the fish can be shocked and netted.

Still, it is possible, using statistical methods, to estimate the true population in a river by a technique called "mark-and-recapture." It works like this: every fish stunned and netted on Day One is marked, either by clipping a fin or inserting a barbed tag. On Day Two, about a week later, the same section of river is shocked, and the number of previously caught fish is noted as a percentage of the second day's catch. Two days are enough for a small stream; in larger waters, several days of shocking are required. The procedure is something like what you might do to estimate the number of jelly beans in a jar when you're not allowed to pour them all out and count them. The rules let you reach in, take out a handful of twenty or so, mark them, put them back, shake up the jar, and take several more handsful of twenty. If you consistently get an average of two marked jelly beans in the next series of handsful of twenty beans, that is, 10 percent of your handful is marked, you can bet the mortgage that the jar holds about two hundred jelly beans (that is, your first handful of twenty was 10 percent of the total). If you have a bigger jar, try to take a much bigger handful, say two hundred. If the subsequent handsful are all over the place, with from none to ten marked beans, you have to keep repeating the process and mark all the beans you catch until you start to get consistent results. Then, you can estimate the total, actual, real number of beans—or, more to the point, fish.

What drove one fisheries biologist to all this trouble—a ten-year survey in Montana—was a gut feeling that something was wrong with the whole idea of stocking fish in a well-populated healthy river. Dick Vincent, of the Bozeman office of the Montana Department of Fish, Wildlife and Parks, was the man who changed the science of managing wild fish. The difference between what he learned from 1967 to 1976 and what all previous studies had shown created a revolution in trout management. He concluded that stocking catchable-sized hatchery trout was not only useless, foolish, unaesthetic, and a waste of resources; it *made things worse*. His study is the most important event in the history of modern fisheries management of high-quality trout streams—of blue-ribbon, destination, important, natural, wild, real rivers. He wouldn't brag on himself if you held a gun to his head, by the way.

Vincent studied a section of the Madison River north of Yellowstone Park. The first surveys had tried to understand and improve the carry-over of trout during winters, when most of the Madison's upstream precipitation is locked in snow and ice. When his study began, fifty miles of the upper Madison were receiving catchable hatchery fish at the rate of sixteen hundred fish per mile (that's almost one a yard). These trout were added to the river from April through August. All these fish were put in the best part—the coldest, most scenic and heavily used section that runs from Hebgen Lake north to Ennis Lake. Farther north, downstream from Ennis, stocking was never instituted: sufficient fish lived there already, angling pressure was relatively light, and the water, rewarmed by passage through the shallows of Ennis Lake, was marginal for trout most of the summer. (Trout will survive, but not feed or grow well, in such warm water.)

Running water in the United States is in the control of water companies, hydropower utilities and irrigators, and the Madison was no different, once it left the sanctuary of Yellowstone Park. Montana's Division of Fisheries negotiated with Montana Power to smooth out its seasonal flow of water, letting more come down in the cold winter months instead of hoarding it until late spring. They expected that this simple management program would improve the river's capacity to sustain fish throughout the year. It did, but only in the little-used and never-stocked section below Ennis Lake. In the good water, the popular section from Hebgen Lake down to Ennis, close study indicated that it did some good but not nearly as much good as below Ennis. It occurred to Dick Vincent that the only significant difference between the two parts of the river was that one was being heavily stocked and the other was purely natural. But this was no basis for a new policy. You can imagine that the pressure that had forced the state to start stocking the Madison in the first place was not about to be mitigated by some inconclusive statistics comparing a popular part of the river with a section of stream that few anglers cared about.

One way to find out if stocking trout hurt the native population was to stop stocking and test again, not exactly a politically sound program. However, one small section of the well-stocked upper Madison was only lightly used by outfitters; perhaps *it* could be used for experimentation without anyone's even noticing. For four miles, beginning at a bridge in Varney, the roads ran farther from the river and much of the riverbank was posted No Trespassing. Although the river was easily accessible by boat or by a little serious walking, fewer fishermen used the area. (On average, trout fishermen will walk about as far from the parking lot as sunbathers.)

The Varney study section had another peculiar advantage compared to the rest of the Madison, one of those happy circumstances that allow, or encourage, the kind of breakthrough study that Dick Vincent initiated. For some forty miles from Hebgen Lake downstream, the Madison runs at an even pace over a streambed composed largely of glacial and alluvial rock and gravel; it stays within a confined bed and is essentially one long, uninterrupted riffle. As the river nears Ennis and Ennis Lake, the slope flattens and the river begins to braid, to cut side channels and meanders, much as rivers do when they reach their deltas at the ocean's edge. It would be possible, Vincent knew, to get better results by electrofishing the multiple (and therefore smaller) channels than by trying to survey a broad and featureless single channel. The river near Ennis has not only manageable side channels and interesting holes and undercut banks for scientists to probe, but also the most enjoyable water for the fisherman who's willing to walk and wade, or float and wade.

Quietly, and initially because a production problem in the local hatchery made a good excuse, Dick Vincent stopped stocking trout in his four-mile Varney section in 1970. The results were astonishing, even to a man who already had his suspicions. The numbers of fish, and pounds of fish per mile, doubled and tripled. Even more important, at least to anglers, the numbers of big trout, three-year-old trout and trout over eighteen inches also doubled. This was, as they say, revolutionary.

But it wasn't enough. After all, the Madison is hardly a natural river. Its flow was subject to the whims of the operators of Hebgen Dam, and, from a biological point of view, it was contaminated by years of stocking. However, a small nearby tributary, O'Dell Creek, hadn't been stocked for years and had a healthy population of wild trout that few anglers could get at because the landowners on both banks had thoroughly posted the land. Though the riparian owners, either dude ranchers or out-of-staters who wanted privacy, didn't permit strangers on their land, they did let Vincent stock some trout for them (and regarded this as a generous gift). The results were instant: two years of stocking cut the total pounds-per-mile in O'Dell

Creek by 60 percent, and hit hardest at the population of two-year-old and older fish, just the ones that interest anglers, just the fish that everyone had assumed could thrash any stocked trout with one fin clipped.

But this was still not enough proof. For one thing, O'Dell is a spring-fed creek, with constant flows and nearly constant temperatures, quite unlike the brawling, sometimes ice-bound Madison. So Vincent went back to the big river, where two years without stocking had improved things, and started putting hatchery fish back in the Varney study section. He managed, with just a year's stocking, to knock the recovering river almost back to where it had been during the years of constant stocking. There are times when you don't need to keep feeding poison to the rat to see if it gets sicker, and this was one of them. The end of stocking in the Varney section of the Madison and in O'Dell Creek came with the 1973 season, and they both recovered magnificently.

The most bizarre result was what stocking had done to the big brown trout. The decline had been most severe in native fish that were sometimes twice the length of the nine- to twelve-inch stockers, and always two and three times the weight of the hatchery fish. Could the relatively small, weak, unadapted, nerdy fish cause the disappearance of big, strong wild-west fish? Every observation up to that time would have made you guess not.

Divers and snorkelers and patient stream-side observers with polarized spectacles had been studying the behavior of hatchery trout mixed in with wild trout for several years, and they always saw the poor, defenseless hatchery fish being chased from pillar to post (or rock to stump), sometimes being driven hundreds of yards downstream before finding a place to rest. What they had missed seeing was that wild trout never chased *each other* around like that. All it takes for a dominant native trout to hold its place is to show itself, make itself and its established rung on the pecking order known, and the weaker wild trout gives up without a struggle. (That is one reason to pay attention to a stream bottom with lots of boulders and similar structure, for as long as trout cannot see each other, they'll be very closely packed into a good feeding lane.)

Like almost all wild animals, trout keep conflict to a minimum. What the hatchery trout were doing was simply wearing out the dominant big trout by not paying attention to the well-understood signals, by forcing aggression and chase, by causing the resident fish to overstep the narrow threshold between energy spent and food acquired. "I think," Dick Vincent once told me, "that those hatchery trout just drove the other ones crazy. The stockers have, so to speak, no manners." The Madison rolls right along, even in the braided channels of the study area; it is a river where anglers spend much time putting flies within an inch or two of the banks, luring the fish that are taking advantage of the decreased speed caused by the bank's friction. A trout obliged to chase another one in such heavy water is a trout in serious danger of losing its food-energy equilibrium.

Montana's rivers, with a few exceptions, have not seen a hatchery trout since 1980; it remains the only state that can make that boast. Stocking of rainbow trout in the Bighorn River did continue in an attempt to increase the proportion of rainbows to browns there. And there will be occasional river stockings to reintroduce fish or to take advantage of new trout water created by dams. But you no longer have to look for the signs of hatchery trout—the eroded tails, sun-burned dorsal and adipose fins, pale colors. Your Montana trout have all been made the old-fashioned way.

No other states have had the fortitude to manage trout populations in all their streams and rivers by managing anglers and catches. Even Colorado, with successful wild-trout, catch-and-release regulations on sections of rivers (the Gunnison, Frying Pan and South Platte), stocked 5.5 million catchable trout last year, more than at any time in the past. A short section of Oregon's McKenzie is now all catch-and-release, wild trout only, but the section holds only the less-popular coastal cutthroats; the rainbow water above Leaburg, Oregon, is as heavily stocked today as it was in the 1960s. Yellowstone Park, federally managed, is all wild fish, as it should be in a place dedicated to preserving the original biology. But as long as people think trout are born to die in a creel, as long as beer commercials end in a frying-pan fade-to-black, it will be a long struggle to return trout fishing to that wildness which really is the preservation of the world.

None of this new management philosophy ensures that you will catch trout. One phenomenon of stocked water is the vulnerability of its fish to anglers, whether the impetuous, innocent stockers or the harassed, hungry natives. The percentage of mortality among wild trout due to anglers in the Madison River actually decreased in the nonstocking years. The numbers of wild trout that died of natural causes (usually during the winter) increased as the population of older wild trout increased, but the numbers of wild trout creeled by anglers stayed about the same. Wildness is not innocence, except in nineteenth-century British poetry.

Most of the Madison is mandatory catch-and-release water, but the Varney section allows the taking of five fish, including one over eighteen inches, each day. One result is that this area, close to Ennis, and subject to considerable predation by anglers, produces somewhat fewer, but much larger, trout than the rest of the Madison from Varney Bridge upstream to Hebgen Lake. Rivers, we should remember, have their own capacities to produce what scientists call "biomass"—so many tons or kilos of life per mile. All things being equal, in that world of limited resources (food, cover, feeding stations) you will end up with the same tonnage of trout whether you kill any or not, but the proportions of smaller to larger fish will vary with angling regulations or natural losses. In a river where a few large fish and many smaller ones are removed regularly, there is more food and more cover for the larger fish, and they continue to increase in size. The British intuitively grasped this relationship between predation and size more than two hundred years ago, when fishing pressure was light. There, the common pike was the major predator on juvenile and young adult trout, and British anglers knew that the rivers with pike in them were the waters that produced large trout. Pure catch-and-release fishing, however good an idea it may seem to guides and anglers, makes for lots of twelve-inch trout. Some regular, controlled, scientifically based predation of middle-sized fish, even if it has to be done by spin-casting fishermen from North Dakota, is what produces the occasional trophy trout in flowing water. Humanitarian impulses are a poor guide to fisheries management.

9

The Psychology of Perception in Trout

Notes toward a better understanding of the art of fly-fishing for salmonids

T he whole question of what trout think they are looking at when they watch a dry fly float toward them is unanswerble. Since trout probably do not think at all, let's rephrase the question. What is it about a floating artificial fly that stimulates the trout to respond by eating it? Some flies look like the real thing, others barely resemble any living insect except in silhouette, and either kind will work some of the time. It is important to remember that the act of fly-fishing is an attempt to get a fish to participate in a ballet that the fisherman is choreographing. The fly is a lure in the fullest sense, not merely an imitation of food but a persuasion to join us in the dance. If all we are doing when we fly-cast is foraging for a meal as our spear-fishing ancestors did, the comment of J. M. Alfred in his brief essay on *The Antiquity of Angling* (London, n.d. [1892?]) is appropriate: "All that can be said with certainty on the point is, that, owing to the relatively low proportion of brain to body in fish, they would be more easily caught than other animals when required for food."

But at certain times and places only one particular dry fly, tied in a form that closely resembles a specific surface-drifting natural insect, will attract fish. These are the easy times. They used to be the hard times, but fifty years of scientific fly-tying has changed the rules for what are generally referred to as "selective" trout. One brief example: for generations, anglers called the hatch of very small mayflies, particularly the infinitesimal *Tricorythodidae*, "the curse" or "the smut." Fly-fishing authors of the last quarter of the twentieth century call the late-summer "Trico" hatch the greatest time of the year for the adept angler (by which they mean someone who has the good sense to read their books). Until this century, the only thing more heartbreaking than trout "smutting" on tiny surface flies was a trout "bulging," which every experienced fly-fisherman today understands to be a trout taking a nymph just under the surface. For centuries, it was regarded as some perverse, mysterious and nonfunctional whim of the trout; anglers did not believe that a bulging fish was feeding at all. No fish is more vulnerable today than a bulging trout within reach of an angler with a box full of the right nymph imitations.

I am not suggesting that I am an expert angler for selective fish, or that one needs to be expert to catch them. By and large, the places where trout are selective are well known; over the season the timing of the hatches of an area's local insect species is common knowledge among guides, fishing companions and clerks in reputable fly shops. If you want to tie your own flies, more than a dozen good books will tell you how, and fly-tying classes are staples of community education programs anywhere there's enough water, and enough trout, to justify them.

Fishing with the most exact imitation dry fly or nymph is sometimes necessary, but to me it is the least interesting form of angling. If you think about it, it is nothing more than bait-fishing made neat and easy. Just because we resort to duplicitous, nearly exact likenesses with the surface fly (something we must do more frequently with sunken nymphs), we cannot claim to have elevated the art of angling, however much our exactness celebrates the art of fly-tying. A fish is no more deceived with a thorax-tie Pale Morning Dun than when it strikes at a fan-wing Royal Coachman—two flies that probably best represent the extremes or literal representation and mysterious attraction among useful fly patterns.

Much is known (and a good deal more is assumed) about the vision of trout. As regards the floating fly, the most obvious fact to know is that the bend and point of the hook are clearly visible to the fish. (For several years after World War II, there was a flurry of invention resulting in flies being tied upside down so that the hook was out of the water, but they never worked any better than ordinary, point-down imitations.) The hook is underwater, where the fish's eye functions best. So the first assumption you can make about trout is that they ignore things. Even a very small hook has a gap considerably larger than the eye of a trophy trout: try to imagine tricking a sentient being into eating a chocolate-covered cherry that has a shiny metal hook as wide as the human eyeball sticking out of it. You would be very surprised if you succeeded.

The second important fact has more to do with the physics of water than with trout vision itself. The surface above a trout has many of the qualities of a mirror, especially when the sun is shining, when the trout sees the fly through a glass, darkly. The parts of a fly that are under the surface film—the bottom of the body, the lower ends of the hackle, would be clearly visible; other parts would be seen as dimples, refracting light, creating a pebbled effect on the mirrored surface. All of the fly above the surface would be visible only as a silhouette, possibly tinted, more of a shadow than an image. Still, even if that is all the trout sees—a gray silhouette against the sky—the image is filled with information, as any color-blind human being or dedicated black-and-white photographer can tell you.

Thus the real issue in dry-fly fishing (and to a lesser extent in sunken-fly fishing) is not so much what the trout sees as what the trout does with the information it receives (or, if you believe as I do that trout are very poor thinkers, what the information does to the trout). Fly-fishing depends as much on understanding how the trout processes information as on which signals—color, shape, size, silhouette and refractive light—are being sent in the message we tie on the end of the leader.

Some laboratory tests indicate that trout can learn to distinguish between wildly different colors—pink and blue, for example. But they make these color distinctions in response to feeding strategies in laboratory aquariums, not exactly the same conditions as distinguishing among subtle natural colors in moving water.

A long time ago, when I worked as an outdoor writer and thus wrote annual advance stories on the opening day of trout season, I pretended to interview a trout—a rookie trout, spending spring practice getting ready for the first day of the season. It could go into the hole, make the pivot, and catch the high fly, but it was nervous about playing before the large crowd expected to assemble. Barring the appearance of a talking trout, we have to deduce what is going on in its small but efficient brain by looking at the scattered clues, and we must be satisfied with an analogue of the truth, not the reality.

Trout are probably not so smart as laboratory rats or pigeons, the two commonest animals used for psychological experiments, but we assume that they all learn in the same manner, by a process of trial and error modified by successes, and that they equate success with a reward. With laboratory rats and pigeons and aquarium trout, the usual reward is a food pellet; with wild trout, a natural insect. When a single larva or adult insect is present in sufficient quantity, it is the only reward that interests the fish at that moment—this is the very definition of selective feeding in trout. The difference between the world of the psychology laboratory and the trout stream is enormous, though, because no one spends time trying to get lab rats to eat rat food. The food is given as a reward for learning something new, like pressing the lever under the green light instead of randomly pressing all the levers in hope that the Great God in the White Coat will feed you. For a trout in a river, reward comes from distinguishing between food and all the flotsam—leaf litter and specks of dirt and bubbles—that continually pass it by. A trout's energy costs are too great to allow it repeatedly to sample the entire universe in search of a meal.

But I do not think, after forty years of occasionally catching trout, that they are operating with a simple stimulus-response mechanism. If that were the case, the right fly would always work, or, being at best a poor imitation of reality, it would never work. (I am not denigrating the achievements of great fly-tiers when I ask whether any of them convince you that, for example, the several dozen feather fibers in a dry-fly hackle actually resemble the six legs of an adult insect.) Something more complicated is going on, and the best analogy is that peculiar branch of learning theory studied by *gestalt* psychologists. Gestalt theory—from the German word meaning the shape of a thing, its totality, its essence—accounts for some truly remarkable human abilities (and for remarkable human frailties—we are beings of great duality). We have all had the experience of recognizing a friend from a great distance: if he is walking or running we can sometimes be quite sure who he is at enormous distances; his posture, his motion, stands for the totality of his being in our mind, and we only need to perceive the peculiarity of a gait, the dip of a shoulder, the toss of a head, to know who it is. Some athletes get to be so well known that we can recognize them in very poor quality movie or television images. Recognizing Joe DiMaggio loping after a fly ball in even the grainiest film is one example of perceiving an unmistakable gestalt. Marathon watchers in Boston, after Bill Rodgers's string of remarkable races, could recognize him instantly, whether he was approaching in the distance or barely glimpsed through the crowd of onlookers at Coolidge Corner. Rodgers was especially easy to identify on the long, steep downhills from Newton to Brookline: other marathoners merely survived the pounding that downhill running gave their knees and quadriceps; he loped like an antelope, apparently ignoring the impact of gravity. This ability to make a whole from a part, a fragment, lets us fill in the missing or broken letters in badly printed newspaper copy, for example. But it also makes for errors, as when a lovelorn human mistakes a stranger, seen at some distance, for the object of his unrequited love. And fly-fishing, after all, is the deliberate causing of errors.

The saddest of faulty gestalt formations results in the hunting accident. Put aside, if you can, the image of the drunken or stupid hunter who indeed does cause many accidents, and look at the typical accident, the accident that has led in most states to the requirement that deer hunters wear an article of blaze-orange clothing. Most accidental shootings are perpetrated by sober people of average or better intelligence who are experienced and successful hunters. What causes these accidents is the hunter's ability to form the gestalt of a deer from only a few clues—the flash of a white handkerchief resembling the deer's tail, the alignment of a deer-colored bit of clothing with a bare branch that momentarily resembled antlers.

When I learned that I, too, could form erroneous gestalts, I quit hunting for big game. The discovery came while enjoying the safest of all outdoor sports—birdwatching. Several years ago, I was charmed every spring evening when I arrived home and noticed that just before dark a screech owl would show its head at the opening of a large bird house I had placed in my backyard, one I had planned to have attract one of the several screech owls we could hear ululating in the nearby woods. Having no house pets, I regarded the owl as my yard pet, as the just reward for my ornithological and carpentry skills. After a few weeks, as the light improved at the regular time of my arrival home, I realized that my owl was nothing but some oddly arranged saltmarsh hay stuffed into the bird house by that bane of all birdwatchers, the common starling. Until then, I had been skeptical about the likelihood that an intelligent person (always defined as someone like oneself, is that not true?) could shoot a human being under the impression it was a deer. If screech owls in bird boxes had been fair game, however, I could easily have shot that handful of marsh grass.

The function of the article of blaze orange (or "hunter orange") clothing is that it breaks the chain of image-processing that results in the mental creation of the gestalt. It works better than any normal color (or white) simply because it is so unnatural that it stops the mind from creating any gestalt that resembles a natural thing. (Blaze orange does not have the same effect on fish, by the way. Hungry trout occasionally bite the floating fluorescent-orange strike-indicators used by nymph-fishermen.)

I believe the trout has a gestalt-forming brain. Surely it cannot be focusing on the whole image of the fly, or else it would see the hook, which resembles nothing in nature. And given the optical physics of water, we can assume that it cannot see the whole dry fly in any case. It is some parts of the fly that matter, and this is true even if the trout will not take a fly unless it is a No. 22 Trico Spinner tied with exquisite attention to the long triple tail and the horizontal placement of the white wings. I have seen a million tricos hovering over a spring creek, and I have seen spiderwebs on nearby fences filled with hundreds of captured uneaten tricos; the best artificial fly looks little more like a real *Trycorythodidae* than (to recall my pet yard bird) a handful of *Spartina repans* looks like an *Otus asio*.

All the best general-purpose trout flies have one important characteristic in common: they provide a variety, a whole menu, of clues that come not only from shape or silhouette or size—all of which are very important—but from the mixed message sent by the best materials in the fly-tier's arsenal. No successful trout flies are made from truly monocolored material, and virtually no flies are made entirely from monotonous artificial substances such as vinyl, rubber, nylon, polyester or thermoplastics.

(The only exception is a wet fly called a San Juan Worm, which has many variations, but essentially is nothing but a hook wrapped with colored yarn, string or monofilament nylon line. It was invented on the San Juan River below the Navaho Dam in northern New Mexico, and may, I insist, *may* represent some of the small leeches, roundworms or platyhelminthic worms that thrive in cold, weedy tail-water rivers. I suspect that the plastic "rubber" worms used by largemouth bass fishermen with such devastating success would work on large trout, but the mind shudders. If you are going to fish that way, you might as well use real worms and eliminate the middleman.)

ART

The closest thing to a monocolored, limited-menu fly is the old Black Hackle, the wingless version of the equally ancient Black Gnat. But the reliable Black Hackle has a body made of that most iridescent and shimmering substance, peacock herl—a single fiber from the dark green sections of peacock tail feathers—wound around the shank of the hook so that every possible refraction can occur in that mixture of light and water which makes trout fishing beautiful in the first place.

To be honest, we dedicated dry-fly anglers spend most of our days fishing for nonselective trout, or else, to be brutally frank, we fish along until we find a trout that is selectively feeding on something like whatever we are using. Since that is the reality, we can appreciate why the flies that over the past half-century and more have been the most popular, useful and productive floating flies in the angler's kit are all ones that display a large menu of food-clues.

I am not going to make a list of the world's dozen or two dozen greatest dry flies; angling has advanced long past the age of Author's Indispensables. But I do want to give you a list of large-menu, multiclue flies that are worth carrying. They all have at least two (and in one marvelous case, three) of the following characteristics:

1. Their hackles are spun with two different colors of feathers;

2. They use deer or elk hair, a particolored, multivalent substance;

3. Their bodies are made of dubbed fur, which is not only multicolored (even if you clip it and sort it with enormous effort to

achieve a monocolor) but so irregular and fine and variable that it cannot help creating a variety of colors when refracting the available light.

The most popular dry fly in North America is the Adams, developed in 1922 by Leonard Halladay of Mayfield, Michigan, and used with great success by Charles F. Adams of Lorain, Ohio, on Michigan's Boardman River. It is supposed to be an imitation of a *Baetis* mayfly with the common name of blue-winged olive (which is also used for an alternative imitation), but it bears little relation to the shape of a true mayfly. It has a thick fur body and an undifferentiated tail made out of a few fibers of grizzly cock-hackle, wings of the same (definitely not blue) feathers, and a substantial hackle tied in front of the wings, where there is nothing on a mayfly but a small pair of legs. Mayfly wings either cock backward in the hatching adult, or else they lie out straight to the sides after it has mated and collapsed back onto the surface water. The original Adams was tied with spent wings, as a spinner, and later was modified, tied with upright wings to approximate, rather poorly, the just-emerged insect with its backward tilted wings.

In addition to the succulent fur body, the Adams has one of the greatest inventions in the history of fly-tying technique: the hackle is mixed of two different colors, grizzly (from feathers of a Barred Rock chicken) and brown (from the Rhode Island Red). Neither the legs nor the wings of a natural blue-winged olive are brown or barred gray, nor does the combination of the two feathers make a blue-gray to the human eye. I would argue the hackle does not do so to the trout's eye, either. Accounting for the trout's taste for the palpably inaccurate Adams has everything to do with how trout process visual information. Floating on the surface, backlit with a confusing light, the Adams presents the trout with several discrete pieces of the puzzle of life due to the barring in the tail and wing, to the mixture of colors and bars in the hackle, and to the variety of color and form in the spun fur of the body. We do not know, and do not need to know, which clues or how many of them are processed by the trout's brain into the gestalt of edible mayfly. It cannot be the totality; the Adams simply does not look like either a generic mayfly or a blue-winged olive. It has to be the individual clues.

Of all the powerful hints from the Adams, I am most impressed by the mixed hackle. (Many feathers used alone have variation within themselves; monocolored hackle is pretty much limited to black and white, and even those will refract light into a more complicated spectrum.) There is a core of dry flies, all of which have mixed hackles, that anglers would be wise always to have in their pockets, even when fishing with the best of guides.

If, like most of us, you buy your flies, there are a few general rules for picking out the particular ones you want from the fuzzy pile in the display box. I wouldn't buy a fly with lacquer or cement in the eye of the hook, not because you can't get it out easily enough, but because whoever tied it was either lazy or never fly-fished. If that wasn't done right, the whole fly was tied too speedily. Any fly, dry, wet, streamer or nymph, should be perfectly bilaterally symmetrical. It won't cast right, it won't float well, it won't swim naturally if it is irregular in outline, lopsided in construction. Caddis imitations bear special watching, as they can be perfectly symmetrical and still not be correct. The flared wing on any deer- or elk-hair caddis should come down, on each side, to the midpoint of the body. You see far too many caddis flies in shops with nice, neat wings that stop short of where they must be when the fly is floating—right on the water, not up in the air over the body of the fly. Nature is a patient and elegant artist; you should demand as much from a fly-tier. That said, these are the dry flies without which I feel unprepared.

ADAMS. Carry the originals and some of the very useful quill-bodied and clipped-deer-hair versions: the Quill and Irresistible Adams. The quill-bodied (the de-fibered central rib of a gray chicken feather wrapped tightly around the shank) has the most mayfly-like body. The clipped-deer-hair body is always, even when tied by the most skilled professionals, too fat for a mayfly. But the so-called Parachute Adams Irresistible, with paired wings made from the tips of grizzly hackle feathers, has the best wing silhouette of the three versions. Parachutes are tied with little or no hackle. I think a Parachute Quill Adams would be the most natural-looking imitation, but it won't float very well. Fly-fishing is always a compromise.

ART

GRAY FOX *and* GRAY FOX VARIANT. These are two of Art Flick's creations. (His *New Streamside Guide*, reprinted in 1982, is the standard book for eastern North American natural insects and their imitations. *Art Flick's Master Fly Tying Guide*, written by Flick and eight other masters, out of print but available in libraries and used-book stores, is the best book for beginners.) The original Gray Fox has that most elusive fur dubbing, fawn-beige from a red fox. The hackle is lightish grizzly and golden ginger mixed. The Variant has a quill body, and has three colors mingled in the hackle: golden ginger, dark ginger and grizzly, a veritable cafeteria of color signals.

ART

MARCH BROWN. The modern tie of this ancient fly uses dark ginger (red gamecock) and grizzly hackle. Art Flick's first version was a bivisible, as Americans call such flies, with the two hackle feathers tied in separately, making a bicolored fly. The "bivisibility" Flick had in mind was that of the trout, who was supposed to be looking for the dark grizzly color, and the angler, who would be able to see the bright ginger-red more easily. This was one of the unlikeliest assumptions in the history of both fly-tying and ichthyology. Today, the two hackle feathers are mingled. First one hackle is wound around the hook, then the second is wound through it in the same plane. The body is a light beige fur, usually fox, sometimes opossum.

ART

HUMPY. Here's a fly that looks like a mayfly only backward, as its wings point down and forward instead of up and back. It may look, to a trout, like a horsefly. It is high-floating (the body and the wings are made of hollow deer hair), nearly indestructible, and has the Adams mixed hackle to top it off. It is usually tied with a yellow floss body, but it is deadly with peacock herl or dubbed fur below the humped-over deer-hair upper body that gives the fly its name.

ART

McKenzie (Green Caddis). This old-fashioned caddis imitation has the mixed brown and grizzly hackle tied in front of the laid-back, flared-out, deer-hair wing. The original McKenzie had a silk floss body, but most are made today with green (and orange, for the McKenzie Special) yarn. Any caddis—and the naturals come in dozens of shades—can be improved by choosing more than one color of feather to make up the hackle or the palmering along the body that all caddis imitations may have. (The caddis is the fuzziest of natural hatching flies, and anything you can do to make the artificial fuzzier is acceptable.) The superb caddis imitations invented by Al Troth, of Billings, Montana, have no hackle per se, but their elk-hair wings are inherently parti-colored. The classic Troth Caddis has peacock herl on the body, lashed down for durability with fine copper wire. Its body and wing materials all send mixed signals.

ART

HOPPERS. All three grasshopper imitations with someone's nickname attached—Dan's, Dave's and Joe's—were originally tied with Adams-style hackles. These older styles are the ones illustrated in the *Book of Fly Patterns*, by Eric Leiser (New York, 1987). A modern Dave's Hopper has no hackle, just some unclipped pieces of the deer-hair head left sticking down to give the sense of movement (by dappling the surface) that is the presumed function of classic dry-fly hackle. Close observers of real grasshoppers will appreciate that there is nothing about a real hopper which requires a bushy hackle at the front end of a phony one; it creates the wrong silhouette for a small-headed creature with very short front legs. Yet it works. It works if the artificial is floating and if it is sunk down in the water where the fish can really see it. That is truly mysterious. The original and classic hopper is Joe's, also known as the Michigan Hopper. It is always tied with a multiple-clue wing of mottled-brown turkey feather. Joe's Hopper also works far to the west of Michigan, where very few, if any, mottled-brown grasshoppers live. In the universe of real grass-hoppers, mottled brown is the rarest color, far behind monocolors ranging from light tan (the typical high plains hopper) to navy brown. Monotone green (at least it is monotone to the human eye) and mottled green are also much commoner than the elusive mottled-brown hopper. Yet it is indisputable that the turkey wing feather works; it must be due to the variety of color signals it shows the trout, not to the imitative effect.

ART

HORNBERG. Here is a classic example of how multiple clues work in a dry fly. Originally, the Hornberg was tied as a streamer fly—a long, streamlined wet fly meant to imitate a silvery-gray baitfish. The Hornberg streamer used soft hackle from hens that would sweep back tight to the body when the fly was pulled through the water. The wings (gray duck flank feather over a dyed bright yellow underwing) were thin and tapered like a small fish. Anglers soon discovered that it would take trout just after it was cast and before it sank. Modifications made it a true dry fly tied with materials intended to increase its floatability. It has the mixed Adams hackle, and it has a very subtle mixed clue in the gray-over-yellow wings. The yellow is visible from the bottom (the trout's point-of-view) and also shows through the opaque, but gauzy, mallard feather when seen from the side or the top. Some writers claim that the Hornberg imitates caddis flies, which do have wings that fold over their backs, not unlike the mallard feathers as they are tied on a Hornberg. It may also be, with its gray sides and yellow underwing, a fairly accurate imitation of some grasshoppers. However, I once watched some very large yellow mayflies (I would guess equivalent to No. 10 hook size) hatching on the third Musquacook Lake in northern Maine. One of the nymphs came up next to the canoe, and then, as mayflies will do, split its skin down the back and started to unfurl its wings and crawl out of its nymphal skin. Just as the back humped up and split, you could make out the yellow mayfly inside the mottled gray skin. If I live to be a hundred, I will never see a better imitation of a Hornberg. On another occasion, on a stream in southern Maine, I was searching the water with a small dry Hornberg. A robin (an excellent woodland fly-catcher when it isn't hunting worms on your lawn) came whooshing down from a stream-side bush and picked the Hornberg off the surface with an audible click of its beak. Neither of my examples says much about what Hornbergs look like to trout. The robin and I both were looking down at the fly, not up.

I wouldn't go anywhere with only these flies, but I don't go anywhere without them. If I had to take just six kinds of flies and the idea was to win a fishing contest, I suppose I would take six kinds of nymph imitations. If the idea was to have fun, I would take a half-dozen types of these mottled, parti-colored dry flies. And because the Adams and something very like the standard, pre–Troth Caddis were the first flies I tied myself, I am always uncomfortable without a few in the box.

10

The Underwater Imperative

*Reflections on the reason for the
delayed development of the art of nymph-
fishing, with comments on its importance to
the business success of angling outfitters*

The basic reason we go fly-fishing is to see a trout rise to our floating fly. (According to several surveys, the reason most men, including bait and lure anglers, go fishing is to get out of the house.) But whether you read how-to manuals, or whether you simply take advice at tackle stores, you will be made fully aware by others of the importance of fishing below the surface with the artificial nymph. The angling world is suffused with nymph-advice. The best-known factoid in fly-fishing is this: "Ninety per cent of a trout's diet is composed of nymphs." One version or another of that simple rule has been explained to me by guides on the Test, the Itchen, the Missouri, the Madison, the Bighorn, the Beaverhead and the McKenzie. My brother-in-law the fly-casting belly surgeon has mentioned it. Whether fly-fishers must let that statistic govern their angling is another question, one they have to resolve for themselves. The trout must eat. We choose to fish.

The nymph—and by that collective noun anglers mean the water-dwelling larvae of various mayflies, caddis flies, beetles, stone flies, dragonflies, mosquitoes and some crustaceans, in short, everything juvenile that swims but fish themselves—may very well constitute 90 percent of a trout's diet, if you mean over its entire life, throughout the entire year, from dawn to dark. Whether it should make up 90 percent of an angler's season depends on when you choose to fish, assuming that you are a creature of volition, not compulsion. If you insist on fishing at odd hours of the day, if you must skip lunch and pound the water at high noon, if you will go out in weather so miserable as absolutely to prevent either the emergence or egg-laying of adult insects, or if you must fish in the dead of winter when, with the exception of some small stone flies and midges, no insect is going to emerge or survive above the surface, then the 90 percent dictum comes true.

Its truth depends also on whether you have come to fish or come to catch fish, which are not always the same things. Paul Roos, who operates a float-trip company out of Helena, Montana, once remarked that when he had learned how to fish the nymph (by which he meant, using the first-person diction of all fishing guides, teaching customers to fish with the nymph) he had greatly improved his business measured in numbers of repeat customers and total days on the river.

"But wouldn't they be happier fishing the dry fly?" I asked him.

"Sure. But most people are not prepared to handle getting skunked."

It can come to that, although in the ordinary season when most of us will fish, through the summer months, there is seldom need to rely on the nymph at all hours of the day. In high summer, more than 50 percent of a trout's diet comes from accidental food that is in fact alien to its environment—terrestrial insects that have fallen into the stream. The ancients knew this, ignorant as they were of the importance of nymphs. They regarded terrestrial food and its imitations as such common knowledge that it was not necessary to include palmer flies (which they believed to represent hairy caterpillars) in their lists of important seasonal flies. Anglers already knew of palmer flies, although they are not mentioned in the earliest list of flies—the 1594 edition of the *Boke of St. Albans*. Walton typically merely copied the earlier lists into *The Compleat Angler,* once again omitting the palmer flies. As with many passages of use in later editions of Walton, it was Cotton who, while merely repeating the old list of seasonal flies, elevated the terrestrial insect to its proper place. He did it obliquely, in passing, while giving instructions for "making a fly, then, which is *not* a hackle or palmer-fly (for of those, and their several kinds, we shall have occasion to speak every month of the year). . . ." The only

ART

terrestrial insect on the ancient lists is the wasp fly for August, which, with its black-and-yellow body, is simply the oldest version of the bee fly or McGinty, an imitation not much used these days. Ernest Hemingway promoted the use of the McGinty, which gives it some literary but little practical endorsement. No one speaks much of palmer flies anymore, though there are whole books written on the dietary importance of terrestrials and how to make artificial ones. The nymph, taking the place of the hackle or palmer fly, is spoken of by guides and sales clerks in every month of the year.

There is something subtly modern about nymph-fishing compared to the wet-fly technique of centuries past, something more modern even than the creations of the nineteenth and twentieth century masters of the dry fly. Nymphing smacks of science rather than art. It is something like the difference between bird-study before and after the beginning of this century. There was very little observation of the behavior of birds until lately; most of the amateur and professional interest in birds in the eighteenth and nineteenth centuries concerned itself with identification and classification. Scientists studied museum skins, and boys collected eggs. But science in this century turned to an interest in the whole animal, in its natural history. Or-

nithologists began close study of the feeding, mating and nesting behavior of birds; lepidopterists spent less time pinning butterflies,
more time studying the food plants of caterpillars. Anglers, too, eyed
the trout with less of a collector's instinct, more of a naturalist's.

A trout's interest in floating, hatching natural flies and in their imitations (whether the soggy wet flies of old or the high-floating dry
fly of the past hundred years) has been perfectly understood by expert anglers since the Macedonians first cast a taking device on the
surface of the water. It happened in front of their eyes. The rhythm
of the emergence of the natural insect was so well understood as to
serve as a schedule for vacation times on the river. But inventing the
nymph imitation required a more clinical attitude, and fishing the
artificial nymph began with, if not the trappings of full-blown science, at least the methods of an ordinary high-school biology class.

A British angler of the Edwardian era, G. E. M. Skues, is credited
with originating the art of tying and fishing the artificial
nymph, a rarity in angling history where so much seems to be either
simultaneously invented or only marginally improved from generation to generation. Skues began with just such a marginal improvement. His seminal *Minor Tactics of the Chalk Stream* describes fishing
the old wet-fly patterns—albeit the most lifelike ones—in a new
way. He cast them upstream like the dry fly and let them drift down
naturally in the current. So managed, they represented that stage between the long aquatic life of the nymph and the brief hour of the
ephemeral adult: Skues was imitating the nymph-in-process—the
hatching pupa—about to rise to the surface and emerge.

The older method, which still works, is to cast the wet fly down
and across stream, and bring it back toward the angler with deliberate motion, twitching it in the water past the trout's nose. Used thus,
either it imitates a very active nymph that deliberately swims to the
surface before hatching, or else it is merely an attractive, stimulating
object. (Some writers have argued that the skittering wet fly might be
imitating aquatic beetles, but that is first-class lily-painting.) Skues's

modest "minor tactic" of dead-drifting the wet fly without added motion was eventually translated into the fully modern and major tactic of nymph-fishing by the simple act of observing what trout ate, what the food looked like, and tying exact imitations. You may wonder why it never occurred to chalk-stream anglers to create the nymph until this century, and the answer is right in Skues's own account in his last book, *Nymph Fishing for Chalk Stream Trout* (1939). Fly-fishing, a gentleman's sport in his youth, was encased in codes of behavior as rigid as the mating dance of the sandhill crane. There was something improper, ungentlemanly, about too-close examination of the digestion of fishes.

Skues would take his day's catch, thoroughly dead by the time he got back to the inn, borrow a china soup plate and a marrow spoon from the dining room (a marrow spoon is thin and long, intended to extract that rich substance from the interior of beef and veal leg bones), repair to his rooms, and there extract nymphs from the stomachs of his trout with the marrow spoon and float them in clear water over the white bottom of the china soup plate. In the bright light of a reading lamp, he made his first drawings and notes of trout food so that he "could simulate the nymphs not only as to colour but as to length, taper, thickness and other detail with a precision previously impossible—*and all this without any of the nauseating mess of an autopsy* [italics supplied]." If British anglers were in the habit of cleaning and cooking their own fish (and they are not and were not—even in the rougher days of Walton and Cotton the "fine dish" of fish was presented entire to the inn-keeper), nymph-fishing, based as it is on intimate knowledge of fish guts, would have been achieved long before the invention of the marrow spoon and the electric light.

It was only the occasional Edwardian angler who essayed the autopsy. J. C. Mottram, in *Fly-Fishing: Some New Arts and Mysteries*, published in 1914, felt obliged to show with diagrams and detailed instructions how an angler might open a trout's visceral cavity, identify the stomach, and gain access to it. Mottram had evidently made the acquaintance of medical doctors, for he suggested the use of dissecting scissors to open the stomach; a knife, he thought, was quite useless. (This suggests that British anglers were not adept at sharpening knives, among other homely arts.) Although he was a dry-fly and palmer-hackle-fly purist—strictly a top-water angler—Mottram remarked quite presciently that "autopsies add much to the interest of fishing and increase the chance of success, and I believe would especially do so when bottom or wet-fly fishing." But though he recognized the importance of nymphs to trout nutrition, he did not pursue their imitation. By and large, he was a fancy-fly man when possible, and an impressionist otherwise, not an exact imitator even when fishing the dry fly. It often happens that someone who is not interested in pursuing practical applications makes a new discovery and does little with it: one is reminded of Sir Arthur Fleming, who was not interested in molds, and initially ignored the significance of the antibiotic penicillin he found contaminating the petri dishes in his laboratory.

Skues, with his too-delicate autopsies and subsequent artificial imitations, was not the first angler to tie good copies of nymphs. Another chalk-stream man, Hewett Wheatley, author of *The Rod and Line* (1849), tied a few nymph imitations long before Skues was born, including one for caddis fly larvae. "A most excellent variety," he explained, "and with which, perhaps, on the whole, reckoning Trout as well as Grayling, I have had the best sport, is with a body made of a narrow strip of wash leather [chamois cloth] wound on . . . which when wet, bears no despicable resemblance to the Caddis tribe." The illustration of his leather nymph shows clearly the darker head so characteristic of caddis grubs. He also tied a Green Drake with its wings just beginning to unfold: "The body is of pale, dirty-yellow, silk chenille, as fine as can be procured, ribbed with brown silk, or a fibre from the common cock pheasant's tail. The wing is the usual mallard's feather stained a greenish-yellow, and so put on as to lie close to the body; just the contrary of what it is after it [the adult fly] has once risen to the surface of the water." Wheatley, one hundred and fifty years ago, was tying a realistic emerger, and fishing it during the hatch in preference to the dry fly!

The trouble with the genuine art of nymph-fishing—and one that still keeps it from favor with the vast majority of anglers—is that you rarely will see the trout take the fly, and, except in unusual circumstances, the fish will rarely hook itself. An angler's need for good vision is about the same for dry-fly- and nymph-fishing, except that with the nymph you are reduced to watching for signals a thousand times more subtle (and as much less enjoyable) than the rise of a trout to the dry fly. The old wet-fly technique, which kept the line tight between the rod and the fly, requires much less visual acuity or concentration. When Viscount Grey of Fallodon (*Fly Fishing*, the 1930 edition) lost his central vision to the point where he could perceive only the motion of the tip of his fly rod and nothing farther away, he returned to the style of wet-fly fishing practiced since time began, swinging the fly on a tight line so that a strike is not only visible, but palpable. Much as he missed the sight of a rising fish, he concluded it was better to fish near-blind than not to fish at all, and better to fish alone with his diminished capacity than to rely on a sighted companion for instructions on where to cast and when to strike: "Nevertheless," he wrote of fly-fishing in his perpetual darkness, "the thing can be done still, independent and unaided, which is an essential part of the peculiar pleasure of trout fishing: and though my baskets are light there come bright gleams of success."

The wet fly, fished on a tight line, swings down- and across stream, and as often as not the fish will hook itself. But the nymph, fished properly, dead-drifts somewhere down out of sight on a slack line, one with whorls in it from the contrary currents of an ordinary stream. The dead-drift technique is required because most natural nymphs are poor swimmers, and even the good swimmers are usually more interested in getting back to the bottom or rising quickly to the surface to hatch than in any recreational natation. Much of the last few decades of writing on nymphing has rattled on about "second-sight" and "instinct." Indeed, with a nymph sunk far below the surface on a slack line, successful anglers developed skills that did not lend themselves to easy explanation. They responded to a host of

clues: vague movements in the water, subtle flashes of light and color
that might be the flank of a fish darting toward the fly or the momentarily open white mouth of a feeding trout. But success for the average, ungifted angler came when he fished the nymph just under the
surface, usually in imitation of a hatching fly that was floating or
swimming to the surface. The rise, the take, of the trout is in this case
clearly visible. This sort of nymphing is merely another version (albeit with a better lure and a more realistic drift of the fly) of the old
wet-fly tactics.

S everal years ago, I had a brief encounter with the nymph and the
trout that remains as vivid a memory as any in forty years of
angling. A friend belongs to an old Cape Cod trout club, one of those
rare examples of private trout water that survived the increasing de-
mocratization of fishing in America—at one time the entire Mashpee
River on Cape Cod was a private preserve, and several small state
parks with trout streams and ponds, scattered from Massachusetts to
New Jersey, are the last stage in the metamorphosis of private water.
This club, one of a handful of survivors, has been protected from em-
inent domain because its waters are the privately owned spring
creeks and reservoirs of a full-blown cranberry farm, and the trout
fishing was an adjunct to the agricultural business. The club's policy
of catch-and-release fishing is not a rigid rule, but more a voluntary
safety measure. Cranberry bogs are treated with persistent organo-
chlorines, and the hatchery trout stocked in the reservoirs and creeks
were presumed to become quickly loaded with dieldrin and chlor-
dane and slowly evolving DDT residues. In this questionable environment, upstream from the largest reservoir, my friend and I
learned something about wild trout and the nymph.

In this source stream, a perfectly clear body of water that ran at no
more than the pace of a good garden hose, there had once been a
private in-stream trout hatchery. The old weir boards had broken out
in flood and ice, a process speeded up by occasional vandalism after
the hatchery closed. What remained was a streambed of quite even

depth and near-rectangular cross section, now slowly returning to nature, a process marked by the growth of abundant stands of watercress in the stream. We walked up to look at the old hatchery, and one of us (probably not me) noticed that there were half a dozen wild brook trout holding near the bottom at the edges of the clumps of watercress. They were small trout, six to eight inches long, about the right size for the stream (any smallish body of water, whether it is an aquarium or a brook, puts limits on the absolute size of the fish that grow in it). The trout were feeding on something that was being washed loose from the watercress, nymphs in the general sense. We could watch the trout turn and move an inch or two, see their mouths open, see the flick of the white-edged pectoral fins as they steadied themselves and swam back to their original lie. My friend, an accomplished angler, naturally had a box of nymphs in his pocket—Breadcrusts and Gold-Ribbed Hare's Ears.

There was no room to cast and no point in casting in the first place. Cape Cod is still so overgrown with scrub oak, poison ivy, catbrier and grapevine that one understands the fear of the Pilgrims for what seemed to them a howling and impenetrable wilderness. The only sensible plan was to creep up parallel to the fish and let a nymph down directly into the water. Because of the angle of the sun, the fish were visible only from downstream, so we took turns being angler and fish spotter. The Breadcrust was of no interest to the trout, so we changed to a very slim Gold-Ribbed Hare's Ear. The angler, as the spotter could see easily, had to put the nymph within six inches of the trout horizontally, and nearly exactly on the same plane vertically, to elicit any interest. Even when it was done just right, as best the trout-spotter could tell, it did not necessarily work. By "work" we meant, as we shared information, simply getting the trout to move toward the nymph, whether it took it or not. Eventually, we hooked and released four trout, each one wild and well marked with the purple-centered spots and colorful fins that make a brook trout the prettiest of the family of salmonids.

It was an interesting lesson about the effectiveness of the nymph (and of cooperative fishing), but we both learned something more generally useful from the exercise. It was one of those days with frequent small puffy clouds scudding overhead, and the only times that the trout would take the fly were those moments when there was a cloud-shadow on the water. They would look at a nymph in bright light, but stop short. In shadow, they would take it calmly.

Anglers cannot summon up clouds whenever they want, but since then, when I locate a fish on a day when the clouds come and go, I try to remember to wait for the passing shadow before casting. When I am that patient, especially with a dry fly, my chances of success are much improved. I think we catch many fish in the shadow of trees not because there are necessarily more fish there, but because the leader is not radiating a spectrum of light, nor is the direct sunshine glinting off the bend and point of the hook. I believe that trout can actually see more acutely in the shade, but they have fewer suspicious clues to run through their data-processing programs. Cloud shade or tree shade especially helps to conceal the leader, which when backlit against a bright sky must look something like a glowing neon tube. Even the thinnest shade can be useful. I recall running five or six miles of the McKenzie River without turning up a fish (fishing with dry flies) until we floated past a small lumber mill below Vida, Oregon. They were burning slash at the mill, and the wisp of smoke over the water was enough to confuse two trout, the only ones we hooked all day.

Even expert nymphers may have trouble at what could be the most productive hours of the day: dawn and dusk. They must look for such obscure signals that nymphing becomes almost impossible in dim light. Nymph-fishing is, for most of us, a way to catch trout in the brightest hours of the day when insect hatches tend to be less frequent than they are in early morning or late afternoon. As evening comes, most anglers, following five centuries of advice, switch to larger and more visible dry flies, even in waters where evening hatches are a rarity. Scientifically, this is exactly the wrong way to proceed.

It is a disheartening fact that the number of nymphs in the drift—floating free above the bottom—is much greater from sunset to dark and at dawn than at any other hour of the day, that is, at exactly the times when visibility makes nymph-fishing most difficult. The reasons are obscure, but biologists know that some nymphs are daytime feeders and some are night prowlers, some admire bright light, some flee it. What apparently happens is that at dawn, and even more at dark, there is some kind of changing of the guard, some scrambling about on the bottom as the diurnal and nocturnal species take up their roles as feeders or resters, and in that turmoil, great numbers of them are swept away for a moment and drift helplessly. It is one thing to know that—and it is well documented in the scientific literature— another to act on it. I have no interest in nymph-fishing in the dark. There is a vast gulf between science and art, between observation and enjoyment, and catching a fish when you cannot see it jump is mere applied biology.

I caught trout for several years on a nymph without understanding what I was doing. Some hatching insects are good swimmers, and one of the best of all is the very active emerging nymph of the caddis *Arctopsyche grandis*, a widespread western American species so common in the McKenzie River that the standard imitations carry the name McKenzie for the green-bodied emergent fly, and McKenzie Special for the orange-bodied mature one (it turns color, but does not shed its skin like a mayfly, after a few hours out of the water). *Arctopsyche* is a net-spinning caddis, which builds the functional equivalent of a spiderweb on the bottom to trap other drifting nymphs, as well as zooplankton, diatoms and phytoplankton (free-floating algae). When it is ready to emerge from its pupal state, it leaves its lair in the stream bottom and swims vigorously to the surface, a genetic

ART

impulse that limits the time it is vulnerable to predatory fishes. We imitated the hatching nymph (technically, the about-to-emerge adult still encased in its pupal skin) with a simple green-bodied, soft-hackled, wet fly and fished it up through the current with short twitches of the rod tip. We had no idea we had mastered the art of nymph-fishing, and of course we really hadn't. The technique only works for a few weeks in May and June when *Arctopsyche* is hatching. The tight line almost guaranteed that the trout would be hooked. But as soon as there were emerging green adults on the surface, or as soon as the orange-bodied ones returned to mate and lay eggs, we switched immediately to dry flies. We came to the river to have fun, and there were always enough fish for lunch, no matter how we angled for them.

Dead-drifting the nymph, which is the true imitative technique for the greatest number of aquatic insects, caught on in England's chalk-stream country long before it was popular in the United States, and I think that is understandable simply because English river rules in the southwestern chalk streams required that anglers cast to visible trout. For most anglers, a visible trout is one that disturbs the surface, not one lurking in the obscure depths; we should remember that rules about seeing the trout before casting to it were made decades before the invention of the glare-piercing polarized spectacles we all own today. Trout taking nymphs just under the surface make a distinct bulge, sometimes even showing the dorsal fin as they roll porpoise-like. Given the requirement to angle for particular fish, and given that this rule usually meant casting to fish that were making noticeable bulges as they rose, you can understand why nymphing first became popular on chalk-stream water and later spread to less regulated streams.

For Americans, who tend to start fishing first and looking second, dead-drifting nymphs is a difficult way to search for trout in obscured water, whether it is deep and dark or vision is hampered by surface reflections and riffles. It became popular in American spring creeks just before World War II, but it remained a minor, little-used tactic on big rivers, especially on destination float-trip rivers, until someone reinvented the bobber.

ART

When I say little-used, I mean that dead-drifting was used with small, delicate, clever nymphs that imitated caddis and mayfly larvae. In the 1930s, a Missoula fly-tier Franz B. Pott developed and patented (U.S. Patent No. 1,949,582) a technique for manufacturing the large varicolored nymphs of stone flies. The Pott's Mites, as the series was named, sold for the astonishing price of 35 cents each, when you could buy good dry flies for a dollar a dozen. Pott was a hairdresser and wig-maker by profession, and his flies were complicated weavings of dyed hair that matched the dark-top, light-bottom color patterns of most stone fly nymphs. He used the ends of a few hairs, cleverly drawn out at the head of the fly, to suggest legs. Most of us who ever used the Mites had no idea we were "nymphing." We regarded them as a lure of some sort, to be used in times of trouble, just as we might put on a Heddon Flyrod Flatfish (a light version of a wood-bodied bait-casting lure) if nothing else would work.

The trick with nymph-fishing is to see something that telltales the strike. People with very good vision can sometimes see a miniscule movement of the line, though more often it is only the floating leader that twitches, and it happens at a considerable distance from the fisherman. By distance I mean something around forty feet. Most anglers think they are casting at least sixty feet of line when they reach their own inherent limits, but forty feet is a long cast for most people. I recall an argument at a Rangeley Lake sporting camp in Maine about casting prowess which we settled by sending the disputants outside to cast from one horseshoe stake to the other, which is exactly forty feet, and neither one could do it. This was before the invention of the graphite fly rod, but more fish are caught inside of forty (or thirty) feet than rod manufacturers like to admit.

Before the reintroduction of the bobber to high-toned trout fishing, some of us fished with two flies, a nymph on the tail end and a dry fly on a short dropper a few feet up the leader, and we kept an eye on the floating dry fly, watching it for any inexplicable change in direction or pace that might mean a fish had taken the sunken tail fly. This doesn't work all that well, for even a short dropper—three or four inches long jutting out from the leader—will absorb the motion of most strikes on the tail fly without moving the floating fly.

In the past decade, American anglers modified the old worm-fisherman's bobber to the fly-caster's use. To make it sound better, these floating devices that show a fish is doing something to the sunken nymph are called "strike indicators." Hewett Wheatley, that endlessly inventive man and certainly the first writer to describe an artificial nymph and an artificial emerger, fished his early nineteenth century nymphs below a delicate float made of a hollow crow's quill threaded over the leader, held in place with a smaller white quill jammed into it as the "stopper."

Today we use a piece of fluorescent orange tape pinched over the leader just above a knot, or we thread on a very small orange foam-plastic round bobber, and thus achieve the same results as we would with a cane pole, a can of worms, and a pond full of willing sunfish. Strike indicators are small and light enough to enable one to cast in an almost ordinary manner, and they are so odd-looking as never to be mistaken for common river flotsam even by those of us, like myself, who are myopic. The combination of a nymph and a bobber is deadly, and it is nearly as efficient in the hands of a visiting tourist as when it is fished by the most experienced local guide. The only problem is getting used to casting the parlay of weighted nymph, perhaps a split lead shot pinched on the leader, and the air-resistant bobber. This requires a soft open loop in the backcast, something quite contrary to what you learn in fly-casting school. My favorite fishing tackle company sells three kinds of bobbers—foam tape, cork and buoyant yarn—in shades of hot pink, blaze orange and shocking chartreuse. According to the catalogue, the yarn is for "flat water where cork indicators may spook fish." I'd just as soon buy a chartreuse yarn bobber as a sweater made of the same material.

I have fished this way (and will again), and on those few occasions when I did, the real purpose was to please the guide. About the only way you can humor a guide, and this is true from Mazatlán to Alaska, from tarpon to trout, is to catch fish. Small talk is fine, tips are appreciated, but the guide has no proof of his competence, no evidence that he is having a good day, unless the customer is catching fish. It is the only compliment you can give him.

A year ago, I made the mistake of arriving on the Bighorn River during the moss hatch. Every summer, when the water recovers from its winter chill, the moss begins to grow in profusion, old strands exfoliate, and small fragments drift along, catching up on flies and lures, making every cast an exercise in fly-cleaning. Although local anglers want the Department of Fisheries to "do something about it," the moss is part of the biomass of this productive river, as inevitable as its fat trout and monstrous whitefish. The moss that day was so miserable, however, that I did not think we were going to catch a single fish, although we were floating the first eight miles of the river below the dam, water that holds eight thousand fish per mile. I didn't care—this was a trip more dedicated to artifact-scrounging on the high plains and visiting the nearby site of Lieutenant Colonel Custer's last mistake—but I had brought a friend along who was rapidly losing faith in the eight-thousand-fish rule, and, I fear, even losing confidence in our guide, the unflappable Joey Caton of St. Xavier, Montana.

We stopped at a very odd little spot, a whorl of a back-eddy that seemed to have no geological or fluvial cause. You couldn't see a rock or a curve in the bank that required the river to make a small whirl-pool, but there it was, and it was full of trout. We could see a dozen, even in the moss-dark water. We rigged up with nymphs, a couple of BB-sized split-shot, and cork bobbers. This was, Joey explained, something he had learned in a master-angler's class: the Short-line Nymph Technique. You had only to cast six or eight feet; the leader, freighted with lead, plunged down with the nymph; the bobber drifted along half-drowned in the surface film; and large brown trout ate the nymph. My friend's nymph, not mine. He saved his day with a half-dozen typical Bighorn brown trout, fourteen to sixteen inches, buttery-fat, yellow-bellied and purple-spotted. It was not as easy as shooting fish in a barrel. I couldn't catch one—less from lack of op-portunity than from utter lack of interest. Still, the day was saved, for both the guide and the guest.

At times I think they ought to outlaw bobbers on water reserved for fly-fishing. Even if you put all the trout back, some fish ought to be able to spend the day, if not their entire life, out of the reach of anglers. More than one of us has caught a wild trout that was visibly recycled, a fish with hook-scars and damaged jaws, a fish that looked rather badly used. As anglers learn how to catch fish for more hours of the day in more months of the year, scarred trout will be encoun-tered ever more frequently, even on the wildest of rivers. There ought to be some mysteries left, some privacies not invaded, some meta-phorical virginity in the river. But that might require, as the fellow said, "being prepared to handle being skunked." At this stage in cul-tural development, neither guides nor anglers are ready.

11

Duffer's Fortnight

A description of the salmon fly,
a giant stone fly of the American West,
and the difficulties often encountered
by anglers in pursuit of it

In the Rocky Mountains, June is the beginning of the season of predictable and regular hatches of mayflies and caddis flies as the earliest rivers recover from the torrent of snowmelt. But fly-fishermen pour into the state in June for another reason entirely, which has nothing to do with technically and intellectually challenging dry-fly action. This is salmon fly season, and it comes as close as anything we have in America to what in Britain has been called, for at least a hundred years, "Duffer's Fortnight." A duffer, as golfers know, is someone who knows the rules, owns his own clubs, but can't really play the game. (That is most golfers, by the way; only about 5 percent of people who play by the rules can break 100 on a par-72 course, and only about 3 percent can break 90—averaging an extra stroke on all but one of the eighteen holes.) "Duffer" is the only word I know that is part of the argot of both those British inventions, dry-fly fishing and golf. In Britain, the two weeks much loved by the less ept angler are those when the mayfly hatches, and the British mayfly (and by that word they mean a specific example, also called the "green drake," not the entire order of Ephemeroptera) is the largest of all mayflies whose profuse hatch will lure the largest trout to the top of the water.

In the West, duffer's fortnight may last little more than a day, and an unpredictable one at that, although with great effort and flexible scheduling, you might be able to extend it for two weeks by chasing the salmon fly hatch up one river and then another. Salmon flies are giant stone flies, with aquatic nymphs the size of small fish and adults as big as your little finger; they are the very definition of a juicy bait. And the salmon fly's effect on trout is legendary. Large trout that have long since been piscivores, satisfying their great but less frequent hunger with a diet of other fish, will come to the surface and swallow salmon flies. They will do exactly the same thing with grasshoppers, but not as predictably; and grasshoppers are around for months in the summer, while the tenure of adult salmon flies is measured in hours. Something about the modern age and its tightly scheduled leisure time makes a predictable insect hatch irresistible to the jet-propelled angler.

The first year I tried to intercept the salmon fly hatch had seen a dry winter and a warm spring, and the combination of low water and early warming had pushed the salmon fly hatch ahead by a few weeks in the tributaries of the Missouri on the eastern, dry side of the Continental Divide. A week or ten days is hardly a noticeable variation in the rhythm of a river, however annoying to the time-bound tourist. I asked my outfitter to keep one day free, with another for travel if necessary, so that we could get from Helena to wherever the salmon flies would be out—any river on either side of the Continental Divide. I had never seen a living adult salmon fly or its smaller cousin, the golden stone fly, for the simple reason that all my angling life I had been either going to school far from salmon fly country or, in adulthood, married to a schoolteacher, making June vacations an impossibility. But by the time I got to Montana, the hatch was over in the Missouri River headwaters—the Madison, the Gallatin, even as far upstream as the Big Hole, a tributary of the third headwater, the Jefferson.

In June the giant stone flies crawl out of the river and then shuck their nymphal skins on the bank. The trigger to this movement is water temperature. Rivers, fed by springs and snowmelt in their headwaters, are always warmer the farther you get from the source. The critical temperature for salmon fly hatches, around fifty degrees, is reached first at the lowest end of the river; under June's high sun the water warms progressively upward, and the hatch marches up the river a few miles each day.

The relationship between variable water temperature and salmon fly development may be the reason (the amount of specific knowledge of the life history of all stone flies is small) that there are no large stone flies in the great tail-water fisheries of the West, the Green and San Juan rivers of the Great Basin, or the Missouri below Holter Dam, between Helena and Great Falls, or the Bighorn, the cold-water outlet of Yellowtail Dam. Water drawn from reservoirs is fairly constant in temperature through the year. The nymphs of stone flies stop growing during the peak of summer warm water. A number of aquatic insects seem to depend on seasonal fluctuations to organize their growth, and stone flies, which are rare in constant-temperature spring creeks and in constant-temperature tail waters, may be inhibited by the very lack of annual cycles of warmth and chill.

We had expected to find salmon flies and golden stone flies on the Big Hole; indeed, the guide was certainly expecting them since the few artificials in his kit were all nondescript, generic stone flies, ranging from an inch to two inches in length. Still, the big flies were long gone, as I heard the proprietor of a tackle store in Divide, Montana, explain to someone on the other end of the telephone. "Yep," he said gleefully, "the salmon flies are gone and so are all the assholes." This unfortunate term, he explained when he got off the telephone and noticed me standing there, did not necessarily refer to tourists like myself, but to the numbers of outfitters and river guides who pursue the salmon fly and golden stone fly hatch, and who generally take up space on a river which, like most local residents, he regarded as his private property to be rented to his own customers.

He sold an exceptionally nice looking line of small caddis flies in his shop, and purely on a whim, I bought a dozen of mixed colors, all sizes 16 and 18, thinking they might come in handy over on the Missouri later that week. This turned out to be a day-saving whim, when my guide and I discovered that the trout of the Big Hole, after the salmon fly hatch was over, had developed an interest in fairly minute caddis and mayfly species and I was the only person in the boat with any reasonable imitations in his gear.

There were two plentiful mayflies on the water, pale morning duns and little blue-winged olives, and a few very small pale caddis, all three of the natural flies about No. 16 in hook size, in other words, tiny. My guide volunteered to take one of his two or three smaller stone flies (No. 8s, the size of a child's thumb) and clip off enough wing and hackle to turn them into the equivalent of No. 16s. This was roughly the same as offering to make me a golf ball by uncovering and unwinding a baseball. I didn't know whether to laugh or sulk. Fortunately, I had the small caddis flies in my gear. Although they were hardly the right color, they were approximately the right size and shape, and we caught enough fish, including two just over sixteen inches, to salvage the day. Later that evening, it became common knowledge in various barrooms from Divide to Dewey to Wise River that the right fly for the day, all the guides and fishermen agreed, was a No. 16 Adams Irresistible, which had taken the most trout and the most big ones. If the Adams (plain) is a poor imitation of a blue-winged olive, the Adams Irresistible is worse. Its clipped-deer-hair body is shaped, even when shaved by the best of fly-tiers, more like a housefly or a hornet than a slim-bodied mayfly. But it has the mixed hackle and the multicolor of deer hair going for it. The reason it worked so well is partly because it floats much better than the original fur-bodied Adams, something important when amateur clients slap flies hard onto the water, let them drag under the surface, and generally have difficulty fishing with sparse flies which have a specific gravity near the neutral point.

I learned something new while fishing the Big Hole on the wrong week with the wrong guide and the wrong fly, and I might not have learned it had I not been mildly upset—although generally speaking, the only thing you learn when you're angry is not to be if you can help it. However, there doesn't need to be such a thing as a wasted day on the water. I was about to learn how to catch trout in a lather—emotional in my case, physical in theirs.

ART

The predominant fly on the water either was, or looked exactly like, the smallest size of blue-winged olive. (The naturals vary from a quarter of an inch to a half an inch long.) There were, fortunately, a few small caddis of the same darkness of hue, and I had a reasonable imitation of those—small, sparsely tied, they could fool a trout who mistook them for upright-winged mayflies having a bad day. Mayflies, when they are having trouble hatching, sometimes maintain a low-winged and struggling attitude as they float in the surface film, and a caddis imitation, particularly if you back-brush its hairwing into a more upright position, will serve. They really ought to sell a small toothbrush when they sell you hairwing caddis fly imitations; nothing primps up their wings like a dab of paste fly-floatant teased into the hair.

On top of everything else, we were having trouble fishing the back-eddies of the river where trout do love to feed. This is never easy, and it takes a skilled and hard-rowing boatman to find and hold a place in the main current where the angler can cast to the back-eddy and get something resembling a decent, natural drift of the fly. The problem is simply that the river is going one way and the back-eddy is going the other, and there is still water in between. Worse, the rate of relative drift is doubled by the contrary direction of the two currents. We kept getting too close, and spooking the fish in the back-current. On one big eddy, forty or fifty feet across, we managed to run the boat down the main current just where it met the slack water. This is an excellent place to fish, but not to float. Then we drifted around the back side and up the back-current right next to the bank, another place where you would rather fish than float. I muttered to myself, I think totally silently, "Well, we've screwed up everything but the middle of the eddy," and I slammed the fly down into the dead center of the whirl.

For a river with a lot of consistent glides and not so many choppy riffles or steep drops, the Big Hole still manages to generate considerable foam, and small specks of long-lasting foam on the dark-stained water are part of the memory one has about the place. Foam collects and aggregates in still water at the center of eddies, and I plunked the small caddis into a patch of foam that was two or three feet across and appeared to be at least an inch thick. The fly disappeared into the indistinct opacity, and, having nothing better to do, I twitched it. One always twitches caddis fly imitations when one has not got a better idea what to do. And a trout ate it. It was an impressive example of how much a trout depends on silhouette and motion to distinguish between the inedible and the nutritional. The fish could not possibly have seen the true color of the fly, and the clever hackling and palmering that usually make interesting lifelike dimples on the surface couldn't have been doing their magic, trapped as they were in the viscous foam.

This same strategy worked all afternoon. If we could find a patch of foam in the center of an eddy and put a fly in it before the boat floated on, something would come up and eat. Such foam looks opaque to the fisherman, as he is above it, between it and the light source, but I suspect it is much more transparent to the trout's eye. The only analogy I can think of is a good French lace curtain, which allows the Parisian housewife to look out without permitting the pedestrian to look in. And the foam will obscure the leader, floating less on the surface, where it is obvious even to the angler, and more in the body of the amalgamated bubbles.

This has turned out to be a useful ploy in other rivers, and on smaller streams where the largest back-eddies aren't much bigger than a bathtub. One of the other places that foam accumulates is just on the upstream edge of a patch of floating debris, or the upstream side of a log lying crosswise to the current. All anglers know that fish live under logs, all things being otherwise appropriate. In heavily fished water, trout are especially fond of lurking during daylight hours under the patches of floating debris that accumulate on tree roots and sweeping branches.

The most harassed fish I know of live in the Swift River, the outlet of the Quabbin Reservoir, Boston's water-supply source some sixty miles west of the city. There would be no Swift River at all—since Boston and its participating suburbs could drink, flush or waste every drop collected in the Quabbin—except that in the agreements preparatory to damming it, the water authority was perpetually obliged to supply ten thousand cubic feet of water daily to the towns downstream; this was done so that the towns would have running water to dump their sewage in, a process which is euphemistically called "in-stream sanitation." Ten thousand cubic feet a day is not much water, but it would make a nice trout stream if it came down gradually over twenty-four hours each day. Instead, the authority runs it through a little hydroelectric plant between 6:00 a.m. and noon most days, and after that the only water added to the river is essentially from leakage around the penstock escaping past the idle generator turbine. The river goes up, the river goes down, and the trout in it spend most of the daylight hours trying to find a comfortable spot to feed or rest. Fishermen complicate things even more. They arrive in the morning, wait for the water to start to rise, and begin to fish, trampling up and down the narrow, shallow river. It is no wonder that the stocked trout spend so much time sulking under debris piles.

The most popular way to catch these trout (the best part of the river is reserved for catch-and-release fly-fishing only) is with something called a Globug, a round "fly" on a lead-weighted hook tied in three vile fluorescent colors—mandarin orange, yellow and char-treuse. These things may resemble salmon eggs slightly, and the eggs of other fish are always of great interest to trout. On the other hand, trout will eat a lot of small, round objects. They will take, and then spit out, small pieces of gravel if you have the patience to toss them in one at a time. In a pond, or a still pool in a stream, you can get fish to come toward you by regularly tossing tiny pebbles, even wild fish that have never seen hatchery pellets.

Aesthetically, there is even less pleasure in fishing with Globugs than with nymphs. But a surface fly drifted down right into the foam that collects above the debris patches will at least bring a strike at the surface, although you are likely to lose the fish to the same tangle that has created its shelter. The Swift River, like all hard-fished streams, tends to be a river of broken dreams, though you apply to it all the wisdom gathered in such distant places as foam patches on the Big Hole. It is a bad fishing trip when you don't learn something, although I wish I had discovered dry-foam fishing by intelligent means and clear thinking, rather than as an undeserved reward for a moment of pique.

We partially salvaged the salmon fly expedition a few days after the unsatisfactory expedition on the Big Hole. I and Matt Kowalski, one of Paul Roos's best guides, took the three-hour drive from Helena over MacDonald Pass to the Clark Fork of the Columbia River, then to the upper reaches of Rock Creek. This river (it is much more than a creek) drains the Sapphire Mountains, another one of those Mon-tana ranges named by mistake for the semiprecious garnets that early miners found. It is a precipitous river, totally closed in by trees on both sides, hard to wade, even dangerous, and unyielding to small boys and other amateur anglers. Whenever my uncle and I fished there years ago, I expected to get skunked. In 1980, Montana put Rock Creek on its short list of Blue Ribbon trout streams, and it at-tracted the attention of thousands of skilled nonresident fly-fishermen. This is a classic example of the deadliness of publicity untempered by catch-and-release regulations. Within a few years of Rock Creek's being blue-ribboned, the state had to institute smaller limits (two fish a day) and restrict the number of outfitters allowed to float anglers down the river. Before rubber-raft trips caught on, most of Rock Creek was out of reach of the ordinary fisherman, but the combination of raft-borne and exceptionally skilled wading fishermen punished the trout—rainbows and west-slope cutthroats—to the point where it was no longer blue-ribbon, pushed it down to the point of mediocrity. Now it is recovering and will improve steadily, absent drought or mining in the headwaters. Cutting the limit has discouraged the carnivores, while limiting the number of outfitters has reduced the admitted stress of repeated catch-and-release trauma to the trout. The only thing Rock Creek will never be is a fine place for boys and other short, inept fly-casters.

The weather looked promising when we came over the hill from Philipsburg and started down the bone-jarring Forest Service road that parallels Rock Creek. In some respects, the road is almost as much of a deterrent to meat-fishermen as the two-fish limit. The Sapphires are rugged, and there isn't enough natural gravel in the valley to make roadbeds that drain well. The dirt road skitters over exposed ledges and shudders through frost-dug potholes that are a front-end-alignment shop's dream.

We hit the river at the first put-in, and the salmon fly hatch was already under way. The rocks on the riverside were bedecked with the dry shucked skins of salmon flies and golden stone flies, and the big flies were crawling on the plated bark of the lodgepole pines at the campground. Stone flies are a primitive aquatic insect, but a little more cleverly evolved than mayflies and dragonflies. Their wings fold back over the abdomen, and the adults are able to conceal themselves, big as they are, in stream-side trees and shrubs, and do their mating in privacy. When stone flies, especially the giant salmon flies, are crawling to the bank to emerge from their scuba gear and take up flying, fishing the nymph imitation is deadly. But few people fly to the Rocky Mountains and drive hours on rugged roads to fish with nymphs. What we needed, that morning, was some warm, sunny weather to prompt the adult females to fly back to the river and lay eggs, something they do clumsily enough in fair weather and cannot do at all in foul.

As if someone had staged the event for one of those public television network nature programs that claim all events are either real or "recreated events based on true examples from nature," the sky was suddenly full of salmon flies a mile downstream. Against the sky, they resembled tiny helicopters with glass rotor blades. They are terrible fliers, the long abdomen droops down, the long but weak and narrow wings thrash wildly. The only insect I know of that looks so incapable of sustained flight is the praying mantis one sees in New England, migrating south in the fall. The mantis has the same belly-down aspect, and the same whirring and inefficient wings.

We got our mile of the famous salmon fly hatch, and no more, for an hour into the trip, a cold front came blowing over the Sapphires and down into the valley. Thunder rattled in the distance, and there is nothing like waving a graphite fly rod around to make you aware of the relative proximity of thunder and lightning. Then gusts of wind started to blow up the river, knocking spray off the tops of standing waves, making fly-casting an aerobic sport. The air was quickly empty of salmon flies, which sensibly huddled against tree bark or hid in the bushes. It wasn't bad catching—a trout every quarter-mile or so—but it was miserable fishing, driving an enormous dry fly into the teeth of the wind or having the wind shift and pile up your back-cast into a jumble. On a float trip, you usually hope it will never end; this one time, I feared it wouldn't.

The only thing I regretted more than the weather was that I did not have a Bunyan Bug in my kit. From the very first day I walked into a tackle shop in Missoula, Montana, I was enamored of the Bunyan Bug, a locally made imitation of the adult salmon fly. There was no point in buying one; I was two months too late for the hatch that year, and I had no collector's instinct. The two shops that sold them, one whose name I have forgotten completely, and Reilly's Cafe and Sporting Goods Store, were the kind of business that did not let small boys buy things they didn't need, and when I picked one out of the bin, or pointed at one under the glass case in Reilly's, I was told it would be useless to try a Bunyan Bug in August. Reilly's, by the way, had to be seen to be believed. It was half barroom–steak house, and the other half sporting goods, including handguns. The bar turned to glass cases halfway down the room, from Highlander beer to Remington pistols. The last time I saw it, it was just another saloon: no food, no trout flies, no ambience. (On reflection and further study, I think my adviser at Reilly's was wrong. Some of the larger stone flies, although not the giant salmon fly, continue to hatch sporadically throughout the summer.)

The Bunyan Bug (it is not made anymore) was invented by Norman Means, a Missoula resident with a touch of press agent's disease, who ran a tackle business under the nom de plume (hackle rather than pen, in this case) of Paul Bunyan. His Bunyan Bug was the first useful imitation of adult stone flies, although it was a horror to cast and so ugly it was almost cute. He took pieces of balsa wood about the diameter of a pencil, fixed them on a hook, painted a lifelike pattern on the wood, and stuck on some flat, spent wings of horse-mane hair. It looked a hell of a lot more like a stone fly, odd as it was, than like any other trout fly in the history of the world. When the Bunyan Bugs were made commercially, Means devised a clever system for "painting" the buggy segmentations on the balsa wood. He had the pattern printed on tissue paper and glued it onto the body with a clear shellac. The tissue paper, its fibers filled with liquid shellac, became almost transparent, leaving only the printed pattern visible to the casual eye. I would have paid considerable money for a Bunyan Bug to take up to Rock Creek.

Bunyon Bug (10 lines #)

ART

In a year of better weather, on the prolific waters of the Madison just above the town of Ennis, Montana, I discovered what truly keeps the salmon fly hatch from approximating the easy fishing of something as regular as a mayfly emergence, as consistent as the green drake hatch. I and a fellow enthusiast for trout fishing and arrowhead hunting were staying with friends who own one of the ranches on the great alluvial fan that looms above the river by Jack Creek, and we thought we had perfectly timed our arrival with the salmon fly hatch. Indeed we had, and that was the problem.

When mayflies are hatching, which for most species occurs daily for weeks, you can expect to see emerging insects every day, and after the cycle begins you will find a mixture of emergers and spinners too. Not so with salmon flies. They had already crawled out of the river when we arrived, and as we came down from Varney Bridge, through Dick Vincent's now-famous study section, the willows along the braided channels of the Madison were loaded with adult salmon flies. Some were continuing their internal development—growing their gonads to ripeness—and others were already copulating as ponderously as elephants. Rocks and vegetation at the river's edge were speckled with the cast-off shells of the nymphal form—the "shuck," as angler's say.

Sofa Pillow Bottle-Brush

10 lines #

ART

Thus we were too late to fish the giant nymph, for they were out of the river, and we were too early to fish the giant dry flies—the Sofa Pillows and Bottle Brushes that attract trout once the egg-laying flights begin. We saw one or two females lumbering over the river and excreting their great dark-purple egg masses, objects about the size and color of the fruit of a Japanese cherry tree, the *murasaki,* the ones that Japanese children love to throw at each other, making small purple spots on their schoolmates' clothing. The trout, perhaps still stuffed and satiated with the huge nymphs, were not feeding much, and weren't looking up at all. Salmon flies hatch in such cold water that the trout's metabolism is slowed, easily sated. We got desperate enough to stop and gather a few dozen salmon flies off the bushes and toss them, one at a time, into likely looking riffles and pools. Not a trout came up to grab them, in spite of our assiduous chumming.

I talked to a few fishermen from Pennsylvania who were camping at the Burnt Tree state access areas between Varney Bridge and Ennis. They had been there for the whole show, having arrived just as the nymphs began migrating to the shore to hatch, and now they were suffering through the doldrums between emergence and egg-laying. One of them had a pocket fishing diary and refreshed his memory in response to my questions. Five days earlier, when they arrived, he had landed seventeen trout, followed by days of six, five, three, one and one. He knew, he said, that he should have gone upriver to keep up with the emerging nymphs, but he kept thinking things would break open where he was, that the adults would start to fly. Surely they did, sometime later, and just as certainly, I was three hundred miles away when it happened. Richard Hafele—author of the single best book on Western fly-fishing, *The Complete Book of Western Hatches*, and the only how-to manual I have ever seen that could justify using the word "complete" in the title—states the problem with these giant stone flies very succinctly: "Those who limit themselves to fishing dry patterns of these stoneflies miss half the hatch. The underwater migration of the nymphs from their rough-water habitat to the quieter water along the banks exposes them to trout for days prior to their emergence. Some of the finest fishing of the season takes place in these pre-hatch days; we would rather be on a stretch of stone fly water just before an emergence than during it." Or, in the simpler notation of the angler from Pennsylvania one may define the state of "just before emergence" with the formula: seventeen, six, five, three, one, one.

Still, I would recommend trying to be on a river for the days of flight and egg-laying. Every fly-fisherman, once in a lifetime, ought to see the air filled with insects as long as cigarettes. We spend so much time with dinky things, with leader tippets the diameter of sewing thread, with flies no bigger than a mosquito. We waste so much time worrying about long and perfect casts and careful, splashless wading. We have all earned one duffer's salmon fly holiday before we hang up the rod. You may not catch anything bigger or better than on any other day; you may get frustrated with the crowds. But you deserve to look up, just once, and see the air filled with juicy baits, and look down at the river and know that no fish in it is so large, so wise, so devoted to eating other fish that it cannot be caught on the next cast. It is just as well the hatch only lasts a day, sometimes only an hour. A month of salmon flies would be too hard on the fish and not good for the souls of anglers. I am not saying we were put on earth to suffer, just that if salmon flies fell on the river every day, we would soon be unable to appreciate the difference between fly-fishing and clam digging.

12

Fishing While Floating

*Comments on the variability of
guides and on float-fishing as an
educational event, with suggestions
for matching the guide's expertise
to the angler's ability*

Float-fishing—guided trips down a river in a boat or raft—is the fastest-growing segment of the fly-fishing industry in America. As just one example, and the numbers would be proportional for Alaska or Oregon or Wyoming, twenty years ago there were fewer than a hundred fishing guides in Montana, and some of them were part-timers, using guide status as a tax dodge to write off their expensive personal toys—their boats and trailers and extra fly rods. As this century ends, there are more than five hundred guides out on Montana's rivers every day of high season, June through August. With prices averaging around two hundred dollars a day, float-fishing anglers pump at least ten million dollars into the economy for guide fees alone, and as much more for food, lodging and transportation. (Ordinary tourists, experts claim, pump eight dollars into the local economy for every dollar spent on a unique local tourist attraction. These experts have never seen five trout fishermen from Pennsylvania packed into a single pickup camper.)

No book instructs one on how to be a float-fishing angler, which is very odd when you consider that books are available on such diverse refinements as: Nymph-Fishing for Larger Trout, Back-Pack Fishing in Alpine Lakes, Belly-Boat Fly-Fishing (a belly-boat is a one-man craft made out of a tire-truck inner tube fitted with a high-tech butt-harness), Fishing with Terrestrial Imitations, and Midge-Fishing Made Easy. Hundreds of books have explained where and how to fish in various countries, states and territories. Anglers seeking any of the different species of trout may purchase instruction manuals dedicated to brook, brown, rainbow and steelhead. For the scientifically minded and manually dextrous angler, dozens more books are available on aquatic entomology and fly-tying technique, some so specialized that they deal with single orders of trout food—not only the popular mayflies, but also with stone flies, caddis flies and midges. Why float-fishing has been left out in this flood of printed information I can only speculate, especially since the potential market is by definition made up of people who can afford to buy books. I think the omission is largely because fly-fishing has always lagged a generation or more behind other human activities in innovation; it is a tardy, tradition-bound sport.

Perhaps the reason why no one has written *The Complete Float-Angler* is that the tens of thousands of us who annually take these trips expect that the guide will know everything (a bold but marginally correct assumption) and that he will tell us everything we need to know (a much greater and less well founded act of faith). Guides are members of one of the few professions that still generate reflexive awe and respect in the consumer—even before they have done anything to prove they deserve it. Pending the inevitable publication of *The Complete Float-Angler*, this chapter will explain how to become expert at the art, to attain a distinctive wisdom quite separate from ordinary fly-fishing.

A proper guide on a proper river will own a drift boat, or, as they are often called from the place where they were first refined, a McKenzie River boat. This is a keel-less double-ended skiff with fairly high sides and upswept bow and stern, maneuverable, shallow-drafted and stable, the best of all rigid boats for running rapids. The customer's most important task is to sit on the center line of the boat.

One does this naturally in a canoe, and one is quickly punished with a dunking if one forgets. In a stable and sturdy guide boat, it is not so obviously necessary. Sitting on the keel line is more a social grace, like using the right fork for your salad. (There are no rules about rubber rafts, except to avoid them if at all possible. Fly-fishing while sitting down, the only position one can take in a rubber raft, is akin to shooting pool sitting down—possible, but inefficient and uncomfortable.) A drift boat can be tipped a little to one side or the other, if either of the anglers (two customers and a guide are the usual complement) doesn't stay centered over the midline. When the boat is canted sideways, the guide, rowing amidships, ends up with one oar effectively longer than the other and has difficulty rowing. This is as annoying and uncomfortable as walking with one shoe on and one shoe off, although some guides, preferring to suffer in silence, will not mention it. Other guides, who suffer very little, will mention it every time either customer shifts off-center. Customers who sit in the middle will have a better day for observing this self-serving courtesy: with a guide who knows his business, the better the rowing, the better the fishing.

At the risk of miffing a few dozen people I know and with whom I enjoy fishing, I will say that Roy Pruitt, a veteran McKenzie River guide, is by a slight but perceptible margin both the best rower and the most persnickety person I've ever met when it comes to keeping the boat on an even keel. I've fished with him in the 1960s and in 1990, and back then and today he's got the only drift boat I've ever seen with an inclinometer, a patented, brass-cased tilt-gauge, installed in the stem of the bow, right square in front of the angler's eyes as he sits down on the front thwart. If this mechanical hint is insufficient, Roy will tell you to move your butt. The reward, however, is immediate and constant. Roy Pruitt works closer to the fish than anyone I know, rows as hard (but more quietly) than anyone I've met, and will slip a boat right down through a tangle of rocks that most guides would cheerfully slide by, preferring to stay out in the main current. The night after the last time I fished with him, I went to sleep with two visual memories: during the transition from wakefulness to dreamless rest, I saw a rainbow trout taking a Green McKenzie at the surface, and I saw the needle of the inclinometer oscillating slightly around the zero degree mark.

Pruitt has a particular talent for fishing two anglers (to use the guide's vernacular), one casting a dry fly, the other using a sunken fly. This is something of an Oregon specialty and an increasingly rare skill among guides. I have known some who flatly refuse to believe it is possible, or if possible, useful. What the guide must do is pick a line of drift with two attributes: first, that the casting angler, standing in the bow, can reach reasonably good trout water, and, second, that the wet-fly angler, seated aft, holding his rod out to one side or the other, is able to fish his fly in equally good spots from time to time. This requires judicious navigation and perfect knowledge of the river. The boat must be constantly rowed in an upstream direction so that it drifts down more slowly than the current, enabling the wet fly to swing below the boat. And the guide has to shift the boat back and forth across the width of the river, working the wet fly (or nymph) first through this, then that, likely spot. It is too much work for too little benefit, I suppose, and it must be acknowledged that the standing, casting angler sometimes objects to sharing the total concentration of the guide and wishes he could always be casting from the best position in the river. Most pairs of anglers (including spouses) would rather divide time in the casting position than fish in mutual but compromised unity.

The older McKenzie River guides came naturally by the technique of using the boat to position the wet fly. Whether fishing with lures, bait or wet flies, they did it routinely when guiding for steelhead in coastal rivers. They became accustomed to regarding the boat as a fishing device, not just as mere transportation or as a platform for a caster. Years ago, my wife and I treated ourselves to a float-trip with Roy Pruitt. (I am not the sort of man who buys his wife an electric drill for Christmas; we both enjoyed the McKenzie enormously, if as nothing more than a murmuring background to a picnic.) She and Roy—she holding the rod, Roy working the boat to let the wet fly drift through a riffle to a drop-off at the head of a pool—caught the largest rainbow trout I have yet to see from the McKenzie, over nine-teen inches, so large that by the rules there, it had to be returned to the river. In those days, the McKenzie River Guides Association had very nice printed certificates naming all customers who have caught and released an oversized trout to honorary membership in that elite group of professionals. My wife still has her certificate, and mentions it on occasion, when the subject of fishing wives comes up.

Two anglers can fly-cast through the same piece of water, if they are willing to take turns. This is their responsibility, however. The guide can't do anything to help people who can't get their acts to-gether—or separate. It's better to take turns standing and fly-casting, but it is best of all not to spend the whole day drift-fishing. If you leave the decision up to the guide, nine times out of ten he will pick a section of river so long that drifting down it occupies the entire day. I have never quite figured out why, except that it gives the guide con-trol over the schedule. Or perhaps guides like to show guests as much of the country as possible, to fish as much water and have as many chances at trout as can be fitted into a day. I have tried all-day drift-ing; I have enjoyed it; and it is the wrong way to fish.

The great benefit of drift-fishing is that, on a good river, it allows you to cover five to ten miles of water, and that means you will float by anywhere from twenty-five thousand to fifty thousand trout, hard as that may be to believe. But with fishing, as with the rest of life, opportunity is not the same thing as success. The problem is that dur-ing most of the day, for all but perhaps a dozen of those fish you will have only one chance, one cast, one drift of the fly. It might seem like a nice idea to kiss every pretty girl in town, but not all on the same day, not while on a dead run down Main Street. There is very little courtship while float-fishing, little interaction between angler and an individual trout, and therefore very little anticipation. If fly-fishing were enhanced by nothing else, simple expectancy makes it the sat-isfying and preoccupying sport that it is. Casting repeatedly to the same trout is comparable to wing-shooting birds over a pointing dog, or hunting wild turkey in the spring season when you hear the bird gobbling as it walks toward you. Those brief moments of expectation (or with turkey, minutes of anticipation) make the sport memorable.

With few exceptions, good trout rivers provide islands, bars and gravelly banks suitable for wading, and you should negotiate your trip with the guide so you can get out several times, not just to micturate or ambulate, but to find a single fish, cast to it, change flies if necessary, worry about it, even fail miserably to catch it. Missing a fish while floating is only a mild and temporary disappointment—you have no chance to redeem yourself and no particular reason to blame yourself—and for the same reason, catching one while drifting by is less satisfying than hooking it while wading: you have not really made the acquaintance of the trout.

Fishing lessons are easier for the student to comprehend from the bank than from a moving boat. There are no special techniques unique to drift-fishing. Everything you do while in a boat is the same as when you are wading, except it happens faster, and speed is no asset to education. All rivers have places where the guide can stop the boat, anchor it or hold it easily in a back-current, places where you can methodically work on a single fish if one is rising, or on a patch of likely water. But you have to tell him that you want to go slow, meet a few of the local fish, take some photographs, enjoy your lunch, and get off the treadmill for a day.

Taking a break and wading also gives a pair of anglers the best moments of the day for sharing the fishing experience. As I said, two fly-casters in a moving boat can choreograph alternate (never simultaneous) casts, but they cannot take turns fishing the same piece of water, they cannot each cast a fly to points *A* and *B*, and they never have a chance to say those most companionable words: "I can't raise that fish—you try him." There is always a likeliest spot in a riffle, often there is a rising fish in a pool, but neither can be shared by fishermen in a moving boat.

The most sensible way to divide the time between casting and doing something else entertaining is to alternate every time someone catches a serious fish. I like to change places after every trout big enough to be worth netting and measuring, as opposed to one so inconsequential that you just reach down, grasp the hook and shake it off. A typical drift boat puts one angler standing in the bow, and seats the second fisherman directly behind him, with the guide rowing from the center seat, the stern section holding gear and lunch coolers, and this is the easiest layout for changing after every good catch. The second angler can get up and start casting while the first is drying his fly, checking his leader, attending to those small housekeeping details that inevitably occur after landing a fish.

If the boat is rigged so that one angler is in the stern, another in the bow with the guide in between, it won't work so easily. Guides are patient creatures by nature (the impatient ones eventually find their true calling and get a job with regular hours), but they can't cope with constantly having anglers crawling over them. Setting rigid schedules—changing on the half-hour or hour—doesn't work either. Even on the best of rivers, there are only going to be a few periods in a day when things go well, and each partner should get as much of the good time as possible.

If the solution is to change places after every extremely serious fish, you have to define seriousness as the day goes along. The last time I went with Roy Pruitt on the McKenzie, my brother-in-law and I changed places after every native rainbow caught—every genuine red-striped, big-eyed fish—regardless of size. It was miserable weather for most of the trip—cold, falling barometer, rainy—and the brief hatches of green caddis and a few small stone flies were over so quickly that we had rather long periods between changing places by reason of trout; we switched more when we changed the criterion to losing a fly in the trees or wanting to change patterns, or simply getting bored with casting and wanting to sit down and think about the cussedness of Oregon weather. But in the few minutes of good fishing we had, we traded often and amicably.

Besides helping the guide plan the day and organizing the social calendar, the customer has to decide whether he wants to be an expert or a student. A drift boat is the best platform in the world for learning the mechanics of fly-casting—you are high above the water and usually free of any impediment to the backcast. Some guides are better instructors than others, some are more didactic, more communicative, more interested in teaching, but almost all guides have some contribution to make if you can convince them you came to learn, not show off. Almost thirty years ago, Roy Pruitt taught my brother-in-law the basics of fly-casting, yet, in guiding me two or three times then, he never taught me anything about casting itself, although he tried hard to put what little skill I had to proper use on the river. The reason was simple: I didn't have the common sense to ask for a lesson. My brother-in-law Ken did, and got two eight-hour days of private lessons that have stood the test of time. On our last trip together, he asked for, and got, a continuous lesson on where and how to fish, including a repetitive lecture on Pruitt's favorite injunction: "refloating" the fly, a McKenzie River specialty.

R efloating is not a practice unique to the McKenzie, but great emphasis is placed on it there, and this has been true since before World War II, when men like the late Prince Helfrich (father and grandfather to eight McKenzie River guides) perfected the technique and taught it to the likes of Herbert Hoover. Refloating is a version of what all instructional books call "mending the line," though that is like saying that mountain climbing is merely hiking on an incline. The purpose of mending a line is simple enough, easier to achieve in practice than describe in theory. Whenever you fly-fish on running water, you cast across water that is moving at a different speed from the water where the fly lands, and most of the time you are casting a straight line; when the line and leader and fly all fall on the water, the difference in the currents almost immediately causes the fly to drag. This is an elementary problem, and the solutions to it are numerous. Some anglers can cast a curved line (the end of the line—and especially the leader—will curve left or right if, at the end of the cast, you move the rod tip abruptly in the direction in which you want the end of the line to curve). Most anglers can cast a line with

shallow S-curves in it; these will absorb some of the difference between the current where the line floats and the current where the fly
(and, one hopes, the trout) will be. Either of two tricks, two ways to
put last-minute shock or stoppage in the casting motion, will put a
series of lazy S-curves in the line: you can lift the rod tip straight up
and back at the end of the cast, or you can let the rod be and pull
back sharply on the line with your free hand.

Mending the line by refloating is another trick altogether. You
make the cast, let everything fall on the water, and then pick up the
line with a sharp upward motion of the rod as if you were starting to
begin a new cast. As the line starts to lift up and back, you snap the
line left or right with a sharp motion of the rod tip. The idea is to
throw a big open curve in the line, the direction of the curve depending on what is necessary to overcome the contrary current between
you and the fly. Most often, you want to throw the line upstream of
the fly, as nine times out of ten, you are casting across a faster current
into a slower one. This refloating motion, this second-step cast, may
sound complex, but it is exactly the same thing you do when the
garden hose gets caught on some low-lying obstruction as you pull it
toward the flower bed, or when the vacuum-cleaner cord hangs up
on a footstool—with a snap of the wrist, you throw a curve in the
hose or cord to move it up and over the obstruction.

Because the whole purpose of mending the line is to prevent the
fly from dragging unnaturally, to preserve the "dead-drift" of all fly-
fishing manuals, most of us mend the line very delicately, and we try
to flip the line without moving the fly. This is not the McKenzie style;
they do not call it "*re*floating the fly" for nothing. The McKenzie refloat is a more violent mend, one that picks all the line up off the
water, pulls sharply on the leader, and usually sinks the fly by dragging it underwater, all as part of the process of throwing the line well
upstream of the fly. With bushy dry flies—caddis and stone flies and
deer-hair-bodied-and-winged mayfly imitations—the fly pops right
back up to the surface. You literally refloat the fly, skittering it along
the surface, sinking it, and changing the lane on the water down
which it will float.

This goes contrary to all the usual efforts, when one tries to present a fly, whether a dry or wet one, softly, and then prays it will not move contrary to the natural flow of the water. The McKenzie refloat changes the rules. You expect and allow for violent movement of the fly right after it lands on the water. You trade this deliberate initial dragging motion for a longer, more natural, dead-drift afterward. The refloat itself, the abruptly moving fly, McKenzie guides believe, attracts the interest of the trout but doesn't scare them. "The idea," as Pruitt explains it, "is to get their attention and *then* get a natural drift." It was for this reason, on our last trip, that Roy said "Refloat, now!" probably two hundred times between Martin Rapids and Leaburg Lake and, once, took the fly rod away from my brother-in-law and demonstrated the technique. He demonstrated the refloat over a very unlikely piece of water, and kept the fly out of the good feeding lane at the base of the High Bank cliffs. Roy is not one of those guides who, like Old Izaak, insist on showing you how to catch a fish by doing the job for you.

Most of us, wanting to achieve a good drift, put the emphasis on the cast and let the float take care of itself. Dick Helfrich, one of Prince's three sons in the guide business, is as serious as Roy Pruitt about refloating. I fished with him a few years ago, and went to sleep that night with the word "refloat" echoing distantly in my ears. During the day, we had run into Roy Pruitt at a lunch spot on the riverbank, and the two of them got to talking about a pair of local fly-fishermen whom Dick had guided earlier that week. He told Pruitt it hadn't been a terribly successful trip: "They could cast," he said, "but they didn't know what to do with the fly afterward. They were so good at casting you couldn't teach them anything about fishing."

It does go against the grain, this refloating business. You must cast beyond the lane where you want the fly to travel, and well above the best part of that water, and refloat the fly back toward the boat. One of the hardest places to get even a few seconds of drag-free float is in the vortex behind a big rock—the slow water behind a rock is always surrounded by the more rapid, accelerated current that sweeps around the obstruction. Refloating to a fish behind a rock may mean casting a dozen feet beyond the spot, into the fast current, then snapping the line back toward you, skittering the fly back into the soft current where, if things have been done properly, it will float for a few seconds before the current on your side of the rock catches the line and snatches the fly away. Long floats are not necessary: trout that choose to feed in such places will be sufficiently alert to take a fly by the time you have counted to "a thousand-two." Everyone knows there are fish behind rocks, but McKenzie guides, in my experience, have the best idea of just where in that vortex they will be—halfway, on average, from the rock to the point downstream where the divided currents rejoin. In rocky sections, a good McKenzie guide will say "refloat" about as often as he pulls on the oars.

Because drift boats are such excellent casting platforms, and because most guides are skilled fly-casters themselves, they tend to keep a boat at too generous a distance from the spot where they expect the customer to cast the fly. I am not quite sure why they do this. A boat drifting down with the current does not frighten fish unless it slides directly over them, so that is not the reason. It is, in fact, amazing how close to your boat you can raise and hook a trout. It is partly the nature of certain rivers—fast-falling and rock-studded—and partly the nature of certain fish—eager and insectivorous rainbows—but I do think most guides put too much strain on the caster and too little thought into their choice of a drift line down the river. On many of my trips on the McKenzie and other rivers, the largest fish have taken a fly within twenty feet, often within ten feet, of the boat.

For your guide fee, you are entitled to ask the oarsman to help you cast within your own capacity, your own range of the lanes where he wants you to fish. Fishing nearer, you may catch fewer trout than your guide would hook if he were casting and you were rowing the boat, but you will catch more fish *yourself* than you would if every cast were to your maximum distance. You are, after all, on vacation. And expert casters (or ordinary casters on a good day) can put a fly out well beyond the point where they can reliably set the hook in a rising fish. Avoiding that extreme distance between angler and trout is a particular benefit of strong, vigorous refloating: it pulls the fly back to a range within which you have a chance of firmly, gently, skillfully setting the hook. The longer the line, the more the slack and curves in it, the harder it is to estimate how vigorously to move the rod to tighten the line.

Once you have sorted out the peculiarities of a river and learned how similar it is and its trout are to running water and swimming fish the world over, you may discover that there is more to angling than fishing all day long. I know some guides who like to go looking for arrowheads and dinosaur bones, for instance, and I spend half the time with them walking near the river, kicking at suspiciously interesting rocks. We might even let the river rest, and take a day to look for the rings of stones that mark old teepee camps, a day to look for even more ancient relics. A dinosaur gizzard stone, a *gastrolith*, sits on my desk, a blue-brown quartz stone polished sixty million years ago as it rubbed against other pebbles, grinding siliceous leaves and stems in the peristaltic gut of a Late Cretaceous herbivore. The rock's true color is a perfect medium blue-dun, the same tint as the rarest of good trout-fly feathers. On its glossy surface are tiny shallow pits where softer particles of genuine gold were scoured down, but not out, so many eons ago. The rock glistens with quartz and gold, with refracted and reflected color. It is the best trophy I ever caught in the valley of the Bighorn River.

I am still looking for my arrowhead, so I will stop at small side streams and dry washes and walk up and scan the eroding bank to see if the winter's rains have uncovered some manufactured flint tool left by the first settlers of the Great Plains. A drift boat is a good way to get into trout country. What you do there should be your own heart's desire.

13

The Theory of Very
Large Artificial Flies

*With an explanation of the reasons
why there are so many very
small natural flies in rivers that
drain lakes and reservoirs*

A few years ago, I attempted to give one of my favorite trout flies to my friend, Alan Kelly, who has a lodge and guide service on the Bighorn River. It was not a successful offering. Kelly's diffidence arose not from an incapacity for gratitude but from his knowledge of the river running by his door. The Bighorn, like all trout rivers that draw consistently cold water from reservoirs, supports an enormous population of very small natural flies—insects less than a third of an inch in length—that are imitated with artificials tied on hooks from size 16 down to 22. The fly I wanted him to have in his armament was more than an inch long and thicker through the middle than the average person's little finger. In total cubic volume (length times width times height), it was a hundred times larger than any Bighorn fly, natural or artificial, and he had trouble concealing his skepticism about it. Expert anglers will X-ray the teeth of a gift horse.

In the case of this fly, scientific instrumentation was hardly necessary. It was an Atlantic salmon fly, the most popular large dry fly in the waters of New Brunswick, and a pattern increasingly popular as a steelhead fly in British Columbia rivers, tied on a No. 4 hook. The current name for the concoction is Bomber, but it was originally and deservedly called Cigar Butt. It is a simple fly, and like all popular flies, has developed a number of variations. I still prefer the original, whether for Atlantic salmon or trout. The body is made of clipped deer hair; the hair is spun onto the hook and then trimmed symmetrically, tapering from a thick middle to slim ends. A single feather (usually a "saddle" hackle from a Rhode Island Red rooster's lower back) is wound from one end to the other and tied off. This is, of course, palmering, though rather scantier palmering than you see on more familiar examples such as the wet fly called a Woolly Worm. A proper Bomber has two sets of horns, a pair of short protrusions at each end. These can be made of some of the deer hair left unclipped, or, if you want to be fancy, short lengths of woodchuck guard hair tied in place. There is no point, in a good Bomber, of talking about wings and tails or even heads and tails. A Bomber is perfectly symmetrical whether you cut it on the long axis or across the middle of the body. All decent trout flies are bilaterally symmetrical, but the Bomber is quadrilaterally symmetrical and has no front or back, top or bottom, except for the eye of the hook and the bend of the point. It looks the same viewed from any angle, and that is true whether you are an angler or a trout. As one ancient author said of the palmered flies in general, "They are never upside down." The Bomber has the added advantage of never being aligned upstream or down. It looks totally out of place on the Bighorn, floating like a battleship among a spectator fleet of rowboats—dinky caddis and smutty mayflies.

ART

Why tail-water rivers like the Bighorn support so many small flies in such profusion requires a doctoral thesis in aquatic biology that remains to be written. However, Alan Kelly has a master's degree in cold-water ecology to go with his years of experience on the Bighorn (first as a consulting biologist to the Crow Nation, which controls most of the land adjacent to the river, and latterly as a guide) and he knows, both academically and practically, the ways tail waters churn out a myriad of small natural flies.

It is in the lakes above the dams that the ecology of tiny flies begins. Reservoir-outlet rivers, like spring-fed creeks, are consistent in temperature, seldom freezing over in the winter and always running cold throughout the heat of summer. Where an outlet river is managed to support a cold-water fishery, water is deliberately drawn out of the lake from depths that ensure it is always chilled. Many of the small species of mayflies that you usually see in small cold streams will find a home in the altered cold main stream of such a river. In particular, the various small mayflies that anglers call little blue-winged olives and pale morning duns are as common in huge tail-water rivers as they are in tiny spring-fed creeks.

Typical tail-water caddis flies, also very small and very profuse, usually outnumber mayflies in daily production of trout baits. It is not so much temperature that controls the size of the various species as it is food. The very small caddis are fattened on food created in the lakes above them. All water produces a host of minute animal and vegetable life, most of it single-celled, almost all of it microscopic in size; the tiny organisms need clear water to allow as much sunlight as possible to reach as deep as possible, all this for the same photosynthesis that is necessary for land-bound plants. This is plankton—the first step in the food chain—and when produced in rivers it is swept downstream instantly if it is floating, or it is scoured off the rocks if it is one of the adherent species. In lakes, plankton grows more profusely and is only slowly carried away in the outlet stream. (As a rule of thumb, a sort of world average, no more than one-thousandth of the water in lakes is carried away daily by their outlet rivers.) Floating vegetable plankton is notably a creature of lakes.

The caddis that thrive in tail waters come mostly from one super-family of the order—the net-spinners. The net-spinning caddis construct complicated little plankton- and debris-seining nets on the bottom of the river, some so finely woven that the mesh will trap large bacteria. Other sorts of caddis are direct-filter feeders equipped with fuzzy appendages on which food is caught and from which it is chewed, or they are grazers, moving about on the bottom like a herd of minute, close-cropping sheep. The clarity of trout water is not due entirely to geological mechanics, but partially to this biological cleansing. All net-spinning caddis begin life with very fine mesh nets because the size of the mesh is directly related to the size of the larva that spins it—to be precise, to the size of the mouth parts which are adapted to extruding the web material and tacking it in place. Like young orb-weaving garden spiders, all juvenile caddis make nets that are fine at first and increasingly wide-gapped as the caddis (or spiders) grow to maturity. But very small species of caddis such as the ones fishermen call the little autumn sedge, little black caddis, or, my favorite, the dinky purple-breasted sedge—caddis which never grow longer than a third of an inch—maintain very fine mesh nets throughout their larval life. These minute nets are perfect for capturing the rich, but fine, broth of diatoms and other plankton swept down from the lake above them. And these dwarf caddis are so efficient at trapping their food that the elevated levels of plankton found just below dams are reduced to normal river amounts by the time you get a dozen miles downstream of the lake. Caddis populations decline proportionally to the levels of plankton, and the frequency of trout diminishes in proportion to the caddis population. On the well-studied Bighorn, fish-per-mile estimates drop from eight thousand just below the dam to three thousand only eight miles downstream.

If you meet a man who prides himself on being able to catch fish on very small nymphs and dry flies and who makes a living teaching tourists to do the same, and if you offer him a fly that looks as out of place as a Bengal tiger at a cat show, you probably deserve what you get. Most Bighorn anglers (even of the amateur variety) are quite sure that large artificial flies will not work, and even surer that large nondescript flies of the sort that anglers call "attractor flies" are worse than useless. (An attractor fly is frequently, but not always, colorful. Its defining quality is that it does not exactly imitate any living thing.) The Bomber I was trying to foist on Alan Kelly met all the criteria of uselessness.

The difference between an attracting fly and a realistic artificial one is not always clear, certainly not to the trout. Whole classes of flies, numbering by now in the hundreds of examples, made of fur and feather and plastic, typify our best human attempts at direct, realistic imitation. Useful attractors look dressier, fancier, less likely, but in fact they are not truly silly-looking. Even though no known insect

Royal Coachman
ART

has the color scheme of a fan-wing Royal Coachman, for example, that fancy fly has a realistic silhouette. (Some thirty years ago, while I was drifting the McKenzie River with a friend from Eugene, Oregon, we both saw a large fly flitting upstream. It had a bright red body, a dark green egg sack at the tail, and white wings. In short, we were watching a natural Royal Coachman, an object unknown to entomologists. We were quite sober, by the way.) Color aside, a properly tied Royal Coachman, whether it is fan-winged or conventionally modeled after the standard hackled flies of commerce, does resemble in its shape any of the large mayflies. The Trude, the next most popular attractor on Western rivers, is equally well shaped to simulate a natural bug; any of the larger caddis or smaller stone flies. I suspect that many of our "realistic" flies work on trout in the same way as the Coachmen and Trudes of this world, they are the right shape, there is something edible-looking about them, and they trigger the only response besides flight which we can expect to elicit in the trout—feeding behavior.

The peculiar thing about these attractor flies is that they are always too big. Anyone who has ever stopped in a Western fly shop in the later summer or early fall has been advised to buy a good-sized Royal Coachman (usually the bushier Wulff Royal Coachman) or a Trude, and either one is out of proportion to the natural insects that are hatching sporadically as the fishing season runs to a close. Late flies (except for some large caddis) are usually smaller than their cousins of June and July, and, if we were intent on matching the occasional hatch, we would choose sizes from 16 on down. Yet clerks with the best of intentions and the best of local knowledge will sell you flies as large as No. 10. And these big flies will work, just as the obscene Bomber will, so long as the trout are looking up toward the surface. Why do trout sometimes eat these outrageously large flies? I have mentioned that close observation of trout behavior, whether truly scientific or merely inquisitive, has produced some of the great breakthroughs in trout management and angling technique. It just may be that we can apply some of the insights of twentieth-century animal studies to this issue.

If you think of innate animal behavior as being made up of urges or propensities waiting to be exercised, then instead of talking about stimulus and response, you can speak of "release mechanisms." The classic example is offered by the egg and the bird. Farmers have known for centuries that one way to get a young hen to start laying eggs was to provide it with an artificial egg. The presence of one of these "nest eggs" (from which comes the metaphor of productivity and wealth in our common speech) caused the young pullet to become "broody," with the inevitable result of interest paid in real eggs. And farmers knew that the larger the nest egg, the more it released the brooding urge in the pullet. The old-timers would use a duck or turkey egg to get a hen started laying. If they used store-bought or hand-carved nest eggs, the duplicitous egg was always at least extra large, twice the size of a natural pullet's egg. Ethologists carried the farmer's trick into the world of wild birds, and found that many species of perching birds and waterfowl will compulsively brood an egg of enormous size, even to the point of absurdity. A fishing friend of mine who teaches animal behavior and anthropology at Harvard has a photograph of a kittiwake sitting on an ersatz egg the size of a cantaloupe. The human being is not above this sort of thing, as evidenced by the behavior of some of us when confronted with secondary sexual characteristics of the gigantic sort. Not merely big bosoms but big eyes are somehow more attractive to men than merely functional ones.

The ethologist's shorthand for this fascination of big eggs to small birds is the phrase "super-normal release," one of those academic phrases that has the attractive quality of being both vague and precise at the same time. Think of it as "big-egg behavior," and you will not forget the important part of the exercise. Now, if you think of a trout as having a predilection for eating a bug called a mayfly or a caddis, and if there aren't enough of them available to trigger selective feeding on a hatch of naturals, you can see why your unnaturally large Royal Coachman or Trude might have the same effect on the fish as the nest egg has on the pullet. The trout has a behavior pattern (feeding) that is waiting for something to start the cascade of steps that make the fish look up, swim up, open up and eat. Why should it be less subject to the power of a super-normal-releasing Royal Coachman than the kittiwake is to the gargantuan phony egg? (If we are fishing on a stretch of no-kill blue-ribbon water, we can say, proudly, that we are engaged in super-normal-release-and-release fishing.)

The important thing is not only the size but the imitativeness of the fly. Kittiwakes will brood a giant egg, but they will not sit on a papaya, a football or a beach rock. Neither will a trout eat a cotton ball, a toothbrush or a jelly bean. Leonard West, a British author of the 1920s (*The Natural Trout Fly and Its Imitation*), was a great believer both in exact, deceptive imitations of the natural fly and in flies that were merely attractive to trout. He long ago wrote the final word on the subject, even though the argument continues: "We may divide flies into two classes, viz., 'attractors' and 'deceivers,' with the reservation that an attractor must be a deceiver, and a deceiver, attractive." I would add only that the flies must be attractive to the angler as well as to the trout. If we have no faith in them, we will not fish with them properly.

The best-known section of the Bighorn River is a deep pool about eight miles downstream from the dam, which can be reached by wading down from a public access parking lot. The pool begins at a sharp bluff that rises perpendicularly from the west bank of the river. The hard stone that makes up the bluff also marks the upstream edge of this very deep, very fish-populated water. The local name of the bar, using (for purposes of rhyming) the British term for caddis flies, is Sedge Ledge. And, truly, innumerable caddis larvae are swept out of the riffles above Sedge Ledge. Just below the bar in the quiet water, numbers of large trout wait and feed on the drifting larvae. When there is a hatch, a few of them will abandon the continuous flow of in-stream food and start to take flies on the surface. It would be a better place to fish if it were not always—from June through September—occupied by at least one or two anglers carefully dead-drifting small Zug Bugs and Red Squirrel/Red Fox fuzzy nymphs down the riffle and over the bar.

Alan Kelly held Sedge Ledge up to me as the perfect example of why my gift Bomber would be useless on the Bighorn, a No. 18 river if there ever was one. And it is true I've never caught a fish on a Bomber at Sedge Ledge, but many trout have fallen for it above and downstream of the ledge. The three times I've floated by it with my friend Joey Caton, we did not stop. Anglers in chest waders were already there, and if there's one thing you should not do from a drift boat, it is interfere with a wading angler. Elsewhere on the river, Joey Caton has seen the notorious, selective, sophisticated Bighorn brown trout eat the Bomber at morning, noon and night. Even he doesn't acknowledge that it happened. I have his word on it, though; I can quote him exactly in reference to the last of several nice brown trout that took a Bomber one afternoon: "I don't believe it."

The faith of an angler is not unlike the faith of the religious convert. All signs are interpreted to conform to the latest doctrine. If you only fish with very small nymphs and tiny imitative dry flies, matching as best you can the insect life of the river, you attribute all success to obeying the rules of your revealed religion and all failure to your own imperfections. This is understandable, but not reasonable. If you are on a river with several thousand trout per mile, and the tens of thousands of fish you float by during a long summer day are not randomly distributed but concentrated in suitable feeding lanes, and if you float for hundreds of yards between rises to your most excellent imitations, you can hardly argue that you have solved the mystery. You will drift a natural-sized, realistic and imitative fly within a foot of at least a thousand fish, you will catch a few dozen and you will say that your ability to match the hatch accounts for what you imagine was your success. I showed the big palmered Bomber to a few thousand brown trout and caught a dozen. I was happy, but hardly a candidate for angling sainthood. There is a wonderful randomness in trout fishing, and we should adopt the statistician's view of very large trials and understand that apparently improbable results are to be expected. If you played a thousand hands of blackjack and won twenty, would you call it a triumph and give the credit to your skills as a gambler? (The purist will argue that if you could win twenty hands in a row, as the best of fly-fishers can take the first twenty fish they see rising, you would, by the twentieth hand, have won $3,932,160 if you parlayed your $2 bets. Purists have vivid imaginations.)

Still, like all caterpillar-looking flies, the Bomber will find its victims. Leonard West shows three "palmers" in his book and accounts for their popularity with what must be admitted is pure pathetic fallacy, that is, ascribing human emotions to animals: "Every windy day numbers of them [caterpillars] must drop on the water, and being fat, juicy morsels, they are immediately seized by trout, which get weary of everlasting duns, stone flies and other aquatic insects." Reservoir tail-water trout usually have an especially limited diet composed of very small items. Because of an excess of dissolved nitrogen gas caused by the outlet system, such streams seldom support any of the larger cold-water stream animals so important to growing big trout—crayfish, sculpins or the large stone flies. Still, I would not have caught my dozen large trout fishing with a real cigar butt threaded over a hook. The Bomber and its little cousin the Buck Bug (one-quarter to one-half the size, and without the projecting horns at each end) are not silly, fatuous, stupid: they are just high-floating, interestingly colored, sparsely dressed versions of the ancient palmer fly, the one regarded by Charles Cotton as good for every month of the season.

You cannot fish a Bomber or a Buck Bug just anywhere in the river, and that is why I love them. They must be fished in active, roiled, riffled water. Even big, slow tail waters have sections with divided and uneven currents; no river runs evenly to the sea. Fishing one of these palmer flies rewards me for doing what I like best, finding the parts of a big river that most resemble the riffle-and-pool streams of my boyhood. I see the Bomber of my seniority as if it were the Joe's Hopper of my youth, and the broad Bighorn shrinks down to the size of the East Fork at Sula Meadows. Sedge Ledge, even though it is a hundred feet across and marks the beginning of a smoothly running pool a quarter of a mile long, is not so different from a small pool where once I saw a dipper-bird, a water ouzel, walk unconcerned by my feet, picking at caddis larva two feet under the surface. The shape of running water is the same everywhere. It varies only in scale.

Whether one has faith in palmer flies in general, or the Bomber in specific, has much to do with one's personal history and geography. Such flies were always popular in the north-central parts of England. Walton, Cotton and the great innovators of the midnineteenth century before the dogma of exact imitation and the dry fly was written in southwest Hampshire, were all riffle-and-pool men. I feel kinship with Michael Theakston, *British Angling Flies* (1853), Alfred Ronalds, *The Fly-fisher's Entomology* (1836), and Hewett Wheatley, a true innovator in both exact imitation and attractor patterns and author of the endlessly wise *Rod and Line: or, Practical Hints and Dainty Devices for the Sure Taking of Trout, Grayling, etc.* (1849). These three all understood the value of the attracting palmer fly, although they differed in explaining its origin, or its peculiar power over trout. Of the well-known northern fishermen, only Francis Walbran (*Walbran's British Angler and Piscatorial Hints by Well Known Writers*, a combined tackle catalogue and collection of essays issued in the 1860s and 1870s) eschewed the palmer fly. However, Walbran did not deny its effectiveness. It was, for him, a matter of personal style, of taste. Theakston, who regarded him as simply "the best flyfisher," is quite clear on why Walbran could not bother with the palmered styles, which were and still are simply called "hackles" on Derbyshire streams:

> The celebrated golden hackle, so fascinating and fatal to many a cunning old trout, has lost its charms to Walbran; and so have most of the land [terrestrial] and other flies that come casually on the water, and are but casually taken. It is too slow a process for Walbran. He is at home only in the midst of the bursting swarms of the aquatic flies; and relies on his imitations of those that are hatching or are on the water at the time he is fishing. . . . When the fish are roused to feed (which they are, more or less, every fishing day) Walbran seems riveted to the streams, and deceives the fish with his imitations of the food they are feeding off; he throws his well dissembled fly on the waters, to take its chance among its living likenesses, and does his work while the fish are doing theirs.

You will never find a better description of the exact-imitation man in action. There is a precision to matching the hatch with a dry fly, or sight-fishing with a top-water nymph, that appeals to people who regard fly-fishing as a contest for the attention of already engaged trout. Unlike trout, Atlantic salmon, as fishermen know to their sorrow, are never "roused to feed . . . more or less, every fishing day," nor are they ever as numerous. I learned to fish with the Bomber while casting to New Brunswick's dour salmon, who take all flies casually, and I am pleased to cast it over amenable trout. Some of us like surprises, and if we are faithful to our attractor flies and thoughtful about where on the river we float them, we shall always find unexpected rewards.

Part of the wisdom of Alfred Ronalds's *Fly-fisher's Entomology*, not only the earliest but in many ways the most sensible book in a voluminous class of angling literature that mixes natural science with fly-tying art, is that Ronalds, for all his interest in aquatic insects, gives good space to the terrestrials, including the palmer flies. By the ordinary standards of biology, Ronalds's book is organized backward, and that is part of its charm and its utility for fishermen in his day: instead of beginning with the natural insects, he begins with the already well-known and widely available artificial flies, and then tells you about the life history and behavior of the insect on which the imitation is based. His work is not organized by the Latinate orders—Neuroptera, Trichoptera, Diptera, Coleoptera—nor is it precise about the genera and species so beloved of scientific anglers and so daunting to recreational fly-fishers. No, he lists forty-seven popular artificials and identifies their natural models, remarks on the season of each and describes such aspects of its life as should matter to the angler. A modern version of Ronalds would be a great help to vacationing anglers, for we typically arrive at a river, visit a fly shop and purchase the imitations appropriate to our week on the water. But dry flies, unfortunately, don't come with directions for use, and few of us take the time to sort through the biological information in the modern anglers' entomologies, searching for clues to insect behavior. Even fewer of us are willing to plead ignorance in the fly shop and ask how the fly must be used. We do not, to put it bluntly, know a damn thing about the life history of *Ephemerella grandis grandis*, or care much. But we should know when we buy the Western Green Drake, an imitation of *E. g. grandis*, that we should use it in the slowest water we can find and let it drift as long as possible without picking it up, for *E. g. grandis* has more trouble getting airborne than any other mayfly.

As befits someone with an interest in taxonomy, Ronalds comes down hard on one side of the eternal argument about palmer flies.

He insists that they are exact imitations of specific caterpillars. Although he does not list the Golden Palmer as Theakston does, he ascribes the Red, Black-and-Red, and Brown Palmers to two species: the first two, he says, are the early and late stages of the caterpillar of *Arctia caja*, the garden tiger moth; while the Brown Palmer is the larva of *Spilosoma lubricepeda*, the spotted buff ermine moth, a caterpillar especially fond of feeding on nettles. But he is not dogmatic about the imitative quality of palmered flies: "The Palmer is never totally out of season," he remarks, adding his own italicized emphasis, "and is *a good fat bait.*" Ronalds recommends using the palmer on the end of the leader, the "tail-fly" of a cast, in British argot, and putting an imitation of an aquatic fly on a short dropper (a "side-leader"), above it, nearer the angler. For the second fly, the angler should try an imitation of an expected aquatic insect, "the fly which *seems* most suitable for the day." The angler can change the dropper until he finds the right imitative fly for the day, while taking advantage of the palmer fly's general nature. "Much valuable time is frequently lost by changing the fly often," Ronalds warns. "It is better to persevere with that which produces tolerable sport, than to do so." I use my Bombers rather in the reverse, putting them on a short dropper well up on the leader, and putting one of the small, likely, imitative flies on the tippet, usually a dry caddis, or something equally floatable in the mayfly line, perhaps a parachute-winged Adams Irresistible. It is easier to cast with the big fly on the end and the small fly on the dropper, but the light tippet is better suited to the small fly, the stiff and heavy short dropper more suitable for a large fly. There are no rules, as long as, like Ronalds, you are content with tolerable sport.

Michael Theakston, a Yorkshireman who fished his own county and neighboring Derbyshire, is the least appreciated of the early angler-entomologists. (His *List of Natural Flies* followed Ronalds by two decades, and was more conventionally organized, beginning with the natural insect and moving on to the artificial.) First, he insisted on using his northern-county dialect names for the insects. The angling world of southern England, and that includes London and the Thames as well as the great waters of the southwestern counties, had already settled on names for the two adult stages of the mayflies: "dun" (which implied rather accurately the duller color) for the newly emerged insect, and "spinner" for the perfect, sexually active stage. "Sedge" was the name for all the Trichoptera, the caddis flies. Theakston, stubbornly parochial, used Yorkshire terms: *his* dun is actually a caddis; *his* spinner is not a mayfly at all but the crane fly. (The usual British name for a crane fly, always wholly confusing to Americans, is daddy-long-legs or Harry-long-legs. *Our* daddy-long-legs spider is in Britain called a harvester.) Mayflies, whether sub-imago or perfect, Theakston called "drakes"—a common enough word then and today, especially for very large mayflies (eastern and western green drake, brown drake, etc.). Theakston says the name comes from the upturned tail of adult mayflies, which resembles the upswept tail of the male (drake) mallard duck. Calling all duns and spinners "drakes" may not have been much of a crime, but in the south, where gentlemen fished and bought books, the mayfly of Duffer's Fortnight (Theakston's green drake) was never called a drake. His terminology was tiresome at best anywhere but in the north, and confusing to the bulk of British anglers. (Curiously, Mary Orvis Marbury, one of America's first fly-tying authors, uses Theakston's argot "dun" for caddis flies.)

This regional peculiarity of speech might have been tolerable, except for Theakston's other distinctive stylistic flaw: he was simultaneously dogmatic and indecisive, capable of arguing both sides of an issue with equal mugwump fervor. His views on the palmer flies are typical of his ambivalence:

> The hackles or palmer flies have been handed through ages from angler to angler, dressed in the same way, and with the same materials, but without any description as to their originals, which seem unheeded or lost in the fame of their counterfeits. It is the general impression they represent, or are derived from, hairy worms, or those caterpillars that are hairy, to which they bear a kindred and very striking resemblance; but the angler never uses the hairy worms as [live] baits, and they are never seen upon the water; if

they were, the hackles (for excellence of imitation) when immersed in the water would take the lead of all artificials.

The hackles have no basis in nature, he continued. They are nothing but "casual or trial baits, which at the best are but a precarious dependance." It was the hatch of naturals to which the fly-fisher should attend:

> The skilful craftsman throws his imitations of the flies among the hatching hordes, that are rousing the fish and baiting the waters for him. He casts them among their living kindred—spread numerous over the waters—while the fishes are taking and feeding upon them all around him. The hackle goes on the water, a chance comer, alone, unknown, and untasted, a solitary stranger, without companion or friend; save its form and glitter—by which it now and then dazzles the eyes of the fish—but is rarely noticed when the living supplies are at hand.

Theakston knew, as we all learn, that the world is not entirely composed of fly hatches, nor, when there is a hatch, are all trout equally mesmerized. And so, he contradicts himself immediately:

> Still it scarce can be doubted that the hackles are the best casual artificial baits that can be used when the fish are not roused to feed on any favourite. Time has hallowed them, and experience has stamped their worth to many a sly fisher, who has often proved them the lions of the day. . . . When the trout is not engaged he may be lured from his lair by any promiscuous fly or insect coming in his way, that is natural to him, particularly if it shew symptoms of life or motion. The hackles are often taken below the surface, where the undulating motion of the water closes or expands their springy fibres. . . . [The hackles are] a numerous assortment of brilliant and enticing artificial baits for small flyfishing, never to be parted with until better are discovered.

The first instructional fishing book written and printed in the United States, John J. Brown's *An American Angler's Guide* (New York, 1845), has a brief section on trout flies, and all the patterns he gives are borrowed from British manuals of the early nineteenth century, with Brown's assertion that they are traditional lures and may very well be useful on this side of the Atlantic Ocean. (Brown, by the way, wrote anonymously, possibly because he sought what all angling writers desire—at least the illusion of unalloyed rectitude and commercial disinterest; he was well known as the owner of the Angler's Depot, a "general emporium for the sale of fishing tackle" on Fulton Street in New York City.) He has absolute confidence in only two patterns of artificial flies: the palmer is "the universal fly," he writes, so important that, alone among all the flies and other lures he mentions, he sets their proper names in italic type: "the *Red Hackle, or Soldier Palmer,* and the *Black Hackle,* or *Black Palmer,* are *"the Flies."*

Unlike standard palmers, including the still-popular Woolly Worm (indistinguishable after one hundred and fifty years from Brown's Black Palmer), the Bomber is rarely taken below the surface—though it is equally attractive to a trout there—because it is almost unsinkable. The smaller Buck Bug, by contrast, is often tied with a weighted body and fished under the surface. The old British style of wet-fly fishing—casting down and across stream and bringing the fly on a swing toward the angler's bank—works nicely with the Buck Bug, and gives the fisherman who is willing to use this "casual artificial bait" an opportunity to disprove two hallowed tenets of modern fly-fishing with a single cast: the dogmas of dead-drift and lifelike imitation. Fishing, like life, is improved by happy accidents such as a brown trout's eating a Buck Bug or a Bomber, by chance encounters and unexpected blessings. That is my sense of things. If you are unhappy with such sentimental thinking, with chance or serendipity, you may nonetheless fish happily with these huge flies. Just tell yourself that you are engaged in field-testing the theory of supernormal release of innate feeding behavior.

14

Not Fine, and
Not Far-Off

*Notes on the lost art of fly-
fishing without fly-casting, with
historical and modern examples*

L
arge flies attract my attention more than they should; I use
them more than is wise. This old prejudice of mine began on
the only day in my life when I outfished Uncle Gordon. We
never competed, we kept no score. When we got home to Missoula
in the evening, we would dump our trout on the lawn by the hose
bibb in his backyard, and we talked little about size or numbers. We
both lined our creels with grass, or with mint if we had been fishing
through a meadow where it grew. Leaves of grass and leaves of mint
each left their distinctive pattern on the fish where the trout rested
against them in the creel; the skin would blanch more where it was
exposed to the open air, and it would stay darker where pressed
against the damp leaves. When the creels were empty, one of us
would wash them both with the garden hose. He and I cleaned the
fish amicably, sharing a single sharp knife.

Gordon had two apple trees in the backyard, and one was an early
bearer, a Gravenstein. It was always August when I visited, before
school began, and windfalls littered the lawn over by the alley fence.
There is a very great dish to be made by some creative chef, trout with

overripe apple and mint, though there may be only one customer for it. To this day, the smell of wild mint reminds me intensely of trout fishing, and fishing without bruising it underfoot seems an incomplete experience.

Only once in all those evenings—bringing the fish inside, putting them in the porcelain sink for the final scrubbing—did my aunt Ruby notice the one big trout, and ask us who had caught it. She fished herself, and understood that my uncle would catch more and larger trout than I did; that was to be expected, and there was no point in commenting on it. But, when we came inside with a dozen fish under eleven inches and one that was eighteen if it was an inch, there had to be an explanation, a story to tell.

We had gone up the Bitterroot without Ruby—she had church work in Missoula—and so Gordon and I and his neighbor Ashley Roche were allowed one of those days when we did not have to pack the watercolors or set up housekeeping at a campsite. Gordon and Ashley wanted to fish several runs on the Bitterroot, starting just above Hamilton, moving on to Bonner. (Whenever we went without Ruby, Gordon always stopped at the closest place instead of going to the farthest and working back toward home.) As it turned out, it was all water that was too big for me. We stopped for an hour here and there, and the men fished the main stream while I wandered along the bank looking for small braids in the channel that were boy-sized, side streams around sandbars and islands, not that I was an expert at small water, just that it was all I could cope with when it came to wading or casting. At each stop, Gordon turned me loose with strict instructions to be back at the car at a given time so that we could move on to the next place. When we came to the last stop I did not have a fish in my creel. Again, Gordon gave me the exact hour to be back at the car when it would be time to start home.

No one had taught me how to fish the edge of a big river, and it is a skill much neglected by most fly-casters. Indeed, more than a skill, more than an art, it requires an optimistic attitude toward what is close at hand, a willingness to forgo what is distant. I despair when I think how many nice trout could have been mine back when the world was uncomplicated if only someone had shown me how to dap a fly without being seen by the trout, how to fish downstream, working a fly near undercut banks, casting down to a rising trout with enough slackness in the line and leader that the fly will drift directly toward the fish. I was a willing victim of the dogma of up-stream conventional casting, and I walked heedlessly, never thinking that trout might as well live on my bank as along the far and unat-tainable shore. This time, an accident of the natural landscape kept me from frightening a big fish before I saw it.

As I worked my way downstream from the car, mindful of the time and knowing that I would have to start back soon, I came on a small Douglas fir that had grown so near the edge of the river that the cur-rent had at last undercut it completely, toppling it into the river at a nearly perfect right angle to the bank. I don't think it had been there long, perhaps blown down by an August thunderstorm. The needles were still bright, and no trash to speak of had piled up against the upstream branches. It had pulled up a good chunk of bank on the inboard side, and the path along the river disappeared into a hole through which a bit of the river flowed darkly. It was almost time to go back to the car, but something provoked me to beat through the blackberry bushes, skirt around the upturned roots of the tree, and look at it from downstream.

Below the tree, a deep, still pool with a slight back-current lay against my bank. The tree looked odd lying flat on the water. Now untugged by gravity, the whorls of branches stood out vertically, per-pendicular to the trunk, more like a child's drawing of a tree than the real thing. From the bank out, ten feet of bare trunk lay on the sur-face of the water; then tiers of branches, a few feet apart, made a series of gaps like the teeth of a giant green comb. Distinct currents swept under the trunk and down through the slots between the tiers. From the downstream vantage point, the limbs of the tree looked like narrow, upright, green hedges dividing the lanes of water. These lanes had not been visible from upstream, where the current pushed the twigs together into a sort of fir-bough fence, nor could you see the effect from the butt end of the tree as you walked around it, for it was hidden by the upturned fan of roots. But downstream, the current straightened out the branches and emphasized the separations between them. And between the first and second set, between what had been the lowest and next-lowest circle of branches when the tree was standing, there was a trout. I would have frightened it away when walking by, except that it was locked in this narrow passage, screened from my view.

I hadn't caught a fish big enough to keep all day, but this one, judging just from the size of the bulge when it rose, was plenty big enough. No one could have cast to it from the bank, since the tree branches were in the way. I stood on the path above the pool, looked up at the tree and the gap between the branches and watched the trout rise again, and thought. I had never thought much while fishing; this was a new experience. If I got in the water and waded out until I was directly downstream from the trout, I could cast to it, flipping a fly up between the branches. I would also be well over the tops of my hip boots. (I usually went in over the tops, but I had never planned to get wet.) I changed flies, taking off the small Adams and putting on the largest hairwing in my fly box. It was a big trout, I had no idea what it was rising to, and it seemed reasonable that I should do everything possible to attract its attention.

The water was shockingly cold. It was always cold when I fell in, but doing it deliberately made it seem colder. I tried casting up to the fish, which rose again. I was no farther away from it than fifteen feet. I could almost reach out and touch the downstream trailing end of the nearest fir branch with my rod tip. But now I couldn't even get started casting because I was up to my armpits in the pool. At that point, I continued to think, which was truly remarkable, because Gordon and Ashley were back at my uncle's 1949 Ford sedan and someone was honking the horn. And what I thought of was an illustration in one of Gordon's fishing books, probably *Herter's Manual of Trout Fishing*.

It was a line drawing of one of the various special ways to cast a fly, the oddest one of all, "the bow-and-arrow cast." An angler, crouched on his knees in a thicket, is about to send a trout fly toward an improbable-looking leaping trout. He is holding the fly pinched between the thumb and forefinger of his right hand; the rod is in his left. The handle of the rod is pointed right at the fish, and the tip section of the rod is bent almost double, the tip pointing back at the fisherman, pulled back by tension from the line. Mr. Herter's fisherman is reinventing the catapult to throw the fly at the fish.

The honking, a few hundred yards upstream, began again with more urgency as I recalled the illustration. I did it all exactly as Herter recommended. With an eight-foot fly rod, standing little more than a dozen feet from the fish, it was not a very difficult cast. I have no idea what the trout was eating before I got there, but he looked at the big squirrel-tail hairwing fly as fit food, ate it, and hooked himself as he turned down and upstream toward the tree trunk.

Everything was going very well except that I was in the water with the trout and had no idea how to "land" it, as anglers say. It was as big a trout as I had ever seen, and all I could do was hold the rod up and let the fish swim against the pressure. Eventually, it started to swim in circles around me, following the current in the eddy of the pool. I had to make slow pirouettes to keep up with it, to keep the rod pointed at the fish. It was then that I realized that my feet were sinking into the soft sand at the bottom of the pool and that it would be a very good idea if I pirouetted in the general direction of the bank. The trout was giving up by then, and as I got a little closer to the bank, as the water receded from my armpits to my navel, I found I could lead the trout as if it were on a leash. It did not seem like a very good idea to derrick the fish out of the water with my rod and swing it onto the bank above me. Even ordinary trout had a habit of shaking loose when I lifted them out of the water like that, and this one was extraordinary. The trout ran out a few feet of line for the last time, I recovered the line and pulled the fish back up, right in front of me. I put my right hand under the trout and threw it as far as I could back over my head into the brush. The leader snapped with an audible *pop* as the fish sailed into the blackberry patch. I crawled up the steep bank with difficulty, much encumbered by wet clothes and filled boots. By then, the car horn was more insistent. It took a few minutes to locate my fish. You'd be surprised how far you can throw a trout when you're scared. I might not have found it except that it was still flopping occasionally, rustling the leaves under the berry canes.

I arrived back at the car as quickly as I could, taking just a moment to lie down and drain the water out of my hip boots. Gordon was behind the wheel, Ashley was in the passenger seat, and I got in the back seat without saying anything. Gordon turned around and began, rather sternly for him, to say something about being more considerate. As I remember, he started to say, "Ashley and I have been waiting. . . ."

I was holding my creel on my lap, and the tail of the trout stuck up out of one side and the nose pushed the lid up on the other side. I had unbuckled the lid's strap, since I thought the trout was too big to be dropped down through the narrow rectangular opening in the lid. Gordon looked at the creel for a minute (Ashley, busily cleaning his pipe, had deliberately removed himself from the situation), and then he looked at the waterline on my shirt above the breast pockets.

"Well, Brother," he said after the pause, "you certainly do have a trout there."

Indeed I did, and although time and chance would bring larger fish, I have never caught one that was so relatively large, so close to the maximum for the river. The Bitterroot does not produce large cutthroats, and even the hybrid vigor of its typical fish, a mixture of west-slope cutthroat and rainbow, rarely produces a trout over sixteen inches.

You may wonder if time has not made this particular fish grow a little; I certainly wondered. Last year, on a desultory summer afternoon, I stopped at the Museum of American Fly-Fishing in Manchester Village, Vermont, and spent a few hours looking through the museum's collection of twentieth-century fly-fishing manuals. (In fact, I was looking for the illustration of the bow-and-arrow cast, and found one, although it did not have the heightened drama of the one I remembered.) On a long shelf, adjacent to the library, I saw a collection of fishing artifacts, including half a dozen wicker creels. One of them, I swear, was the exact duplicate of my old one. Some creels were manufactured with a ruler embossed on the leather lid-hinge, and three of the ones in the museum had the law-abiding measure printed on them. Creels came in two basic sizes: one was about a foot across the back side, and the hinge had a ten-inch rule printed on it; the smaller ones were ten inches across the back, with an eight-inch ruler. Mine, I remembered well, was the eight-inch-ruler model. I borrowed a tape-measure from the curator and measured the curve from one side lip of the eight-inch model down to the bottom and back up to the other side. It was just a little under seventeen inches. The rectangular hole in the lid, the one through which you dropped your trout, measured just one and a half inches by two inches. A large, but not unheard-of, Bitterroot trout would have easily pushed up the lid on both edges; and certainly, a healthy seventeen-inch trout would not have slipped easily through the hole. Given the slipperiness and flexibility of a fresh trout, I suppose I could have jammed it through the hole and bent it nearly double and fastened down the lid of the creel, but this was a trophy to be carried gently in a casket, not a murder victim to be stuffed in the trunk of a car.

It's been forty years of fishing, and I have never used the bow-and-arrow cast again. This is partly due to growing up and learning how to cast in a number of other effective and devious ways, but it is also because I have never again seen a fir tree lying so perfectly across a current to remind me of the technique. Many times, on small waters, a catapult-cast would have worked better than anything I was doing, but I never thought of it until much later.

I have, slowly, gotten better about paying attention to my own bank, not worrying so much about what is going on across the river. Something about fishing near to your own feet doesn't appeal to modern anglers, although all the old books have descriptions of creeping up on unsuspecting trout. Of all the tricks that anglers use, concealment is the least preferred today.

I am not quite sure why we prefer distance to discretion, casting to camouflage, but we do. I think it is our admiration for physical skill (our own, at least in our imaginations) and our disdain for physical caution. "Bushwhacker" is not a term of approbation, but we would catch more trout if we had the stomach for ambush.

Fishermen were not always so adept at distance-casting and, when what are today very ordinary casts were impossible for them, they were great skulkers and sneakers. The widespread adoption of the rotary fishing reel in the early nineteenth century allowed anglers to manage considerably more line than before, when extra fly line had to be "reeled" by hand around two pins in the rod handle. And heavy, tapered, oiled fly-casting lines were coming into use, made of braided silk impregnated with hardened but flexible linseed oil—the same process as was being applied to make that new invention, linoleum floor-covering. These could be cast farther than the old, less dense, horsehair and silk lines of the previous decades. By midcentury, wise fly-casters had noticed that their fellow anglers were spending too much time casting much too far. John Beever (*Practical Fly-Fishing Founded on Nature*, n.p. [Edinburgh?],1849) is the earliest remonstrant against this excessive reliance on new technology and improved technique: "Nineteen out of every twenty fish, taken by the fly, are killed with a line under ten yards long from the top of the rod. . . ." The angler should "remember that other fish are rising at the same time in narrower places, which he can cover with ease."

No place is easier to cover than your own bank, and if it is steep or undercut, it is also the best concealment. Solid dirt interferes with a trout's vision. Good bait-fishermen know this (surely another reason why fly-casters ignore it), but few masters of the angleworm are left in the world. As more people take up fly-fishing on large and well-populated trout water, as they learn how to cast far and fine under expert tutoring, the old arts disappear; indeed, some of us who know them perfectly well will forget them, caught up for the day in the mystique of fly-casting.

One of the more difficult rivers for the walking angler is the Beaverhead above Dillon, Montana. Most of the bank is lined with willows, and some of it with deep thickets of that tree—green hells that keep you from even finding the river if you strike out through one unaware of the twists and turns in the channel. And where the bank is clean, the river is not always easily fished. The few places on the Beaverhead where you have an open backcast tend to be places where the trout are tucked tight up under the sweeping willows across the stream. Boaters, who do most of the fishing on the Beaverhead, have access to numbers of small islands in midstream where they can get out and wade, and cast with open water before and behind them.

I mention these conditions on the Beaverhead by way of making an excuse for what I did there. It was the most successful hour of fishing of my life—sometimes I think it was a little too good. It came down to that very modern question: Had we come to fly-cast, or to catch fish?

It was August, hopper season for most of us, although the Beaverhead continued, as tail waters will, to support hatches of very small mayflies and caddis. I had asked in Dillon for the directions to a place where I could fish from the bank, and someone suggested the Henneberry Bridge public access, one of those Montana Fish and Game sites marked with the state sign of an oversized jumping trout and a truly gigantic bare hook. I found it easily and then got bogged down in the usual confusion in verbal angling directions. The man had said to "go on down" from the access, and I thought he meant to go downstream. He meant either "on down south" (the Beaverhead runs almost due north) or back down the road from the parking lot at the end. If you go that way, staying on the public parking lot side of the bridge, there are several long runs—riffles and pools—with an open backcast for fishing. I found them later in the day.

I parked at the bridge, crossed it, and went downstream, the opposite of my informant's intention. The river disappeared from view a hundred feet below the bridge, screened by a dense stand of willow. Having no idea where to go and no stomach for creeping along through the mosquito-loud brush, I decided to walk along in the open prairie until I caught at least a glimpse of the river. After a fifteen- or twenty-minute walk (if ambulating in chest waders is walking), I came to where the river popped out from behind the willows and meandered into the open toward the tire ruts I was using as a path through the prickly pear.

At least a hundred yards of naked bank confronted me. Nothing grew on it but bunch grass, a few stubby patches of sagebrush and a single wild rose right at the edge of the river. I walked over to the upstream end of the opening and pondered the current. A long, deep section with a distinct eddy swirled in toward my bank. The eddy began halfway down the open bank, which was slightly undercut by the slow back-current. I could see a few flecks of foam edging their way along the vertical bank toward me, moving against the direction of the main river. A two-man raft was pulled up on the bank at the bottom of the pool, several yards below where the back-current started; and the guide and his customer were eating lunch. (Show me a man wearing a Florida-style sun helmet in Montana, and I will show you an out-of-state customer; the guide wore the usual baseball cap.) I waited for them to leave, because a devious plan was starting to form in my mind, and privacy seemed appropriate.

If the back-current was as steady and slow as it appeared to be from a distance, and if the steep slope of the bank continued down into the river, as it was likely to do, I was looking at the best piece of trout water I'd seen in days. One of its attractions, not to be lightly dismissed on a hard-fished river, is that someone in a boat would have considerable difficulty drifting a fly up the back-current while the boat was sliding downstream. And the river was not more than twenty yards across, narrowed as it was by the deep pool in the meander. Floating anglers would be rather closer to the fish than they ought to be. The terrain was all in favor of the bank angler, as long as he didn't mind fishing like a farm kid walking along an irrigation ditch.

After the floaters pushed off, I gave it five minutes by the watch and then walked down to the end of the pool, keeping well back from the bank. I put on a grasshopper imitation (I should have put on a Bomber, just to be contrary in the extreme), and reeled all of the line and three feet of the leader back up through the guide at the tip of the rod. This left six feet of leader hanging off the end of nine feet of fly rod. All I had to do was stand back at arm's length from the edge, slide the fly down the bank, let it start floating on the hidden surface of the stream, and walk it down the current, keeping an eye on the leader. The trick was to leave just enough slack so that there was a little bend in the leader. This gave me a chance, even with middle-aged reflexes, to keep the rod tip straight over the fly and thus not impede the fly's natural drift.

It hadn't floated a foot when the leader went straight. I had forgotten that it takes a little extra effort to set a big hook in a big trout, and I didn't tighten hard enough. The trout got off immediately. Not to worry: I dropped the fly in again, and it drifted along another two feet as I walked it down the current. The leader straightened again, and I set the hook with more vigor in what turned out to be a twenty-two-inch brown trout. It swam out into the main current, jumped once (big brown trout do not "tail-walk" across the water), and went to the bottom. I led the fish downriver and unhooked it at the floaters' lunch spot. In the next half-hour, in the same pool, taking time to let it calm down between fish, I took two more trout that appeared to be siblings, possibly triplets, of the first one. At a minimum, I had caught ten pounds of trout, perhaps as much as twelve pounds, packaged in just three fish. The last two I unhooked in the water without taking time to measure them against the rod's guides. By then, the grasshopper was thoroughly chewed, missing one of its wings, and slime-soaked. I tried the trick again, and this time the grasshopper sank, caught in a down-swirl next to the bank, and I had to feed a little line out to keep the leader slack. Another trout hit, and I struck too hard and broke off the fly. It felt like it was an even bigger, almost immovable trout.

That was enough. I had proved that human beings were smarter than brown trout. Nothing else. I had caught fish, but under my own bank. I did not get to watch the fly drift, I could not see the hole open in the surface and watch the fly drop into it like a golf ball into the cup. So, the fishing was not wholly satisfactory, but it was the best I could do.

One alternative to bank-walking, if you insist on casting fine and far-off to a trout lying in a back-current against the far bank, is to pitch the fly and a few feet of leader right straight into the bank. With luck, about one time in twenty, the fly will drop naturally into the water, and the leader will pile up behind it in a series of S-curves. The fly will drift along, and a trout will see it before the drag sets in or the leader floats over the fish. Bouncing the fly itself off the far bank, when you do not have tricky currents to overcome, is a nice old technique. It is by its nature a dry-fly, top-water ploy, for you intend the trout to believe that something living has just dropped onto the surface. All terrestrial insects float until they are spent and waterlogged; there are no heavier-than-water bugs.

Making a carom shot off a far bank is really a long-distance form of dapping. The first printed reference I have seen to this technique is in George C. Bainbridge's *The Fly Fisher's Guide* (Liverpool, 1816): "An excellent mode of enticing a good fish is to throw the fly against the opposite bank, so that it may drop gently from thence to the water." Bainbridge is one of the best of the devious authors. As well as being an inventive caster, he was a close student of the wariness of trout. He noted it was necessary not only to stay low, but also that "it is certainly of some importance to avoid [wearing] glossy or bright colors, and above all, metal buttons."

Bainbridge was surely casting no more than twenty or thirty feet of line; with modern equipment, you can double those distances. But when you are forced to reach out to your natural limits and at the same time leave enough slack to delay the moment of drag setting in, the fly often lands in the middle of two or three coils of leader, and you haven't got a prayer. Worse, when things otherwise go well, it is difficult to calibrate your strike to account for the slack in the line and leader if the fish takes the fly; you are likely to snap the tippet or fail to set the hook at all. No curve-cast or slack-cast I have made has compensated for the doubled effect that occurs when an eddying back-current moves contrary to the main stream. Although you certainly are fishing like a sportsman when you cast across two currents to the far bank, you are likely to get your fish more by accident in such conditions. When you go bank-walking the fly along, you angle with malice aforethought.

Most of us will not wear out the knees of our waders while fly-fishing; we don't creep much, nor will we choose to parade a fly down an undercut bank with just part of the leader hanging out of the tip-top of the rod. We would rather stand up and cast delicately, even fashionably, to distant fish. Cowboys or fly-casters, we like to be tall in the saddle.

15

Rainbow Trout
Abroad

*A report on angling for
American fish in Derbyshire, and
an illustration of the immutable
sociobiology of salmonids*

L ike other anglers (and all human beings), I am a creature of
habit, and what I deem to be verities are no more than the
sum of my experiences. As an example, I believe it is unwise
to travel any difficult path to fish for brown trout. This is not because
that trout is flawed, but because after forty years I am still in love with
native cutthroats and rainbows, still searching for wild American fish
in freestone American rivers.

For that reason, and in spite of my affection for the old British
writers from Cotton on down, it never seemed worth the trouble to
fish in England for their trout, just as I take my Shakespeare where I
find it and have felt no irresistible urge to see Stratford-on-Avon or
the putative site of the Globe Theater now buried under some
twentieth-century office building. But I changed my mind when I
heard about the River Wye.

The Derbyshire Wye (to distinguish it from the larger Wye which
makes up the southern end of the border between England and
Wales) has two attractions for an American angler, one historical, the
other biological. The Derbyshire Wye, as far as the written record

shows, was the first river in the world where the use of the artificial fly was commanded, this as early as June 1865. In modern times, the river has become the only stream in Britain with a self-sustaining population of wild rainbow trout. While every state in the union with trout water, save Alaska, now hosts British brown trout, only to Derbyshire has the migration gone east. It seemed a fine idea to visit our American cousins in their new home and to celebrate the Mount Sinai of dry-fly fishing.

The best angling sections of the Wye and the nearby Derwent have been for many centuries the property of the dukes of Devonshire. (Why the major landowner in Derbyshire is the Duke of Devonshire is not clear in the record. The family name is Cavendish, and most of the historical wealth came from factories and coal mines in neighboring Yorkshire.) The Derwent, beloved of Charles Cotton, rises in the village of Buxton and then flows through the Chatsworth estate of the Dukes of Devonshire, on which grounds is built a country house so improbably large, so opulent, so laden with history (Mary, Queen of Scots, was once paroled there) that it is simply called "The House."

The duke business is not what it used to be, and like so many great British estates, The House is now open to tourists for a substantial fee and is a major tourist attraction. The vast, rural grounds include room for a small luxury hotel (The Cavendish Arms) and also an example of that ubiquitous British eyesore, the trailer park. The Cavendish Caravan Park is exceptionally well hidden from view behind the walls of the old kitchen garden. The Duke and Duchess of Devonshire are persons not only of reasonable wealth, but of extreme good taste. As one example, in addition to sequestering the caravans, the small village of Buxton, source for many years of intensive labor on the estate, was given outdoor streetlights only in the 1960s, in part because the duchess thought such artificial illumination would spoil the view. The view is worth saving. Neither clean, well-lighted nor dark, satanic factories blot the landscape. Hedgerows along the highways screen traffic from a visitor's view. It is the same countryside, with the same clouds and rays of sun, as you expect after looking through a book of landscapes by Constable.

The Cavendish Arms hotel plays a rather larger part in angling than it should, for, though it does have lavender-scented sheets, it is no sportsman's lodging. It caters to the Tory upper middle class, business travelers and visitors to The House. Its attraction to anglers is that the hotel desk dispenses fishing privileges to well-paying guests. (Local anglers can purchase season tickets to the duke's waters, but tourists must go through the hotel.) The duke's property is equipped with, besides accommodations for tourists and the sprawling House: roe deer, Merino sheep, ring-necked pheasants, black ponies, Holstein milk cows and a formal flower garden about the size of a soccer field ensconced in an arboretum the size of a small state park. This adds up to a place suitable for entertaining nonangling spouses. My wife is capable of watching me fish for hours, but it is a sometimes unamusing spectacle.

The Derwent has a reputation for producing large brown trout, although most of the fish that anglers see are stocked-out brown and rainbow in the twelve- to fourteen-inch range. The larger fish are holdovers, and dine exceptionally given that they are living in a freestone, non–chalk-stream, river. This is partly due to the presence on the estate's southern boundary of the Buxton municipal sewage plant, from which, after treatment, the effluent tinkles down into the Derwent over a series of aerating steps. (The usefulness of a mild dose of such nutrients in a freestone river is not to be underestimated. The productivity of the Battenkill, in New England, increases considerably after it assumes the lightly treated discharge of Arlington, Vermont, a few miles downstream of Manchester; so, too, the famous rainbow trout of the Bow River of Alberta, Canada, would be much fewer in number and grow more slowly without the contributions of the citizens of Edmonton. Sometimes the best of ecological intentions go awry: Michigan's Au Sable supported gigantic brown until trout fishermen persuaded the local municipalities to stop injecting treatment-plant discharge into the stream.)

The Derbyshire Wye, a dozen miles away from The House, has purer and naturally harder water than the Derwent, due to its limestone spring sources. It has smaller trout on average and is thus less in demand with anglers. As tourist access to the Wye is also limited to house guests of the Cavendish Arms, and as the Derwent is only a few minutes' walk from the hotel, not a £15 cab ride, the Wye gets even fewer visitors than the estate's home river. Both streams are restriced to fly-fishing today, and the smaller and wilder Derwent has the additional limitation of a prohibition on wading, a rule in effect since early in the nineteenth century. This is no impediment, as the bank-side angler can cover the whole river with very ordinary casting. That the Wye should be the ancestral home of fly-fishing-only rules is an accident—a conjunction of biology and technology.

The British mayfly, known in the north counties of Derbyshire and Yorkshire as the green drake, is, like its American cousins the eastern and western green drake, one of the largest mayflies. It is one of the few stream insects, and the only mayfly, big enough and sturdy enough to be used as live bait. In the colder and higher country of the Peak District, mayfly season is a few weeks later than in the southern and western rivers, so it was the first week of June 1865, when the hatch of flies had begun and the local anglers, all fee-payers to the Duke of Devonshire, gathered at the river and began plucking the living insects off the stream-side vegetation, impaling two or three on a hook, and dapping them on the water. So it had been done in England for five hundred years that we know of, so the Macedonians, inventors of the artificial fly, would have done two thousand years ago if their natural fly had been equally sturdy. (The oldest texts do include recipes for tying artificial Green Drakes, but these were wet flies, intended either to match the emerging fly struggling out of its pupal skin or else to simulate drowned adults, and were inferior lures to the real insect.)

Among the anglers on June 5, 1865, was James Ogden, the proprietor of a fishing tackle company in Cheltenham, by the metropolis of Gloucester. Ogden, a brilliant "fly-dresser," as the British say, came supplied with a creation of his own, a true dry fly imitative of the green drake. For several years Ogden had been selling what may have been the first commercial flies in the world meant to float on, not in, the surface film. His new effort, the dry Green Drake, was cleverly made with the upright silhouette and three-whisk tail of the species. High floating, its feather wings and pale straw body tinted by the dyer's art to exactly match the creamy green hue of the newly hatched dun, it was an astonishing success. Ogden had invented the artificial fly that would make Duffer's Fortnight, the few weeks of mayfly season, part of the British angler's vocabulary.

Dry British Green Drake
(10 lines #)

ART

Fishing with the natural fly was always considered somewhat less than desirable by river proprietors. Not only did the dappers with their real flies kill many fish, but gathering the bait gave them reason to trespass. The natural insects, while making their last metamorphosis into sexual adulthood, move away from the river and rest on nearby vegetation before shedding their skin for the last time and returning to the river to mate, lay eggs and die. Fishermen had an excuse to hop fences, to beat through the nearby fields and hedges and flower gardens while searching for more live bait, to behave rather like rude schoolchildren. When the duke's steward met Ogden at Bakewell on the Wye, and watched as Ogden made an exceptional bag of trout with the artificial drake, he forbade, on the spot, the use of the natural fly. The result was predictable: when Ogden returned the next morning to fish again, the other anglers mobbed him like crows after a hawk, not because he represented fishing snobbery, but because he was the monopolistic inventor and distributor of an expensive item they would have to purchase, or manufacture themselves, if they wished to fish the duke's water during the green drake hatch. He was driven from the stream by these angling Luddites, and did not return that season. The duke, however, pleased with the excuse to ban dapping with live flies, gave Ogden a week on his most private and personal water.

Earlier in the nineteenth century, anglers in the south, particularly on the Itchen in Hampshire, tied upright-winged mayflies that floated, dried them by repeated false-casting, and fished them dead-drift down over rising trout. Ogden's contribution, and a painful price he paid at first, was to cause a local authority—the duke with his *droit de seigneur*—to elevate dry-fly fishing from an arcane art to a statutory requirement.

American fish and game departments are often loath to emulate the Duke of Devonshire. In America, sport fish and game animals belong to the state, not the landowner, and by extension trout are the property of all citizens. Though subject to regulation, they may be, as it is usually written in the law, "reduced to possession." Until very recently, fly-fishing has been regarded as elitist and the imposition of fly-fishing-only rules as antidemocratic. The universal result, however, of both fly-fishing-only and the often-associated catch-and-release rule has been increased "angler effort," sometimes to the point of absurdity. The paths along the Swift River in Massachusetts are worn twice and three times as deep in the fly-only, release-only, section as in the several miles of good trout water farther downstream which remain open to dappers and danglers of bait. One attraction of fly-fishing water is the assumption by the angler of a level playing field, of a fair chance, not unlike the attractiveness of well-regulated horse racing to the bettor. Purchasing a fishing ticket at the Cavendish Arms provides the levelest of all playing fields: a share of the season-long limited access, prohibition of bait, and exclusive use for the day.

Tom Richardson, the river-keeper on the Wye, when reached by telephone, suggested which section of the river was fishing well, and gave me directions that included, after descending through Monsal Dale, having the taxi take a hard left turn to the Netherdale Farm, where he would look for me near the footbridge. Netherdale Farm, it happened, grew goats. Goat keepers are almost irresistibly attracted to trout rivers. Something about the clarity and cleanliness of trout country must attract the entrepreneurial and health-conscious goat-breeder; along the Wise River in Montana, about as far as one can get from a marketplace, there is also a goatery, and others lie along the banks of the McKenzie in Oregon and the Bitterroot above Missoula. There are state universities nearby the latter ones, a potential market for the acquired taste of goat cheese or the putative benefits of goat's milk.

The Wye-by-Goatside had the instant charm of all fair, small streams: it was the kind of water that explains itself, exposes itself on first view. Just below the footbridge by the goat farm ran an open, braided riffle. Just above the bridge, the river deepened into pools shaded by willow and rowan (mountain ash) trees. The river, as good ones do, came out of the green-cast shadow and into the sunlight. The Wye had the characteristic of all stocked trout water—a randomness to the pattern of rising trout. In the pool above the bridge as it exited the lane of trees at least three brown trout were cruising back and forth and up and down, taking some nymph just under the surface, bulging the water but not breaking it. They had no fixed home, no holding lie, but circulated through the pool in pairs and threes, foraging for food. I do not mean to imply that wild trout and well-established resident stocked fish never cruise, but there is something about apparently aimless wandering, and most particularly about trout moving in pairs and threesomes, that suggests they are only recently arrived in a river and have found the best spots are already occupied.

It was early in the day and late in the year. Although the weather was sunny and mild, no insects hatched; there was nothing to do but fish the nymph. There was an even more sensible thing to do, but I was not prepared. One should have been ready to take Richard Bowlker's three-hundred-year-old advice, and "fish the minnow or worm" until the flies were hatching. Although real minnows and real worms were forbidden on the Wye, numerous artificial flies im-

Muddler Minnow
ART

itate them nicely. (There are no garden-worm flies, except the jesting "garden hackle," but there are several odd-looking things that resemble leeches and wireworms and platyhelminths—the water-bred flatworms of high school biology classes.) You really should never go anywhere without streamer flies that imitate minnows or sculpins, and since the restrictions on the Wye were only for fly-fishing, and not for dry-fly fishing (including, as they do in Britain, fishing with a nymph but calling it a dry fly), I should have had some small Muddler Minnows, which are excellent imitations of the sculpins of Britain, the ones called, from the shape of their fat heads and the usual calumny about giving short weight by pressing on the scale surreptitiously, "Miller's Thumbs."

Pheasant Tail (6 lines #)
ART

I am seldom fully armed with nymphs, and had only a small collection of Gold-Ribbed Hare's Ears, a single Frank Sawyer–inspired Pheasant Tail left over from a day on the Test and Itchen, and a half-dozen generic undecipherables, veterans of the American West. Unfortunately, the Pheasant Tail, quite small, a No. 18, was the only thing in the box that was of any interest to the fish above the bridge, and, as will happen, it was lost in the fifth brown trout that took it. I fished on up for another hour, amusing, but not interesting, the trout that came near to my other nymphs or dry flies but always stopped short. The fish farther up held in very discrete lies, all of them under sweeping branches, all difficult places to drift any fly, some impossible for a floating fly.

The footbridge by the goat emporium turned out to be a link in a public trail that runs through the Peak District, and although there were several fish in the pool that ran down to, and just under, the bridge, it was difficult to fish for them. Friendly trail-walkers (I should say the friendliest Britons I have ever encountered, in the sense of unreserved and outgoing personality) would stop on the bridge and point out to each other that the man was fishing, and then they would point at the fish. As the low October sun was behind them, they managed to cast large and waving shadows over the trout, invariably putting the fish down for a few minutes. Fortunately, the public trail was well fenced and the private nature of the riverbank well posted, with access to the river only through a narrow turnstile in the latticed wire fencing, or else I believe all of the walkers would have come down to the pool for a closer look at this interesting sporting activity. I retreated upstream, hoping that some change in the trout's diet, possibly a hatch of flies, would have occurred. The friend who had told me about the wild rainbows in the Wye had fished in the fall himself, and found a steady hatch of caddis on his visit. Something like that was needed, as I did not have the right nymph, and there was none of the feeding excitement necessary to draw the trout upward from their sequestered lairs.

Richardson the river-keeper came down around lunchtime to collect his copy of the hotel day ticket and, more usefully, to see if there was anything he could do in the way of advice. When I mentioned the problem with the nymphing fish, I asked him to look through the dry-fly box (yes, just one box—this was not the most well equipped expedition in the history of angling) and see if anything looked likely. He thought the caddis would do well, "*if* there was a hatch." These were little Elk-Hair Caddis, quite unlike the British downwing tie, but he easily identified them as, in his vernacular, "sedges." The little Tricos, sizes 22 and 24, he thought would have done wonderfully a few weeks earlier, but there had been hard frosts, and he believed the tiny flies were gone for the year. The fly that caught his eye surprised me. He poked a finger at the three No. 16 Orvis Mahogany Spinners in the corner of the fly box and said: "Those ruddy ones are just the thing, right in the film, or just under it."

I told him I rather expected that they were early-season flies. After all, I thought to myself, Juliana Berners, who was a north-country lady, had said five hundred years ago that the Ruddy Fly was excellent in May. "Good all year is that fly," Tom said firmly.

He had to leave to be about his business elsewhere: "Poachers," he explained. Before he went I asked if he thought there were rainbows about, and he said, Oh, yes, all downstream from the bridge were rainbows. "All wild?" Yes, they only stocked the brown trout that summer.

"Do you really have to stock? Wouldn't it be nice to have all wild fish?"

"Oh, indeed it would. But it's poachers, you see. Perhaps you don't have poachers where you come from—and our gentlemen must have their fish, too."

Almost the moment he was gone, as I walked back down to stream-side, I looked at the pale gray bark of a small mountain ash that grew at the very edge of the river. There were three mayflies sitting on it, and all three had the clear wings and the rufous body of, depending on which century it was, the Ruddy Fly or the Orvis Ma-

Mohogany Spinner (Senest)
ART

hogany Spinner. They had been there all morning while I had been lurking about the stream-side trees and bushes, using the foliage for cover and camouflage, and I had not noticed them. It is often the case that the word precedes the perception. I suspect that if someone had just said: "Ruddy Fly" to me sometime earlier in the day I would have seen them then.

With great difficulty (but no great skill, the river being so narrow at that point), I managed to float a Mahogany Spinner under the willow branches far enough and long enough to catch one of the retiring brown trout that had been rising under the sweeping tree. It was a wild fish, I think, about a foot long, not too fat, bright, clean-finned and living in exactly the right place. I unhooked it, held it under the belly until it swam off and watched it head right back to the dark water under the willow. It was not a bad fish at all, for a brown trout.

The limit, for day-ticket holders, was four brace, eight fish. I did not have to kill mine, but in a moment of excessive optimism I had offered to give a couple of fish to the taxi driver. On the way over, he had remarked that it must be nice to fish the private water on the Wye—he fished a little himself—and something about the way he said it made me think he wanted a fish for supper. When I asked him if he did, he had said it would be lovely. I put back fish all morning on the assumption that anyone who could hook the first five fish he cast to would be able to pick up two fresh ones that afternoon for the taxi man's dinner. Even though we had an early train from Chester-field back to London, it should not be a problem to meet him at the goat farm at three o'clock with a brace of Cavendish Hotel, Duke of Devonshire trout.

The open, braided riffle below the bridge looked promising until the schoolchildren came trooping up the path from the direction of Buxton, twenty or thirty of them marching behind their teacher, all of them beknickered and cheerful. They were being quite good until it came to a choice of walking over the bridge or wading the shallows just below it. All ten or fifteen brace of the children decided that a cooling wade was the way to improve their nature study. I decided to let the riffle at the bridge rest, and wandered on down where the river narrowed, slowed and deepened, only to find the same kind of dour trout that had been upstream, fish still nymphing, and still uninterested in anything I had left in my small box.

It was nearly time to go as I walked back up to the riffle and sat down at the edge and watched the water near the grassy bank. Very small trout, still with the vertical bars of juveniles, scudded up and down over the gravel, ten and twenty of them at a time, schools of parr. I put on a caddis and cast out just a few feet farther, past the tiny ones, and caught the next size larger, five inches of beautiful rainbow, the parr marks faded, the rainbow faint but clear, the fins sharp-edged, the eyes big and clear, a true and honestly wild fish. It was big enough to eat, particularly in a country where men fish assiduously for dace and minnows, but it was not large enough to be a gift fish.

It occurred to me that for some reason I had been fishing all day as if there were a rule about casting only to visible, rising fish. There was no such law. The only peculiar rules of the Wye are the prohibition against wading and the restriction of the angler to a single fly. There was nothing in the ticket rules about upstream casting or sight-fishing. And, if the edge of the riffle held these small wild rainbow trout, there should be something better out in the deeper runs between the gravel bars and the occasional beds of watercress. Rainbow trout do not need a great deal of depth, nor are they as committed to shade and cover as the brown trout.

So thinking, and keeping one eye on the road over by the goat farm to see if the taxi cab was upon us, I put on an elk-hair caddis, said an agnostic prayer to whoever is in charge of rainbow trout, and started working the caddis as any sensible American would—down over the dark spots that might mark deeper water, through small riffles that stilled quickly as they dropped over bars into deeper runs. When I could control the fly, when it was floating well below the line but not dragging crossways, I twitched it a few times, remembering how caddis flies will flutter upstream just before their wings are dry and they can lift off the surface.

The rainbow came up out of a dark area in the farthest riffle from me, the one closest to the goat pasture across the river, and took the fly down with just a little extra, almost angry, motion. It came to hand fairly easily, only stopping once to try to bury itself in a patch of watercress. It was perfectly colored, blue-gray shading to green above the bright rainbow, clean white below. It would easily weigh a pound, but it, too, was not a gift fish. At some point in its life, the trout had suffered an injury just ahead of the tail fin, some loss of blood supply. Either another fish had grabbed it, or some careless angler, releasing it when it was smaller, had held it by the tail for a moment, damaging the caudal arteries, dwarfing the fin. It was a sixteen-inch trout with an eight-incher's tail. All the edible flesh was there, but I could not kill it for someone's dinner. I wrenched the fly out without touching the fish and watched it until it slipped away toward the center of the river.

Then I heard the taxi horn, and my wife and I started for the footbridge. I apologized for not catching the taxi driver something. When we parted at the train station in Chesterfield, I tipped him too much.

16

_____

Return to the River

*Natural and man-made
changes on the East Fork
of the Bitterroot River*

In August 1975, I went back to Missoula to visit Uncle Gordon and Aunt Ruby, to go fishing. It was a stop on a business trip— Missoula was more or less in between Boston and Portland, Oregon, and it seemed like a wasted opportunity to fly over the Rockies without stopping. I got a room at the Florence Hotel downtown before I called Gordon. He was a little offended that I didn't want to sleep in the cellar bedroom, but he understood that I was trying to make things easier for them both.

We had only one day to fish, and I knew where it would be spent. "We should go up to Sula Meadows," I said to him over the telephone. "It's a long drive, but it's the best place." It was also on my mind that Gordon was over seventy, and Sula was an easy place to fish; short casts would do it; wading was optional.

"You always liked it, Brother."

We got a late start the next morning. I walked over from the hotel, across the Clark Fork bridge, by Svensen's ice cream parlor, cut behind the high school to University Avenue, and headed down to Eddy Avenue, carrying a pair of hip boots, a fly rod in its case, and a little travel bag with a reel, two fly leaders still in their cellophane wrappers and a box of dry flies. The flies were all the usual Montana suspects: some Joe's Hoppers, a few Adams, homemade nondescript hairwings. I also brought a couple of strangers, Bombers, small ones about an inch long left over from a salmon-fishing trip to New Brunswick. The cutthroats at Sula were never so sophisticated that you absolutely had to fish with tiny dry flies or nymphs.

After breakfast, it took Gordon an hour to find all his fishing tackle, his hip boots, the right hat. Ruby packed us a lunch, and that took forever, too, matching tops with the right thermos bottles, finding the wicker lunch hamper in the cellar. I realized that Gordon hadn't been fishing that summer, and that seemed odd.

The road up the Bitterroot was just as I remembered it from the last time, a dozen years earlier. The river showed itself a few times from the highway, low water curling around large sand-and-gravel bars. It had not been a dry summer, but the lower Bitterroot is always drawn down in August. We drove through the cause—miles and miles of irrigated alfalfa fields that lined the river.

I was not paying attention when Gordon turned left off the highway somewhere south of Hamilton. We crossed the Bitterroot, which did seem wrong, and started to climb up out of the valley. I thought there was something he planned to do, some reason for it, until Gordon pulled over on the shoulder and looked at me and said, "I don't know what's gotten into me. We're on the Anaconda road." Indeed we were, halfway up the foothills of the Pintlar range, on the way to Georgetown Lake and Anaconda.

He turned the car around, and we got back on the main road and drove south again, through Darby and Conner, on past the Spring Gulch campground. The highway was pinched in now, between the East Fork and the hills. "This looks more like it," he said. On our right, on the west side of the highway, some clear-cuts marred the scenery, cuts on such steep slopes that the land had been terraced before it was replanted. The terraces made sinuous tracks across the fall line of the hillside.

We made the correct left turn at Sula Meadows, the little gas station and store just visible through the trees a few hundred yards farther up the highway. It all looked wonderfully the same as we came out of the narrows and into the open valley, "Ross's Hole" on maps. The valley road hugs the southeast edge, skirting the hay meadows, and we followed it up and took the first right turn, the gravel road down to the wooden bridge where we always parked.

Something looked wrong, and at first I couldn't put my finger on it. The big cottonwood trees that should have marked the bridge long before you got to it were gone. So was the old bridge, as it turned out, replaced by a concrete one. The deep hole that lay under the wooden bridge was missing too, and the water flowed evenly, shallowly. My God, I thought to myself, they sure tore hell out of this just to put in a little farm-road bridge. Above and below the bridge, it looked as if someone had put a Caterpillar dozer in the river and ripped its heart out. The undercut banks with their drooping grass were gone, and so were the small stream-side willows and the big overarching cottonwoods. The river ran over clean gravel and large stones, bank to shallowly sloping bank. Fifty yards downstream from the bridge there had always been a deep pool, the one where I saw my first dipperbird, but it didn't show itself when I looked down to where it should be. The water seemed to run at an even pace, there was no stilling, no small riffles dying out into a waveless pool.

We strung our rods. I'm not sure whether Gordon realized how bad it looked to me, whether he was surprised or not. You can only see a few hundred feet up or down from the bridge, for the river curves away out of sight. Gordon said he thought he would try it upstream. That was always the way; he liked to fish up, and I didn't mind fishing down. "We'll give it an hour," he said, "and then we'll run down to the campground for lunch."

Downstream it didn't get any better. I walked for a half-mile, almost to the Sula store, and the river was dead, running quietly, without feature, between bare banks of dry stone and gravel. There were no fallen trees, no snags, no undercut banks, no pools, no dipperbirds, and, although I realize a fly rod is a very poor scientific instrument for sampling fish populations, there were no trout in it, either.

Gordon was already at the car when I got back to the bridge, leaning against the right front fender, his hip boots turned down at the knees.

I slid my rod into the car, pushing the butt against the firewall, leaving the tip trailing out the rear-door window. We always did that when we had just a few minutes' drive, and that was all it would be, down to Spring Gulch campground for lunch. I went over to the bridge, braced my knees against the concrete guard rail, and stared down at the river. When Gordon walked over, I noticed he was moving a little gingerly on his feet. And while we were standing there, a pickup truck came down the road, stopped, and the driver got out and joined us. All three of us looked at the river.

I don't know who this man was. Usually, in Montana, you introduce yourself, but I wasn't feeling very sociable. I just looked at the stranger and asked him what in hell had happened to the river.

"Floods," he said. He told me it had been flooding badly every spring for the last few years, too much runoff, and the river had been eating into the hay bottom. The ranchers were losing too much hay land to the river, so they had gotten a dozer and straightened it out.

I said they were sonsabitches. I never before had sworn in front of Gordon. I didn't care if this stranger was one of the ranchers or not. He said it wasn't the ranchers' fault. "Forest Service," he explained, and then he spat in the river. The Service had gotten the idea that beavers up in the headwaters were bad for trees, he said, so they had dynamited and trapped and cleaned the beavers out, and the spring runoff just came pouring down.

In fact, I learned much later, there had been a small skirmish with the beavers. The Forest Service roads up into the timbered slopes above the East Fork were built cheaply, with culverts instead of bridges across the feeder streams. The beaver loves the culvert because it means the road builder has done the hard work and all the beaver has to do is block the narrow pipe and he has a completed dam. So, to save their logging roads the Forest Service trapped out the pest beavers.

But the real story of the runoff was much more complicated. It began with clear-cutting the forest. The view from Highway 93 as you approach Sula from Conner was not the best public relations for the Forest Service in the early 1970s, and it still isn't. The steep slopes on the west side of the Bitterroot River have some monumental clear-cuts near the highway. I knew this before I saw them in 1975; they were ugly enough to be photographed and published in the *New York Times*, though I hadn't heard about the war on the beavers. In fact, there were even more monstrous clear-cuts than the ones visible to passing motorists on the main highway. These were upstream on the East Fork drainage, hidden by the rugged folds in the mountains. Back in the hills were 4,634 acres of clear-cuts plus miles of access roads. Some of the tributary streams had been treated so brutally that Bob Hammer, the Forest Service hydrologist in Hamilton, still calls one of them, Lodgepole Creek, "Oh My God Creek." And nature treated the East Fork as badly as the Forest Service; fires burned another nineteen thousand acres in the drainage, so fire roads and salvage lumbering made it all worse.

What the cutting and burning had done to the watershed was simple: spring and summer rains, instead of falling on old trees and a spongy forest floor with a hundred years of litter lying there to soak up the water, fell on soil compacted by logging, scarred by hard roads, baked hard by wildfires and fires set by scientific foresters, and replanted with inconsequential seedling trees. Before the clear-cuts and the fires, the total July runoff averaged 13,820 acre-feet. (An acre-foot is a dam-builder's measure, an area of one acre covered by one foot of water, or 43,560 cubic feet of water, which works out to 325,828 gallons of water in an acre-foot.) After the damage, July runoff averaged a total of 21,351 acre-feet. August runoff was equally torrential, if less in total volume, rising from an average of 5,752 acre-feet to 8,983 acre-feet. Those are 54 and 56 percent increases. Daily runoff records from the East Fork's gauging station near Conner, below the Spring Gulch campground, show the problem even more clearly than the monthly averages. When the rains fell, the runoff came down precipitously, the daily flows rose several feet overnight and then fell as quickly. The Forest Service, in the typical logic of an agency trying to cover its ass, called these torrents a blessing:

"substantially increased streamflow has resulted, particularly in the summer months when demands for irrigation water are greatest and minimum flow is needed to sustain the fish population."

I did not know any of this when I listened to the stranger on the bridge, and I believed his cockamamie beaver story. "Then they're all sonsabitches," I muttered. The retired supervisor of the Bitterroot National Forest, speaking to a columnist for the *Daily Missoulian*, expressed my anger more eloquently. Commenting on the difference between the selective logging practices of his era and the brutal clearcutting decisions made by his successor, he said, choosing his words with care: "If public horse-whipping were still a part of public discipline, that would be the least punishment that politicians and reluctant agency regulators could expect." Such elegant language escaped me, and I just repeated myself. "Sonsabitches," I said again.

"I wouldn't be hard on the ranchers," the stranger said evenly. "It wasn't their fault." I responded with something reasonably polite, and he left.

Gordon and I drove back down the highway to the campground on the edge of the river. The East Fork had ripped through it, too. About half the giant Douglas firs I remembered were gone, and all the picnic tables and concrete fire rings looked as if they had been recently replaced. The highway bridge just upstream of the campground looked different to me too, newer and fancier in some unclear manner. We ate our lunch, and Gordon said he probably wouldn't fish anymore; he couldn't find the innersole inserts for his hip boots that morning, and the stones on the riverbank had bruised his feet. Years before, I knew, he would have walked with ease on the thick hay that grew between the barbed wire fence and the bank, stepped softly on the soft mint that covered the edge between the high-water line and the summer flow of the East Fork.

I said it was all right, it was going to be late enough when we got back to Missoula, we could call it a day. Silently, I told myself that I had already seen enough. After I put the lunch basket back in the car, I was taking my fly rod apart when Gordon smiled suddenly and said to wait a minute; we should stop one more place, he had forgotten about it, he'd just remembered it, and we should stop there for a while.

I had forgotten too, my memory clouded by my reaction to the miserable condition of the river in Sula Meadows. About a quarter of a mile downstream from the campground there's a little place to pull out onto the gravel shoulder at the bottom of a sweeping right-hand curve in the highway. As you look upstream a hundred yards, the river comes down over a ledge and through a narrows between the highway and the foot of a sharply rising cliff on the far side. It's an odd place to fish; you need a sense of humor even to consider it. The bank from the highway down to the river is fifteen feet of quarried granite rip-rap, machine-placed, barren, very steep. I recognized the run of the water. We always stopped there for one last fish on the way home from Sula Meadows and Spring Gulch. You have to walk back up the highway from the pull-out and stand right on the edge of the gravel shoulder and fish almost straight down.

I can tell you exactly how to find the good part of the hole. You walk up until you are across the stream from the vertical ledge and look for a pale yellowish rock in the water, six feet across at least. It must be a piece of trucked-in rip-rap that got loose and tumbled into the stream, there aren't any other yellow rocks in the river and none in the cliff across from the highway. It's a big rock, but even in low water it's always covered, though in the clear summertime East Fork it's always visible. The trout are not by the yellow rock. They are near the next big rock downstream from it. This second rock is only six or eight feet out from the bank. There is a trout in front of this rock and another one below it, downstream. The one in front lies hidden deep in the soft cushion that the rock makes in the flowing water. The one below the rock is out of sight in the slow return current, in the vortex behind the rock. The big, gray rock just down from the pale yellow rock—remember that. And also, you must remember to watch your backcast, because logging trucks and camper vans and pickups and sedan-loads of tourists are going to pass about five feet behind you as you stand there casting down onto the river. I would go alone if I were you. My wife has seen me fish there, and thinks I am crazy to do it. I understand her concern, but we drive hundreds of thousands of miles in our lives, and we do not flinch every time we meet an oncoming vehicle that is as close to us as one is when we are standing by the edge of the road. I never notice the traffic when I'm fishing there. Watching a dry fly concentrates the mind.

East Fork cutthroats are not very big, but they are lovely, green-backed, delicate fish, carrying the tiny black spots of a typical Pacific Slope cutthroat. I caught two while Gordon watched, the fish in front and the fish in back of the rock, on two casts. They both took a small Bomber, coming straight up from the bottom like little submarine-launched missiles, taking the fly and continuing up with it into the air, and falling, surprised, back into the river. The trout there come in a hurry because any food that sweeps down by the yellow rock is moving along at five or six miles an hour, and there is no time to be choosy—the main current is too strong for the trout to fight it for more than a few seconds. I killed them both because, you see, we were going home to Missoula to have trout for dinner.

I offered to drive back, and Gordon let me. He was a little tired, he said. I'm not sure what else we talked about, but I do remember, down somewhere between Hamilton and Florence, that he said without any introduction: "Don't let those two trout fool you. This country's not what it used to be." That was the first gloomy thing I'd heard him say, ever.

"They did tear up the meadows, didn't they?"

"That, too."

I realized he meant all of Montana, not just the valley. I suppose it is not the country it used to be, although I love it still. There are locked gates and NO TRESPASSING signs now, which I understand, little as I like them. But there are hundreds of new public access sites, if you don't mind fishing near signs telling you where to park. There is more information and less serendipity, now.

That fall I got two large packages in the parcel post. Gordon had wrapped up his fly-tying materials—saddle and neck hackles, wing feathers, duck skins, fur scraps, dozens of boxes of fly hooks, thread, floss, tinsel, fly-tying vise—and sent them all to me. He even included, for no reason I could imagine, all of Aunt Ruby's Eagle Claw bait hooks, the ones she used with grasshoppers and salmon eggs for bait. There was a note inside one package. He wrote that he didn't need the equipment anymore and knew I would like to have it. It was as sad a gift as I ever hope to get.

Then, in that winter, Gordon developed the full-blown symptoms of Alzheimer's Disease. My mother said, with our family's typical circumlocution about all medical matters and in particular about mental states, "Gordon is not always exactly sure where he is." The neighbors had noticed it even before our last fishing trip. He gave the Petersens next door a house key because he had locked himself out once or twice and couldn't remember where he hid his extra key. I assume, now, that the early stages of the disease accounted for the wrong turn up the Anaconda road, the missing innersoles for his hip boots, and the apparent equanimity with which he looked at the destroyed East Fork in Sula Meadows. He died in a nursing home in Hemet, California, a long way from the Bitterroot.

I resist believing that Gordon was not sure where he was. He remained, by all accounts, sweet-tempered right up to his death. That is not always true with his condition, but not even Alzheimer's could reverse his gentle disposition. I do like to think that if he could keep his sunniness in that dying light he knew exactly where he was: he was up on the Bitterroot, the country was the way it used to be, and the trout were taking the dry fly. I am sure he was alone at the end, fishing by himself. Ruby would be down at Spring Gulch, reading *Science and Health with a Key to the Scriptures*. And Brother? Oh, I would have been then where I am now: out of sight, around the bend, a long way downstream.

17

New Rivers,
Old Bones

*Some final thoughts on
the nature of trout country*

T he last time I stopped by Sula Meadows, my wife was traveling with me. She understood without any explanation how
sad a place it had become. We had walked by the Beaverhead
and the Little Blackfoot, Flint Creek, Rattlesnake Creek over by Dillon, and she had seen the pure high-country meadows of the upper
Big Hole.

I did want to show her a west-slope cutthroat trout, and so we
stopped just above the campground at Spring Gulch and walked
down to the east bank of the river below the highway bridge. It was
high noon on a hot August day, and in the shadow of the bridge, a
flight of caddis flies swirled close to the girders. Maybe there aren't
always trout under a bridge, but in season, shade-seeking caddis flies
swarm there to mature and mate.

At the bridge, I learned it was time to say goodbye, once and forever, to the East Fork of the Bitterroot. Nothing happened that
should stop you from enjoying the river, for most of it is as it was and
should be. But for me it was the end.

We both watched the water, but saw no sign of trout. The myriad caddis flying in the shadow and the many more crawling on the underpinning of the bridge were all the information I needed to imagine the right way to catch a trout for her, to bring it over the clean gravel into the sunlight on the edge of the pool, to show it to Florence. I expected a trout, nothing less. One of the charms of the upper East Fork had always been that it was nearly devoid of fly-grabbing whitefish (perhaps entirely so, I never saw one or caught one above Conner). I tied on an Elk-Hair Caddis—my favorite kind, the style with a peacock-herl body reinforced with thin gilt wire—and started fishing at the lower end of the pool, working upstream and farther across with each cast. A trout took the fly near the far bank, just below the shade of the bridge. It was a cutthroat, but a small one, and though it had vivid gill markings and small black dots stippling its green sides, it did not have the heft or seriousness of a good fish. I released it without taking it out of the water and told my wife the next one would be better.

Old artificer, crafty man that I was, casting was no problem that day. Even the bridge was no impediment, for a low, slanting backcast, followed by the same low loop in the forward cast, unrolled well below the bottom of the bridge. Moderate skill was and always will be more than adequate to that small river. At the very head of the pool, at the last and best spot upstream in the perpetual shadow of the bridge, I could see where the better fish would be. Even though the bright light on the water upstream of the bridge glared in my eyes and obscured my vision, much as it will as you come to the end of a highway tunnel, I could easily see the slow current by the bridge abutment.

It was difficult to get the caddis fly to drift naturally in that slacker water. The quicker current in the center of the pool worried at the line and dragged the fly across the surface, creating a small wake on the smooth glide by the bridge. A little drag on a caddis fly is sometimes helpful, but it is better, more natural-looking, if the fly is moving upstream. This drag was an ineffective down-and-across motion. Without even stopping to think about it, quite reflexively, I cast the fly a little farther, bounced it off the concrete foundation, and let it drop on the water at the end of the slackened leader. A fish took the fly a moment later, as if it had to do so, and hooked itself turning down- and upstream.

Florence, who takes photographs of such important events, prepared the camera while I led the fish, unwilling as it was, down into the well-lighted pool. I told her I thought it was a better fish and worth the film. In fact, I could tell it was much better, and I played it carefully because you cannot always land a fish when you want one for a photograph.

As it tired, as I drew it in toward us, something seemed wrong with it, the color seemed odd. My mind was not able, on first view, to process the signal. Near at hand, a few moments later, the fish revealed itself for what it was, a very healthy, very colorful, yellow-bellied, vermiculated, purple-spotted, brown trout. I was almost ill. God knows, I have fished hard for brown trout on two continents and one sceptered isle, but I did not need to see one sixty miles upstream from the Clark Fork. It is an entirely personal prejudice, and I try to apply it only to fish, but I still make a distinction between native things and interlopers, between rivers as nature made them and rivers as men alter them. This distaste may be nothing but a lamentable inability to change with the times. In spite of that conservatism, I did not mind that I had better flies (an Elk-Hair Caddis is an enormous improvement over what I used to tie at Gordon's desk: the sizes are more realistic, the wing-shape more natural, the attractiveness more compelling), nor did I in the least regret the casting ease of a graphite rod, or the inevitable change from the angler's youthful enthusiasm to his mature cleverness. It was the right trout, but in the wrong place. A rose bush in a hayfield is just another weed. When I held its mouth open to unhook it, the sharp teeth on the lower jaw and the tongue made scratches on my left thumb that annoyed me for a week.

We journeyed on, after that, and fished for brown and rainbow trout (both feral, but neither native) on the lower Missouri River and farther east on the Bighorn. That is now my countryside of dreams, the dry side of the Rockies. Given a choice, I will keep going back to the Bighorn valley. It is near enough to where I was born, close enough to where my father courted my mother over at Lame Deer on the Northern Cheyenne reservation, to seem like home. Hardin is a town of few trees and fewer comforts, but I am accustomed to a world where the tallest building is an alfalfa-seed elevator, a town where you drink with your hat on.

I think it is the transitory nature of the Bighorn country that appeals, now that I know that the West is not, as Gordon said, the same as it used to be. I resign my boyhood to memory, and accept life as it is.

One band after another of humankind has wandered through the plains of eastern Montana—archaic Indians and post-contact Plains tribes, trappers, cattlemen, homesteaders like my grandparents, tourists like myself. We are drawn, after many a detour, to the high rolling plains that step up into the Bighorn Mountains. The oldest types of human relics in North America are scattered thinly over the foothills, artifacts dating back to the time when the first immigrants from Siberia pursued the last mammoths, stabbing them to death with long, fluted spear points. There they drove the now-extinct straight-horned archaic American bison over cliffs, and dismembered the animals with sharp flakes of flint down in the dry beds of the canyons. Even during the long and inexplicable dry spell that depopulated the Great Plains for centuries (roughly from the fall of Troy to the sacking of Imperial Rome) the Bighorns, high enough to catch the ephemeral rain clouds, stayed moist enough for man and beast and even for trout. The great game fields in the foothills and along the rivers, once elk and bighorn sheep and buffalo pastures, eventually became some of the best cow country east of the Rockies.

It is a place of constant change. Even the Crow Indians and the Northern Cheyenne are newcomers. They got to Montana centuries after Columbus reached Cuba, long after Captain Rolfe discovered the pleasures of both tobacco and Pocahontas on the distant Virginia shore. By all accounts, the Crows came into the valley just fifty or sixty years before Lewis and Clark. These new Plains Indians moved west with the aid of that all-leveling invention, the black-powder gun. They drove the old people, the spear-carrying *gens de serpent*, the Snake Indians, back into the permanent desert of the Great Basin, and then settled along the rich valleys watered by the Big-horns, places with grass-names: Lodge Grass, Rotten Grass, and the place where Custer discovered reality at last. We call it the Little Big-horn, the Cheyenne and Sioux called it the Battle of Greasy Grass.

I read the landscape and see change, and it comforts me, oddly enough. The high Yellowtail Dam, finished in 1965, created the trout fishery below it by trapping the silt and chilling the water. As a trout river, the Bighorn is exactly half my age. The dam, the reservoir and the resulting trout are no more permanent than any other piece of civil engineering, and someday, centuries from now, the lake will be solid with silt, growing trees and grass along the banks of the river that still runs through it. With the lake full, the trout will no longer thrive on the top of this peculiar and artificially enhanced food chain. I believe there will always be trout somewhere, though not here, not down in the valley where once an ordinary plains river ran, stocked with catfish and paddlefish and golden-eye minnows. But that inevi-table eutrophication will take centuries. Barring some catastrophe, either one of nature (the dam sits not far from one of the massive faults that mark the uplifting northern edge of the Bighorns) or some equally disastrous flaw in the engineering process, there will still be cold water and trout in the Bighorn during all our lifetimes and on through the generations to at least the biblical number of forty.

Every time I go back I spend less time on the river, more hours up in the high country between the reservoir and the Pryor Mountains. There are bluffs back in there with hundreds of teepee rings on them, rings so old that even the few worms that survive below the bunch grass and prickly pear in that arid climate are slowly undermining and burying the stones that once held down the buffalo-hide cones. Flint shards—the remnants, the *débitage* of tool-making—lie scat-tered on the ground bleached white, the stone losing its silica in the sunshine and the rain, transmuting from glassy-sharp and useful cut-ting edges into soft, porous curiosities. The flakes of flint ("chert" as they say in America) are almost always outside of and in between the teepee rings. Anyone who has played at knapping flint will understand why: new flakes are sharper than razors.

Near the largest set of teepee rings, by the western edge of the Crow Reservation, a small spring-fed brook called Hoodoo Creek has cut a deep ravine in the soft soil. The locals say the name is a reference to the fear that the Crow Indians once had of the Pryor Mountain country, a place they thought was inhabited by dwarves of some malignancy. You can find it easily on standard topographical maps, it is at the intersection of 108 degrees, 7 minutes west longitude; 45 degrees, 7 minutes north latitude, and it has east-slope cutthroats in it, small ones, scaled down to the size of the water, metal-bright fish with the dense and large black spots and garish scarlet gill stripes of the species. The creek tumbles over a series of impassable waterfalls before it reaches the Bighorn Canyon reservoir; no stocked fish can come up into Hoodoo country and spawn. The trout are as pure, as safe from cross-breeding or competition, as if they were on another planet. When we go down and fish for them, my friend carries a .44 magnum pistol with soft-tip loads for the possible grizzly bear and bird-shot loads for the predictable rattlesnake. I do not like the revolver much, but it is, at least for this century, his country.

Farther north, with no bears but many rattlesnakes, he and I and my wife will walk along the summer-dry bed of Beauvais Creek. (Anglers floating the lower section of the Bighorn downstream from St. Xavier will pass Beauvais Creek's meeting with the river, and see trout rising in the back-eddy that forms above the sandbar deposited in flood-time by the creek's flow.) We look for dinosaur bones and gizzard stones. Once you had to put quotation marks around "gizzard stones," because there used to be an argument about whether these highly polished pebbles really had been manufactured in the guts of the herbivorous dinosaurs of the Cretaceous era. They are shinier pebbles than ever you picked up on a beach or a creek bottom, but some scientists, many of whom live on disputation as much as discovery, scorned the diagnosis. The evidence, including the recovery of polished pebbles from the interior of fossil dinosaurs, is now clearly on the side of the old dinosaur hunters who knew, the minute they saw one, that these polished pebbles and small rocks were not the product of mere geological forces.

An outcrop of Late Cretaceous rimrock is exposed above the bed of Beauvais Creek, a dark red sandstone that lies on top of distinct bands of volcanic ash deposited in lacustrine and marine layers, red over gray over white over gray again. A hundred miles north of the Bighorn valley, Montana has better exposures of this Cloverly group. They are up on the Missouri Breaks, near where I was born. The famous dinosaur fossils come from up there: Hell Creek, near Jordan, is home to the first-ever and now the most-complete-ever fossil of *Tyrannosaurus rex*. My family left there long ago, but somehow it was imprinted on me, and wandering along this southerly uplift of the Cloverly, it feels like home again.

The country around Hardin has seen many transients. Even the plants are wanderers. In June, when the sego lily and the brilliant cerise, leafless and low-lying bitterroot are both in bloom, so, too, rise the yellow flowering heads of western salsify. They look like giant dandelions. Their cousins, meadow salsify, flower on the waste ground between my house and the highway, back in Massachusetts. No one had to import salsify to Montana. It is a European herb that has traveled north on the summer wind, seed by seed on parasol wings, from the Spanish settlements to the high plains. It beat Lewis and Clark to the territory.

The springs fed by the Bighorn Mountains become rarer as you move north from the foothills, and by the time you reach Beauvais Creek and the Cretaceous outcroppings, it is a drier, hotter, less hospitable climate than the country with the teepee rings and the acres of scattered stone flakes a dozen miles south, closer to the source of waters. There are no concentrations of the artifacts of old wanderers, no obvious living floors or scrap heaps of the Stone Age. One or two homesteaders tried and failed, leaving cellar holes and a few rusting remnants of late Industrial Revolution detritus. If you look hard, you can find the hidden campsites of some dinosaur hunters, Barnum Brown from the American Museum of Natural History at the turn of this century, John Ostrom of Yale in the decades just past.

One of Brown's finds from Beauvais Creek is mounted on the wall of the Late Dinosaur Room at the American Museum of Natural History in New York. It is labeled simply as a Nodosaur, an example of a large family of armored herbivores. It has a specific name: *Sauropelta edwardsi*. The plated body has been flattened by the pressure of time into something resembling a giant armadillo squashed by a semi-truck and trailer. The preparer's notes indicate that it had gastroliths, gizzard stones, in its "gastrolith canal."

We find gastroliths by the dozens, down in the dry bed of Beauvais Creek. They wash out of the Cloverly, up on the rim of the canyon, and tumble down over the Bearpaw shale and finally come to rest on the sandy bottom. They stand out, they are easy to find, for this country is so unpolluted by man (so inhospitable to anglers, hunters or picnickers) that there are no shards of broken glass, no shiny plastic, no new, unrusted tin cans to glisten in the sunlight. Everything that glitters, all the reflected points of light, are the best-polished gizzard stones. We would have great difficulty finding one by the side of a road or nearer a town, even on the littered ground about a long-abandoned homestead cabin. Here, they show themselves to the curious.

And we are not the first people to look for them. From time to time, perhaps one in every dozen polished stones, we pick up a fragmented gastrolith with the peculiar shape of a stone deliberately and carefully fractured by the hand of man. A bit of one end has been chipped off to create what flint-knappers call a "platform," a flat surface against which to strike a precise blow to remove a flake. The pieces we find are usually the rounded outer surface of the old pebbles, knocked cleanly off from the core with a single sharp impact on the platform. On what was once the interior surface we can see a shallow bump, and sometimes a series of concentric arcs spreading out from the place where the blow was struck. These arcs are the record of the shock wave as it traveled through the glassy chert or agate of the gizzard stone. The apex of the little bump on the stone marks the exact place where the old one struck the platform; it is narrow at the point of impact, and spreads down and out from there. People who admire these things call this bump the "bulb of percussion," and recognize it, wherever in the world it is found, as the hallmark of mankind's deliberate tool-making.

Some of the flakes we find have clear evidence of wear, of use as tools. There are fine serrations fractured into the still-sharp glassy edges. Long ago the flake had cut meat and sinew, skinned out a carcass, scraped a bone. I find it pleasant to walk along a creekbed and see that men not so different from myself had interest of their own in these by-products of dinosaur digestion. There are no suitable native rocks for flint-knapping anywhere near Beauvais Creek, they had to be carried in, and so they were, more than sixty million years ago. Much later, they were picked up, flaked and used, sometime after the last great glacial epoch when the old ones walked here from Siberia. And now we hold them, and think about time, trout, the antiquity of rivers and the ephemeral nature of dwellings, of both teepee rings and log cabins.

The Cretaceous—back when the nodosaurs and their allies were picking up rocks of all sorts, only some of which survived the grinding of the gastrolith canal and even fewer of which took the high polish that makes them easy to find when we want a souvenir—was also the time when trout were coming up out of the ocean, becoming freshwater fish. In genetic time, the smooth belly of a trout held up for a picture near the mouth of Beauvais Creek is as old as the polish on the blue-brown, gold-bearing rock picked up the next day, fifteen miles up the creek from the river. And my hand, though softer, is the same as the hard and skillful one that hammered a piece of polished red chert into a blade a few thousand years ago, used it, and then discarded it on the sandy bottom of the dry wash.

These things interest me as much as the trout, now. I want to know where the river comes from and where it is going, who lived there once, who farms there now. I admire the alfalfa, and look with some mild displeasure at the irrigated fields of sugar beets. They are the worst, almost the only, polluter of the upper Bighorn. Beets are a row crop, dirtier than hayfields, for the irrigation water runs through loose, plowed soil and muddies the river when it returns. But this will pass, too. The sugar refinery in Hardin is already closed tight, and the beets are trucked all the way to Billings, and that refinery has been shut down once or twice. It is no business of mine to lobby against sugar beets, but sooner or later the price-support for domestic sugar (and sugar beets) will end. The fields will be put back to hay, and the runoff to the river will be less filled with chemicals and soil. We can wait. The trout and the anglers will outlast the beets.

These days, I need to know the names of the wildflowers and the species of the dinosaurs whose bones erode out of the rock. The boy is transmuted; obsession with trout has been replaced with a stronger and yet more diffuse affection for trout country. I want fish, but also mint, dipper-birds, bitterroot in bloom and ospreys kiting over the river. And I still desperately want that missing arrowhead.

I fish most often with companions, now. The urge to share stories is stronger than the need for solitude. Most of my fellow anglers are alive, but not all. This winter I plan to take a razor blade to the old chamois cloth in the garage and slice some thin wash-leather strips and tie a caddis-worm and fish for brown trout some August day with Hewett Wheatley, who in 1849 described the nymph in *The Rod and Line*. I do not fish joyfully with a nymph or eagerly for browns, but Mr. Wheatley is worth the trouble. If it works, I will give one to a friend (some of my best friends are nymph-fishers), and tell them that the fly makes "no despicable imitation of the caddis tribe." It will have to be a friend, not because the fly is valuable, but because the language is inflated. And some June, when the bitterroot is in bloom and the Canada geese on the river are flightless in their summer molt, I will get back to the Madison or the Beaverhead with a Bunyan Bug in my kit and fish the salmon fly hatch the old way, with the right, foolish-looking fly, and remember Ashley Roche, and Missoula the way it used to be. Gordon I remember often, now more for his smile than any memory triggered by the mothball smell of dry flies or the pungency of rod varnish, or wild mint and trout lying on a back lawn. Trout smell the best, I should tell you, when they have been dead just the right amount of time.

In good light and in fair weather, when it comes up and takes the dry fly, the trout is a wonderful thing. But it is not enough. I sit and watch more, just for the love of running water, and I walk farther now than before. There are springs to see, and the shadows of small wild trout flicking across the bed of a side creek. I carry a wading staff and poke at interesting rocks. Sooner or later, one of them will be the tip of a half-buried lance point.

Every year, fishing takes me farther from the river.

A NOTE ON THE TYPE

This book is set in a typeface called Méridien, a classic ro-
man designed by Adrian Frutiger for the French type
foundry Deberny et Peignot in 1957. Adrian Frutiger was
born in Interlaken, Switzerland, in 1928 and studied type
design there and at the Kunstgewerbeschule in Zurich. In
1953 he moved to Paris, where he joined Deberny et Peignot as a member of the design staff. Méridien, as well as his
other typeface of world renown, Univers, was created for
the Lumitype photo-set machine.

Composed by Graphic Composition, Inc., Athens, Georgia
Designed by Anthea Lingeman

Same start for both with
parallel ends

Double has one
more turn

· Single and Double
SURGEON'S or WATER KNOTS

To join two ends of gut

BARREL or BLOOD KNOT